D1544872

Regents and Rebels

Studies in Social Discontinuity

General Editor   *Charles Tilly, The New School for Social Research*

Studies in Social Discontinuity began in 1972 under the imprint of Academic Press. In its first 15 years, 53 titles were published in the series, including important volumes in the areas of historical sociology, political economy, and social history.

Revived in 1989 by Basil Blackwell, the series will continue to include volumes emphasizing social changes and non-Western historical experience as well as translations of major works.

Published:

The Perilous Frontier
Nomadic Empires and China
Thomas J. Barfield

Regents and Rebels
The Revolutionary World of an Eighteenth-Century Dutch City
Wayne Ph. te Brake

Nascent Proletarians
Class Formation in Post-Revolutionary France
Michael P. Hanagan

In preparation:

Modern French Anti-Semitism
A Political History
Pierre Birnbaum

Coffee and Contention
Political Change in Modern Brazil
Mauricio Font

Rites of Revolt
The War of the Demoiselles in Ariège, France (1829–1831)
Peter Sahlins

Regents and Rebels

The Revolutionary World of an Eighteenth-Century Dutch City

WAYNE PH. TE BRAKE

Basil Blackwell

Library of Congress Cataloging in Publication Data

Te Brake, Wayne Ph.
  Regents and rebels.
  (Studies in social discontinuity)
  Includes index.
  1. Deventer (Netherlands) – History.
  2. Netherland – Politics and government –
  1714–1795. I. Title. II. Series.
  DJ411.D5B73 1989   949.2'1   88-34975

  ISBN 1-55786-040-8

British Library Cataloguing in Publication Data

A CIP catalogue record for this book is available from the British Library.

Typeset in 10 on 12 pt Ehrhardt
by Vera-Reyes, Inc., Philippines
Printed in Great Britain by
T. J. Press Ltd, Padstow, Cornwall

For my mother,
Helen Segaar te Brake,
and in memory of my father,
William te Brake,
ordinary people with extraordinary ideals

Contents

Editor's Preface

Charles Tilly, New School for Social Research

THIS SERIES

Studies in Social Discontinuity present historically grounded analyses of important social transformations, ruptures, conflicts, and contradictions. Although we of Basil Blackwell interpret that mission broadly, leave room for many points of view, and absolve authors of any responsibility for propaganda on behalf of our intellectual program, the series as a whole demonstrates the relevance of well-crafted historical work for the understanding of contemporary social structures and processes. Books in the series pursue one or more of four varieties of historical analysis: (1) using evidence from past times and places systematically to identify regularities in processes and structures that transcend those particular times and places; (2) reconstructing critical episodes in the past for the light they shed on important eras, peoples, or social phenomena; (3) tracing the origins or previous phases of significant social processes that continue into our own time; (4) examining the ways that social action at a given point in time lays down residues that limit the possibilities of subsequent social action.

The fourth theme is at once the least familiar and the most general. Social analysts have trouble seeing that history matters precisely because social interaction takes place in well-defined times and places, and occurs within constraints offered by those times and places, producing social relations and artifacts that are themselves located in space-time and whose existence and distribution constrain subsequent social interaction. The construction of a city in a given place and time affects urban growth in adjacent areas and subsequent times. Where and when industrialization occurs affects how it occurs. Initial visions of victory announce a war's likely outcomes. A person's successive migrations have cumulative effects on his or her subsequent mobility through such simple matters as the presence or absence of information about new opportunities in different places and the presence or absence of social ties to possible destinations. A population's previous experience with wars, Baby Booms, and migrations haunts it in the form of bulging or empty cohorts and unequal numbers of the sexes. All these are profoundly historical matters, even when they occur in the present; time and place are of their essence. They form the essential subject matter of *Studies in Social Discontinuity*.

Edward Shorter, Stanley Holwitz, and I plotted the studies in Social Discontinuity in 1970–1; the first book, William Christian's *Person and God in a Spanish Valley*, appeared in 1972. Over the years, Academic Press published more than 50 titles in the series. But during the early 1980s publication slowed, and then ceased. In 1988, happily, Basil Blackwell agreed to revive the Studies under my editorship. Wayne te Brake's *Regents and Rebels* belongs to the first cohort of the renewed series.

THIS BOOK

Two hundred years after the French Revolution of 1789, celebrations, publications, and debates in abundance have drawn new attention to the founding period of representative governments in the West. Not long before 1789, the nearby Dutch Republic underwent a series of struggles that shared many a theme with those that were soon to stir France. The bicentenary of the Dutch patriots' movement, or revolution, passed with little fanfare, no doubt forgotten because in 1787 a Prussian invasion of the Netherlands on behalf of the dispossessed House of Orange crushed popular demands for political change.

Wayne te Brake gives us good reason to regret that neglect – not because the Dutch Patriot's Revolution of 1786–7 actually succeeded, but because it teaches us so much about popular struggle in the age of revolution. Although Te Brake, ever prudent, does not risk the comparison, the Dutch experience offers an opportunity to think about alternative paths the American and French Revolutions might have taken. Conjure up a more commercial, urban, and prosperous America or France with more durable guarantees of municipal autonomy, and imagine an even more bourgeois revolution than actually occurred. Postulate successful repression of either revolutionary movement in its early phase, and use Dutch history to speculate on how differently we would now tell the tale.

Te Brake does, in fact, offer a striking and germane comparison. For in 1795, under French influence, a more successful revolution did occur in the Netherlands. The events of 1786 and 1795 were not simply two identical actions, differing only in the character of external intervention; toward the end of his book, Te Brake shows us clearly how conditions had changed during the intervening nine years. The earlier mobilization itself significantly affected the identification and internal organization of competing parties in the Netherlands, as did the reaction that accompanied the Prussian invasion of 1797; the revolutionary process of 1786–7 damaged the structure of patronage that had previously attached local powerholders to the Stadhouder, greatly increased the importance of popular assent (or at least its appearance) to the effectiveness of any political change, and gave far greater salience to ideological divisions within both local and national politics.

Wayne te Brake's thoughtfully comparative book builds most of its comparisons around a very solid core; a thorough reconstruction of social organization and politics in a small commercial center, Deventer. Deventer serves its purpose well, because the divisions and changes that racked the Netherlands during the 1780s took dramatic forms within the city, including the veering of guild artisans from a revolutionary to a counter-revolutionary position. At the level of a single city, Te Brake can make us aware of individual actors, their connections, and their rivalries. Among other things, he clarifies the critical position within local life occupied by the artisans and shopkeepers whose revolutionary role other observers of the eighteenth century have repeatedly noticed. Then he returns to comparisons with nearby Kampen and Zwolle, cities that took alternative paths through the revolutionary period, but experienced many of the same divisions. Moving from city to province to nation and back, Te Brake pinpoints with rare precision the relations between local and national politics, between parish factionalism and large struggles for power, between everyday rivalries and sweeping revolutions.

Preface

This work is the product of many years' effort to approach the history of the Dutch Patriot Revolution from a comparative perspective. Stimulated by R. R. Palmer's *The Age of the Democratic Revolution*, I set out as a graduate student at The University of Michigan to analyze the patterns of popular collective action in the Dutch Revolution of the 1780s, much as students of the French Revolution had been doing for years. I soon realized, however, that the dynamics of the Patriot Revolution were strikingly different from the French, and that the available archival records were of a completely different sort. Events on the periphery of Dutch politics, not at the center, commanded my attention; petitions and local militia lists, not police interrogations, afforded a fuller picture of the process of popular mobilization.

The first fruit of my labor in the Dutch archives was a dissertation on the Patriot Revolution in the province of Overijssel. Undertaken at a time when work on the Dutch Patriots – not to mention the so-called land provinces – was hardly fashionable, this research was a venture into uncharted waters which promised the rewards of discovery as well as the perils of intellectual isolation. But for the encouragement and generosity of the late Professor D. J. Roorda, I might have lost the courage of my convictions and sought out a more traditional topic for research. His sense of the importance of political geography and local history guided me through the thicket of unfamiliar names and dates at this early stage, and his careful reading of the first draft of my dissertation saved me from many a foolish error. I wish he could have seen this more mature version of that early work.

Transforming my dissertation into what I considered a satisfactory book involved not only refining and expanding the original data on popular mobilization in Overijssel, but defining more clearly the broader regional, national, and international context of revolutionary conflict in the Dutch Republic.

Conceptually, the key was to adopt municipal revolution as a unit of comparative analysis within which it was possible to ask critical questions regarding the political activity of ordinary people – questions that did not presume a standard form of revolutionary conduct, but rather demanded a systematic explanation of the obvious variations. This, in turn, required me to specify more clearly the pace and direction of the long-range political and social transformations that help to account for the variable pattern of revolutionary conflict in the cities of Overijssel. The result, then, is a book that is more systematically comparative even though it focuses on a single city.

I am pleased to acknowledge the support and encouragement of a large number of institutions and individuals without which this book could never have been completed. At various stages, my research and writing have been financed by a Fulbright–Hays Dissertation Research Fellowship from the United States Office of Education, a summer stipend from the Research Foundation of the State University of New York, a Research Fellowship for Recent Recipients of the Ph.D. from the American Council of Learned Societies, a President's Award for Junior Faculty Development from the State University of New York at Purchase, and a Senior Research Fellowship from the Netherlands–America Fulbright Commission along with supplemental funding from the Nederlandse Organisatie voor Zuiver-Wetenschappelijk Onderzoek (ZWO). Looking back, I am impressed by the generosity of this support.

During my various sojourns in the Netherlands, my work was facilitated by the good will and cooperation of a large number of archivists and librarians. I wish in particular to acknowledge the support of the directors and staffs of the Gemeente Archief and the Atheneum Bibliotheek in Deventer, and of the Economish-Historisch Bibliotheek and the Koninklijke Academie van Wetenschappen (now the Meertens Instituut) in Amsterdam. Each of these at one time or another provided me with a pleasant working environment and offered me invaluable assistance in locating and gaining access to critical documents. The Gemeente Archief in Zwolle and the Rijksarchief in Utrecht, moreover, made special efforts to microfilm materials from other archives or libraries. I am also grateful to the municipal administrators of several smaller communities who allowed documents from their archival collections to be transferred to more convenient archive depots in Amsterdam.

Over the years, I have been blessed with an ever-expanding network of Dutch friends and colleagues. When many of them turned out on a cold winter's night in 1985 for a surprise celebration of my academic tenure, I was touched by this reminder of the warm homes, the hearty meals, and the late-night companionship, not to mention the sage advice and constructive criticism, I have always received in abundance in my ancestral homeland. Without meaning to slight the many others, I wish especially to thank Johan and Corrie Matter and Pieter and Maaike van Dijk, who have been faithful friends from the very beginning, and Rudolf Dekker and Lotte van de Pol, my collaborators at Erasmus University Rotterdam, who helped to sharpen my thinking on a broad range of historical problems.

On this side of the ocean, my mentors, colleagues, friends, and family were important in more ways than they will ever know or I can ever acknowledge. Though few had ever heard of Deventer or the Dutch Patriots, they were willing to bear with me and hear me out as I worked my way through the various stages of this project. I wish especially to thank David Bien, who first encouraged me to strike out on my own in Dutch history and to think in comparative terms; and Charles Tilly, who helped immeasurably to clarify my thinking about revolution and social change and has more than once provided a stimulating intellectual home away from home. Together Professors Bien and Tilly taught me to ask the questions that this book seeks to answer and have guided and encouraged me to the very end. One can hardly imagine a more congenial and complementary pair of intellectual mentors.

As I prepared this manuscript, I benefited from the advice and criticism of friends and relatives alike. Gail Bossenga read the middle chapters at an early stage; Bill te Brake helped me think my way through virtually every aspect of the argument and its presentation; Marjolein 't Hart and Walter Lagerwey both read the entire manuscript with great care on very short notice. At SUNY Purchase, my colleagues have graciously indulged my frequent requests for leaves of absence while my students have challenged me to communicate my ideas clearly and concisely in a non-specialized language. In Ossining, my friends on both sides of the walls of Sing Sing have consistently supported my professional life while encouraging me to invest myself in unexpected and rewarding ways in the lives of the people around me.

And among the people around me, none are so indispensable as my wife and children. Nelva has seen me through it all, knowing with uncanny precision when to encourage and when to challenge. Martin, Maria, and Nicholas have respected my professional space when necessary but have intruded just enough to keep that space to a proper minimum.

Ossining, New York
W. Ph. te Brake

Abbreviations

The following abbreviations are used in the notes. For full details of archival sources see the Bibliography.

AGN	*Algemene Geschiedenis der Nederlanden*
BMGN	*Bijdragen en Mededelingen betreffende de Geschiedenis der Nederlanden*
GA	Gemeente Archief
NNJ	*Nieuwe Nederlandsche Jaarboeken*
RAO	Rijksarchief in Overijssel
VMORG	*Verslagen en Mededelingen van de Vereeniging tot Beoefening van Overijsselsch Recht en Geschiedenis*

Outline Chronology

1528	Overijssel is incorporated by Charles V, King of Spain and Holy Roman Emperor, into the Hapsburg domain in the Netherlands.
1560s	Religious protests and the first revolts in the northern provinces; repression by the Duke of Alva.
1579	Union of Utrecht created as a defensive alliance against Philip II, King of Spain; guarantees provincial sovereignty.
1581	Act of Abjuration by which the signatories of the Union of Utrecht forswore their allegiance to Philip II.
1584	Stadhouder William I of Orange is assassinated.
1591	Deventer is "liberated" by Maurice, son of William I, and becomes a constituent part of the Dutch Republic.
1609–21	Twelve Year Truce in the war with Spain.
1630	Deventer Atheneum is established.
1648	Treaty of Munster by which Spain recognizes Dutch independence.
1650	Stadhouder William II's attempted *coup* at Amsterdam fails; following his untimely death, the office of Stadhouder is left vacant in most provinces.
1652–3	The Grand Assembly reaffirms the principle of provincial sovereignty and strengthens provincial control over the standing army.
1672	William III is appointed Stadhouder of Holland and Zeeland as French troops invade; the provinces of Utrecht, Gelderland, and Overijssel are occupied by troops allied with Louis XIV of France.
1675	Utrecht, Gelderland, and Overijssel are readmitted to the Union on the condition that they accept provincial Governmental Regulations designed by William III.
1702	Following the death of William III, the office of Stadhouder is again left vacant in most of the Dutch provinces; in Overijssel, the

	provincial Estates abolish the Governmental Regulation.
1703	In Deventer, guildsmen intervene in a factional conflict within the local oligarchy; in an "extraordinary election," they appoint a new Magistracy and Sworn Council.
1709–10	"Contracts of Correspondence" help to restore harmony within the oligarchy in Deventer.
1713	The Treaty of Utrecht ends the last of Louis XIV's wars with the Dutch Republic; the Republic begins a period of neutrality in European affairs.
1747	French troops once again invade the Republic; William IV is appointed Stadhouder in those provinces where the office had been vacant; the Governmental Regulation is reinstated in Overijssel.
1748–9	Popular protest brings political reform and strengthens the position of William IV in the provinces of Groningen, Friesland, Holland, and Zeeland.
1751	William IV dies; regency is established for his young son.
1766	At his majority, William V becomes Stadhouder of all seven Dutch provinces.
1770s	Issues of national defense and foreign policy begin to divide the Prince of Orange from the self-styled Patriots; in Overijssel, J. D. van der Capellen leads the opposition to William V.
1778	Van der Capellen is suspended from the Ridderschap of Overijssel.
1780	Britain declares war on the Dutch Republic; the Fourth English War begins to precipitate a national political crisis.
1781	The publication of *Aan het Volk van Nederland* crystalizes the political opposition to William V.
1782	In the wake of popular agitation, the Dutch Republic recognizes the United States of America; massive petition campaigns in the cities of Overijssel attack the Prince of Orange and his allies; Van der Capellen reclaims his seat in the Estates of Overijssel; the Patriots at Deventer appoint a Burgercommittee to coordinate their activities.
1783	More petitions in Overijssel keep the Orangists on the defensive; the Patriots at Deventer organize a Vrijcorps and challenge the Stadhouder's political patronage by encouraging the Sworn Council to hold a "free" election of Burgemeesters; E. H. Putman, an outspoken Orangist, is removed from the Magistracy of Deventer; the provincial Estates of Overijssel are paralyzed by the issue of *overstemming*.
1784	The Fourth English War is ended with the ratification of the Treaty of Paris; Van der Capellen dies after a lingering illness; the threat of war with Joseph II and Orangist "riots" in Holland spur the creation of *vrijcorpsen* throughout the Republic; the Dutch Republic

concludes a defensive alliance with France; the first national meeting of Vrijcorps delegates is held at Utrecht.

1785   The crisis over the issue of *overstemming* within the Estates of Overijssel is finally resolved in favor of the cities; a provincial Vrijcorps Association is created in Overijssel; the *kleine steden* of Overijssel begin to assert their "rights" *vis-à-vis* the Estates as well as the Prince; petitions in the *hoofdsteden* of Overijssel demand constitutional changes in provincial and municipal government; the Stadhouder leaves The Hague and takes up residence in Gelderland.

1786   Special commissions publish Draft Regulations for the *hoofdsteden* of Overijssel; the Patriots' first municipal revolution installs a new popularly elected government at Utrecht; Patriots are routed by William V's troops in the small cities of Elburg and Hattem in Gelderland; an Orangist Burgercommittee is organized in opposition to the Patriots' proposed constitution for Deventer; the Magistracy of Zwolle votes to halt the process of constitutional reform.

1787   *January*: Amid popular protests, the Sworn Council of Zwolle suspends the Governmental Regulation and removes Orangist Burgemeesters from office; Overijssel becomes the first revolutionary province when the majority of delegates to the provincial Estates vote to suspend the Governmental Regulation.
February: Following a large petition campaign, the Sworn Council of Deventer removes Orangists from the Magistracy, and the revolutionary regime begins to repress the Orangist Burgercommittee.
April: The Patriots engineer a *coup* and attack Orangists at Amsterdam; similar Patriot victories follow in other cities in Holland, but the Patriots do not yet control the provincial Estates of Holland.
May: the Estates of Overijssel adopt a new Governmental Regulation, appoint new provincial officials and create a special Defense Commission; a clash near Utrecht between a contingent of William V's troops and Patriot forces ends in a celebrated Patriot victory.
June: More municipal revolutions assure Patriot control of the province of Holland; Princess Wilhelmina is arrested by a Vrijcorps patrol on her way to The Hague; Deventer is reinforced by Vrijcorps volunteers in anticipation of an attack by William V's troops in Gelderland; five Orangists are killed in a clash with the Patriot Vrijcorps in Deventer.
July: The King of Prussia, Princess Wilhelmina's brother, demands an appropriate "satisfaction" from the province of Holland for his sister's "humiliation" by the Patriots' Vrijcorps; civil war seems imminent.

August: Vrijcorps Association in Overijssel makes plans for a provincial army.

September: Prussian troops invade the Republic from the east; French military aid for the Patriots' regime is not forthcoming; most cities, including Deventer, fall quickly to the invaders; Orangist crowds attack Patriots especially in Gelderland and Zeeland; the houses of leading Patriots are attacked in Deventer while the Orangists elect a new municipal government; the Stadhouder returns to The Hague.

October: Amsterdam, the last Patriot bastion, capitulates to the Prussian invaders; the Estates of Overijssel vote to reinstate the Governmental Regulation; many Patriots flee into exile in France and the Austrian Netherlands.

1788   The Prince of Orange is called on to mediate disputes between guildsmen and the Orangist Magistracy in Deventer; attacks on Patriots continue in Zeeland.

1795   French revolutionary army invades the Republic; municipal revolutions occur in many Dutch cities; William V flees into exile in England; the Batavian Republic is established.

Map 1   The Dutch Republic in the Eighteenth Century.

1
Introduction

It was the best of times, it was the worst of times, it was the age of wisdom, it was the age of foolishness, it was the epoch of belief, it was the epoch of incredulity, it was the season of Light, it was the season of Darkness, it was the spring of hope, it was the winter of despair, we had everything before us, we had nothing before us, we were all going direct to Heaven, we were all going direct the other way – in short, the period was so far like the present period, that some of its noisiest authorities insisted on its being received, for good or for evil, in the superlative degree of comparison only.

Charles Dickens, *A Tale of Two Cities*

With this single stunning sentence, Charles Dickens has introduced generations of readers to the drama of the period we today commonly call the age of the democratic revolution. In a story that plays on all the superlatives of its introduction, *A Tale of Two Cities* brings to life unforgettable characters whose passionate lives span two decades of the most dramatic history in the modern era. Though, in the final analysis, I believe Dickens's nineteenth-century lens to be a distorting one, it nevertheless emphasizes two complementary perspectives that I should like to develop in this book. In the first place, Dickens locates the central action of his book in cities, even though he recognizes and explores the essential connections between, say, peasants and *sans-culottes*. He also roots his vision of the revolutionary world of the last quarter of the eighteenth century in a comparison of the great cities of London and Paris. While the setting, the characters, and the events of the present work are not so memorable as Dickens's *Tale*, the central developments of this story are essential to the tumultuous era which has captured the imagination of devoted Dickens readers for more than a century, and the analysis of the revolutionary world of eighteenth-century Deventer can lead to a more nuanced and less dichotomous view of the ending of the old regime in Europe.

To move, however, from Paris and London to Deventer, in the small Dutch province of Overijssel, is not only to step outside the focus of Dickens's drama, but to take a giant step beyond the pale of traditional historiography. Like Dickens, historians of the revolutionary period have tended to emphasize events in major cities – Paris and London, Boston or Philadelphia, Brussels or Amsterdam. And despite the recent resurgence of interest in regional and local studies, most historians have generally stayed close to the most familiar centers of action – either within France or within the "most important" provinces of lesser polities, like Brabant, Massachusetts, or Holland. For better or worse, the revolutionary experience of peripheral communities like Deventer is largely the domain of amateur and apprentice historians writing in arcane provincial journals.

Nevertheless, most eighteenth-century Europeans lived in smaller towns and villages which experienced revolution in a distinctive way. In Deventer there emerged in the 1780s an unprecedented sort of controversy and conflict that not only undermined the legitimacy of the oligarchic old regime but promised to establish the contours of a new, more democratic political future in which government would be seen to rest on the consent of the governed. The vast majority of the people of Deventer – from dandies to day laborers, from shopkeepers to shoemakers – were involved in this essentially revolutionary process in one way or another, and though the conflict came to divide them deeply, they seemed to share the conviction that the future was theirs to shape and define. As it happened, however, outside intervention ended the conflict abruptly in 1787 – two years before the beginning of the revolution in France – and restored a semblance of the political *status quo ante*. Consequently, Deventer's revolution has been largely forgotten along with those in countless other eighteenth-century cities where the interests of more powerful outsiders seemed in the end to prevail. Thus, to focus on the revolutionary world of a small provincial town requires not simply an open mind, but a more fundamental redefinition of what is interesting and worthy of study. To that end, it is necessary to begin by clarifying our sense of some key terms and objectives: "municipal revolution," "comparative analysis," even "revolutionary" situations and outcomes.

Municipal revolution – a term that, for most historians, conjures up visions of the late spring and early summer of 1789 when, in cities and towns throughout France, common people forced their municipal governments to establish or accept revolutionary committees, thereby transforming both local and national politics. In the political vacuum created by the collapse of centralized, autocratic authority, French communes provided the ideal political space within which politics could become a revolutionary activity for ordinary people who were normally excluded from the domain of aristocratic and autocratic politics. As Lynn Hunt sums up the consequences of the municipal revolutions in 1789, "changes in local communities were essential to the creation of a new national political community; without them there would have been no national revolutions in the major centers of power."[1] In short, municipal revolution represented a distinct and critically important phase in the French Revolution.

If that is true for France, more can be said for municipal revolution in the Dutch Patriot Revolution of 1786–7. In the Dutch Republic, too, revolutionaries challenged the old regime in its urban context,[2] but in the loosely confederated Republic, municipal revolution took on a special significance. Having issued from the successful sixteenth-century revolt against centralizing Hapsburg authority, the Dutch Republic had remained fundamentally decentralized; its constitution of government guaranteed the sovereignty of each of the seven provinces (or "allies" as they usually referred to one another), and within the sovereign provinces, virtually independent cities often dominated the provincial Estates. Especially in the urban and commercial west, cities were politically dominant, but even in the more rural eastern provinces, the votes of the enfranchised cities and the land-owning nobility were generally balanced equally in the provincial estates.[3] It is not surprising, then, that in the 1780s the Dutch Patriots saw cities as central to the success of their political movement. If one could control the cities of a province, one could most often control the provincial Estates, and if one could control the Estates of the various provinces, one could finally influence foreign and defense policy (though little more) at the Estates General. In a profound sense, municipal revolution was the heart of the Patriot Revolution, the necessary precondition to political reform at the provincial and national levels.

This book is an analysis of the development and consequences of one of the Dutch Patriots' many municipal revolutions. Though it focuses on a single case, on the city of Deventer, it is nevertheless intended to be essentially a study in comparative history. This means, in the most obvious sense, that I have tried whenever possible to compare developments in Deventer to those in other eighteenth-century cities, especially the other two enfranchised cities in the province of Overijssel, Kampen and Zwolle. But more fundamentally, I have tried to answer broadly defined questions that are central to the comparative analysis of revolution, and in particular to the understanding of the so-called democratic revolutions of the late eighteenth century. As Marc Bloch described the process of comparative analysis more than 50 years ago, it is only when we have broad comparative questions in mind from the outset of research that our local histories will avoid the pitfall of ascribing truly general phenomena to peculiarly local causes.[4] Conversely, as Bloch's logic suggests, it is only through systematic comparison that we will discover what was unique in events like the American, French, or Dutch revolutions.

Now, despite the comprehensive framework proposed more than 25 years ago by R. R. Palmer and J. Godechot,[5] the comparative analysis of eighteenth-century revolutions has, in fact, not progressed very far. Palmer, in particular, lamented the fact that Europe's smaller polities do not enter more fully into our general histories, for he found their experiences to be "illuminating."[6] It is not surprising, then, that some scholars of Europe's smaller countries, like Dutch historian C. H. E. de Wit, have enthusiastically embraced comparison as a means of upgrading the significance of the smaller European revolutions:

> There is probably no event before the French Revolution as "illuminating" as the first Dutch Revolution: it confirms the thesis of *The Age of the Democratic Revolution* that the French Revolution was only one, be it by far the most important, of many Western revolutions, that these Western revolutions arose from circumstances and ideas analogous to the French, that the Dutch Revolution and counter-revolution were prototypes for the French, and that the principal outlines of the French Revolution appear in the Dutch Revolution.[7]

Still, it is clear enough from most of the work being published today that most scholars would argue, along with Albert Soboul, that differences outweigh similarities and that comparison is, therefore, meaningless if not destructive:

> To put the French Revolution on the same footing as "the revolutions in Switzerland, the Low Countries and Ireland" suggests a peculiar concept of its depth and significance, as well as of the violent changes it brought about. Such a concept of the French Revolution deprives it of all specific content – economic (anti-feudal and capitalist), social (anti-aristocratic and bourgeois) and national (one indivisible nation) – and nullifies a whole half-century of revolutionary history, from Jean Jaurès to Georges Lefebvre.[8]

The reasons for this apparent impasse are undoubtedly many and various, but one problem seems obviously to be related to the unit of analysis: comparison at the "national" level is not likely to be fruitful when the polities in the comparative pool vary as greatly in size and character as do, for example, the kingdom of France and its tiny neighbor, the city-state of Geneva. Indeed, to speak of *the* French Revolution and *the* Genevan Revolution in the same breath is simply to beg the old "apples and oranges" objection to comparative analysis. The basic assumption of this study of revolution in Deventer is that municipal revolution is a category or unit of comparative analysis more appropriate to the widely varying conflicts in revolutionary Europe. Within the north Atlantic world, municipalities represented an arena within which politics could become a public, on-going activity for people normally excluded from the charmed circle of aristocratic government; cities provided a space for the development and sustenance of a new kind of popular politics. Choosing municipal revolution as the unit of comparative analysis, it is possible to examine a common set of important comparative questions relating to: (1) the organization and composition of popular revolutionary coalitions; (2) the issues around which these coalitions were mobilized; and (3) the conditions under which these coalitions successfully challenged established regimes of whatever stripe.[9] If we follow the precept of Marc Bloch, however, the goal of this comparative analysis of municipal revolution should not simply be to make all eighteenth-century revolutions look alike, but to understand more precisely, within the context of broad similarities, the peculiarities of the Dutch, American, Swiss, or French revolutions – that is, to explain their differences.

Thus, in a profound (and, one hopes, meaningful) sense, this is intended to be not so much a local study of the Dutch Patriot Revolution as an analysis of eighteenth-century revolutionary conflict in the Dutch municipal context. While it is the complex interplay of issues and actors within the urban political space that is of special interest to me, any local study of revolutionary conflict must necessarily take into account the way in which broader constellations of power – provincial, national, and international – could variously influence the character and fate of revolutionary conflict – this in order to avoid the sort of historical nominalism to which microhistory is easily susceptible. After all, it is clear that the American Revolutionary War helped immeasurably to precipitate political crises in England, France, and the Dutch Republic, just as French and Anglo-Prussian intervention were decisive in the outcomes of the American and Dutch revolutions, respectively.

In order to accommodate this multiple interest in the local, national, and the international dimensions of the revolutionary world that enveloped the city of Deventer in the 1780s, I have found it necessary to distinguish between "situations" and "outcomes" that we might term "revolutionary."[10] In many theories of revolution, important questions regarding the extent and character of the changes produced by revolutionary conflict are settled pre-emptively, as a matter of definition. Thus, "true" revolutions are often said to produce sweeping changes in economy and society as well as politics. As obvious as this equation of revolution with fundamental change may be as an empirical observation of the so-called great revolutions, it is, nevertheless, problematic as a tool for the study of actual revolutions. It diverts our attention from the often long and painful political struggles for state power that are obviously central to revolutionary conflict while it forces us prematurely to make long-range judgments of social and economic results or outcomes. In revolutionary situations, as Dickens shows us in *A Tale of Two Cities*, real people are often involuntarily faced with serious dilemmas, and how their actual choices are related to long-range transformations is by no means obvious – it needs to be opened up to systematic and comparative analysis.

In this study, I would like to help to put politics and struggle back into the center of the eighteenth-century revolutions by regarding revolution as an essentially political process which, under varying conditions, can yield differing outcomes. Adapting the political-process model of revolution to the Dutch context,[11] I will define the Dutch revolutionary situation as the condition of multiple sovereignty that began when the Patriots first made good a part of their claims for political power over the determined and forceful opposition of the established Orangist regime in 1786; it ended when the last bastions of Patriot power surrendered to the Prussian invasion in 1787. How and why the Dutch Patriots ultimately lost this determined and increasingly violent struggle for state power and whether the revolutionary conflict produced sweeping or important changes are, thus, open questions that need to be answered on the basis of continuing research. For our purposes, it is sufficient to see the overall political process as a revolutionary conflict that is particularly interesting and worthy of closer scrutiny both because of its location – in the decentralized political context of the Dutch Republic – and because of its timing – two years before the fall of the old regime in France.

Putting all the above considerations together, I should like to suggest that this is, at bottom, a work in social history. Though there are many competing claims for the definition of the term, one that I find particularly compelling and useful suggests that the task of European social historians is to reconstruct how ordinary people lived or experienced the large structural changes, like the formation of national states and the development of capitalist economic relations, that are fundamental to the course of modern history.[12] Clearly the revolutionary struggles of the last part of the eighteenth century constitute an important link in the larger historical development of modern Europe; indeed, many countries date the beginning of their "modern" history somewhere in the critical decades between 1760 and 1815. My concern here with how ordinary people lived the revolution is, thus, part of a larger concern for how Europeans in varying political, social, and cultural contexts experienced the larger historical processes. Revolutionary conflict serves as a useful frame for this kind of social history, not only because it often lays bare developments and struggles that are not readily visible in less agitated circumstances, but also because revolutions, even when unsuccessful, accelerate and, as I will argue here, alter the direction of long-term social and cultural transformations.

Part I sets the context of Deventer's municipal revolution. Chapter 2 situates the city in the broader regional, national, and international context of eighteenth-century Europe. Though this chapter will naturally serve to introduce the reader to the generally unfamiliar structures and institutions of this provincial Dutch town, the larger goal of this discussion is to chart the pace and direction of changes in Deventer's economic, political, and cultural life since the last part of the sixteenth century – that is, to show generally how the people of Deventer had experienced the big changes of the early modern period. Chapter 3 locates Deventer's conflicts within the broader provincial, national, and international context of the age of the "democratic revolution." An essential introduction to unfamiliar events outside the focus of traditional historiography, this chapter will show how Deventer was, in the 1780s, enveloped in a world of revolution – a revolutionary world of which even this small provincial capital was a distinctive and integral part.

Part II analyzes the internal dynamics of Deventer's revolutionary conflicts. The focus of this analysis is the story of the dramatic rise and decline of the Patriots' local revolutionary coalition – a story that not only echoes many of the familiar eighteenth-century themes of popular politics and democratic ideology, but also highlights some of the peculiar features of revolutionary conflict in the Dutch Republic. Chapter 4 examines the rapid mobilization of a broad reform movement (1782–5) following upon the dramatic politicization of the local population during the Fourth English War. Chapter 5 looks more closely at the evolution of political discourse during the critical constitution-making phase of Deventer's political struggle, late 1785 to late 1786 – the period during which political harmony in the face of a common political enemy gave way to serious internal dissension. Chapter 6, then, analyzes the acute social and ideological divisions that animated Deventer's bitter political conflicts from late 1786 through the restoration of the Orangist regime in late 1787 – the critical period in which Deventer, as a virtually sovereign, self-governing city, constituted a revolutionary world unto itself. Altogether, this section of the book will show how the conflicts of the 1780s were at once the reflection and the culmination of the broad social, cultural, and political developments discussed in chapter 2.

Part III examines the limits that external circumstances – the real world of power politics, not the theoretical world of municipal sovereignty – imposed on Deventer's municipal revolution. Chapter 7 explores the various coalitions and networks that connected specific groups within the divided population of Deventer with political allies outside the city's walls, for it was the relative strength of these broader coalitions which ultimately determined the outcome of Deventer's revolution and thus limited Deventer's ability to determine its own political future. Finally, chapter 8 assesses the long-term impact and significance of Deventer's revolution in light of its immediate counter-revolutionary outcome and the more "successful" Batavian Revolution of 1795. Here I will argue that while the story of Deventer's municipal revolution can never match the drama of Dickens's *Tale*, it can be considered no less instructive of how ordinary people lived the big changes in European history, and how their revolutionary conflicts were an integral part of the revolutionary transformation of Western culture and society at the end of the eighteenth century.

NOTES

1 Lynn Hunt, "Committees and communes: Local politics and national revolution in 1789," *Comparative Studies in Society and History*, 18 (1976), p. 322.
2 The standard histories of the Dutch Patriot Crisis are H. T. Colenbrander, *De Patriottentijd. Hoofdzakelijk naar buitenlandsche bescheiden*, 3 vols ('s-Gravenhage, 1897–9), P. Geyl, *De Patriottenbeweging 1780–1787* (Amsterdam, 1947), and

C. H. E. de Wit, *De Nederlandse Revolutie van de Achttiende Eeuw* (Oirsbeek, 1974). In English, see R. R. Palmer, *The Age of the Democratic Revolution*, 2 vols (Princeton, NJ, 1959–64), vol. 1, pp. 324–40, and Simon Schama, *Patriots and Liberators, Revolution in the Netherlands, 1780–1813* (New York, 1977). For a critical review of the historiography of the Dutch revolutionary period, see E. O. G. Haitsma Mulier, "De geschiedschrijving over de Patriottentijd en de Bataafse Tijd," in *Kantelend geschiedbeeld. Nederlandse historiographie sinds 1945*, ed. W. W. Mijnhardt (Utrecht/Antwerpen, 1983).

3 On the structure of the Dutch republican state, see Robert Fruin, *Geschiedenis der Staatsinstellingen in Nederland tot den val der Republiek*, 2nd edn ('s-Gravenhage, 1922), and S. J. Fockema Andreae, *De Nederlandse staat onder de Republiek*, 2nd edn (Amsterdam, 1962).

4 Marc Bloch, "A contribution toward a comparative history of European societies," in *Land and Work in the Medieval Europe*, Torchbook edn (New York, 1969).

5 See especially Palmer, *The Age of the Democratic Revolution*, Jacques Godechot, *La grande nation, L'expansion revolutionaire de la France dans la monde 1789 – 1799*, 2 vols (Paris, 1956), and Jacques Godechot, *The Counter-Revolution. Doctrine and Action, 1789–1804* (London, 1972).

6 Palmer, *The Age of the Democratic Revolution*, p. 323.

7 De Wit, *Nederlandse Revolutie*, pp. 149–50.

8 Albert Soboul, "Preface to the English-language edition," in *The French Revolution, 1787–1799* (New York, 1975), p. 10.

9 See, for example, the unpublished papers by Wayne P. te Brake, Gail Bossenga, and Janet Polasky as well as the comment by Lynn Hunt presented to the American Historical Association in December 1982 in a session entitled "Municipal revolution in France and the Low Countries, 1785–1793."

10 I am especially indebted to the theoretical work of Charles Tilly: *From Mobilization to Revolution* (Reading, Mass., 1978), and "Revolutions and collective violence," in *Handbook of Political Science*, vol. 3, ed. F. Greenstein and N. Polsby (Reading, Mass., 1975). See also Rod Aya, "Theories of revolution reconsidered: Contrasting models of collective violence," *Theory and Society*, 8 (1979), pp. 39–99.

11 For an evaluation and critique of the political-process model, see the Introduction to Theda Skocpol, *States and Social Revolutions. A Comparative Analysis of France, Russia, and China* (Cambridge, 1979); see also, Jack A. Goldstone, "The comparative and historical study of revolutions," *Annual Review of Sociology*, 8 (1982), pp. 187–207.

12 Charles Tilly, "Retrieving European lives," in *Reliving the Past. The Worlds of Social History*, ed. Olivier Zunz (Chapel Hill, NC, 1985).

PART I

The Context of Municipal Revolution

2

Deventer under the Old Regime

When Gerhard Dumbar, Jr, Secretary of Deventer and one of its most learned citizens, set out to describe his native city as it was in the 1780s, he was apparently determined to begin on an optimistic note.[1] Dumbar was part of the European generation that was fascinated with vital statistics, and having studied the elaborate statistical tables that had been compiled for Deventer in recent years, he was impressed by what he thought was the exceptionally large percentage of people who died at an advanced age. Despite its typical Dutch dampness and its narrow streets, then, Dumbar proclaimed Deventer to be an exceptionally healthy place to live. By emphasizing its healthful qualities at the outset, Dumbar clearly hoped to alter current perceptions of Deventer as a city in decline and thus, perhaps, to halt the steady emigration of young people and even to attract new economic vitality to the city. But ironically, by calling attention to the large number of elderly folks living in Deventer, Dumbar may unwittingly have underscored the notion that Deventer was old, stodgy, and more than a bit down on its luck.

At first sight, Deventer undoubtedly looked quite stable and respectable. Indeed, it was, in the eighteenth century, a city not unlike many other provincial capitals in northwestern Europe. With a population of just over 8,000, it was hardly a metropolitan center to rival Paris, London, or Amsterdam, but to the people of Overijssel, Deventer was known as the first in rank of the three "great cities" which were situated along or near the IJssel River to the east of the Zuider Zee. Within its *Vrijheid* or immediate jurisdiction, it was largely self-governing,[2] while on a regional scale it functioned as an important marketing, administrative, and cultural center with special ties to the eastern section of the province called Twente. But like the Dutch Republic as a whole, it was relative to an even more illustrious past that Deventer was almost inevitably considered, at the end of the eighteenth century, to be a city in decline.

As Gerhard Dumbar himself described it, Deventer was a city with a rich political, cultural and economic history. And it was still replete with reminders of the glorious days of the Hanseatic League, of Geert Grote and the Brethren of the Common Life, when Deventer, in the late middle ages, had clearly earned the designation "great city." At the end of the eighteenth century, the most visible testaments to this illustrious and prosperous past were its sheltered and spacious harbor, its three great churches, all of medieval construction, and the magnificent Weighing House situated at the end of a large public square called the Brink (see plate 1).[3] All of these bore silent witness, however, to a quite distant past. By the eighteenth century Deventer's economy had been transformed by fundamental shifts in the patterns of international trade, and its reputation as an international center of renewed Catholic spirituality and learning had been decisively fractured by the exigencies of the Protestant Reformation and the Eighty Years War.

Deventer's demographic history illustrates more precisely the nature of the city's decline and the kinds of problems it faced in the eighteenth century. Although completely reliable figures are not available, it is clear that Deventer's population had declined substantially since the sixteenth century – that is, dropping while other parts of the Republic, and especially the province of Holland, were undergoing very rapid expansion.[4] On the eve of the Dutch Revolt against the Spanish, the population of Deventer is estimated to have been between 10,500 and 11,000 persons.[5] Given a population of approximately 8,200 in 1795,[6] we can estimate an absolute decline of between 20 and 25 percent in just over two centuries. In this, Deventer does not appear to have been alone, for its sister cities, Kampen and Zwolle, suffered complementary declines which combined to produce a pattern of de-urbanization for the province of Overijssel as a whole.[7] At the point of its inclusion in the Hapsburg domain in 1528, Overijssel had been among the most urban of the Netherlands provinces, with more than 40 percent of its population living in the three *hoofdsteden* (Overijssel's principal cities) according to one estimate.[8] By 1795, less than 20 percent of the province's population lived in Deventer, Kampen, and Zwolle.

The de-urbanization of Overijssel was a long and uneven process which resulted in part, at least, from the rapid growth of the eastern region of Twente from the middle of the seventeenth to the middle of the eighteenth century.[9] But for Deventer, absolute decline appears to have come quite suddenly during the early years of the revolt against Spanish hegemony.[10] Under Hapsburg rule, Deventer had been a heavily garrisoned city, the largest and most important in Overijssel, and especially between 1587 and 1591, when warfare most seriously affected the area, Deventer suffered greatly under Spanish occupation. Large numbers of people apparently fled the city to avoid the intolerable conditions caused by siege warfare, just as others had fled earlier to avoid religious persecution, and many of those who left appear not to have returned following Prince Maurice's capture of the city on behalf of the rebel cause in 1591. By

1599, we can estimate on the basis of tax records that Deventer's population had declined by as much as one-third to somewhere between 7,000 and 8,000 inhabitants.[11]

Whether Deventer's population continued to decline before it stabilized and recovered is unclear, but we do know that in the period from 1675 to 1795, for which we can make reasonable estimates, its population actually grew at a moderate rate even though, like the other cities, it failed to keep pace with the growth of Overijssel as a whole.[12] Vital statistics available for most of the period after 1755 indicate, even more precisely, that all of the city's basic demographic indices – birth, death, and marriage rates – were declining in the second half of the century.[13] Thus, when crude death rates were held high temporarily by an outbreak of smallpox in 1781 and 1782, an excess of deaths over births caused a slight natural decrease in population, but this was clearly more the exception than the rule. In fact, Dumbar's suggestion that Deventer was a relatively healthy place to live may not have been terribly wide of the mark. After all, in contrast to many pre-industrial cities which were notorious consumers of population replenished only by substantial migration from the countryside, Deventer's vital statistics seem to suggest that the city could generally sustain itself demographically.

To judge by its demographic history, then, Deventer was facing real, but not dramatic or sensational problems at the end of the eighteenth century. In any case, since the middle of the seventeenth century, the overall impression the city's demographic history projects is one of long-term stagnation or even modest growth rather than absolute decline or imminent crisis. By extension, in order to sketch more broadly the essential historical background to Deventer's political conflicts in the 1780s, we will surely have to take note of the dramatic importance of the sixteenth-century revolt against Spain which established the framework of the Dutch old regime, but within that framework we will also have to be alert to more subtle, structural shifts in the economic, cultural, and political fortunes of the city and the people who lived there.

WORK AND WELFARE

Under the relatively benign overlordship of the Bishops of Utrecht, Deventer grew during the middle ages to be an important link in the international commercial network of the Hanseatic League.[14] Located at the intersection of important overland trade between Flanders and northern Germany and river traffic along the IJssel River between the North Sea and the Rhine, Deventer's commerce benefited on the one hand from direct trade connections with Bergen in Norway, and on the other hand from the traditional preference for overland trade routes that avoided the perils of the open sea. Its commercial prosperity continued well into the sixteenth century, but by the time of the

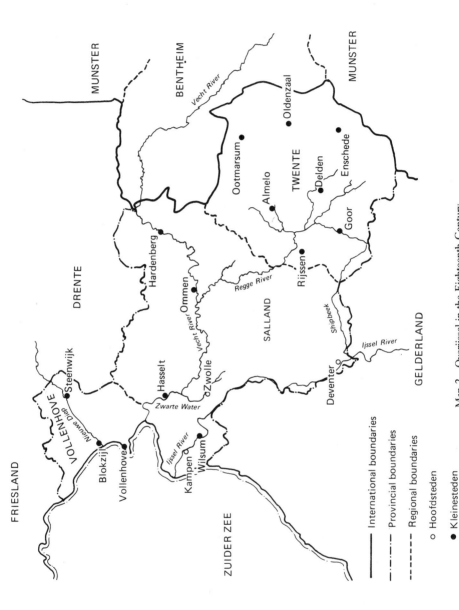

MUNSTER

BENTHEIM

MUNSTER

Vecht River

- Oldenzaal

Ootmarsum •

• Almelo

TWENTE

• Delden

Enschede •

• Goor

Hardenberg •

Ommen •

Regge River

Rijssen •

DRENTE

Vecht River

SALLAND

Shipbeek

Ijssel River

Steenwijk

Hasselt •

Zwolle

GELDERLAND

Zwarte Water

Deventer ○

VOLLENHOVE

Nieuwe Diep

Blokzijl •

Vollenhove •

Ijssel River

Kampen ○

Wilsum •

FRIESLAND

ZUIDER ZEE

International boundaries

Provincial boundaries

Regional boundaries

○ Hoofdsteden

• Kleinesteden

Map 2   Overijssel in the Eighteenth Century.

Dutch Revolt Deventer was beginning to be affected by structural shifts in the international economy which eventually transformed it from a center of international commerce into a provincial dependency within a larger urban, commercial system.[15] Though the rapid rise of the Antwerp market in the beginning of the sixteenth century surely signaled the changes that were to come, it was the phenomenal growth of Amsterdam by the beginning of the seventeenth century as the center of a vast international commercial network that finally relegated Deventer to a clearly secondary position.

Although Deventer's transformation into a secondary regional market was surely hastened by the devastations of the Eighty Years War, the decline of its international commerce was otherwise quite predictable. At the same time as competition from Amsterdam and English merchants reduced Deventer's direct connections with Scandinavia, its long-range overland trade routes to the east were made obsolete by rapid expansion of direct trade between Amsterdam and the Baltic through the Sound.[16] What is more, the gradual silting of the IJssel River made it impossible for the ships of the more modern international trade to reach Deventer's harbor. To be sure, Deventer still was an important link in the vast international network of commerce centered in Amsterdam, and thus at the core of Europe's burgeoning economy, but its function within that network was circumscribed and clearly of secondary importance. Thus, the ships that called at its harbor were only those associated with the so-called "*binnenlandsche vaart*," the domestic or regional river traffic that extended as well into Westphalia and the Rhineland.

While the growth of the Amsterdam entrepôt transformed Deventer into a provincial market town in the early years of the Dutch Republic, the process of protoindustrialization affected it no less in the last part of the seventeenth century and into the eighteenth.[17] As merchant entrepreneurs in many parts of Europe sought to expand industrial output by the multiplication of small producing units, primary industrial production often shifted to the countryside where, outside the restrictions of guilds, cheap, part-time wage labor was readily available. In the Dutch Republic, there were two major concentrations of rural protoindustrialization, both involving textile production: in the southern Generality Lands (in Brabant) there emerged a major extension of the older urban wool industry of Holland, and in eastern Overijssel (in Twente) a large-scale production of linen and various mixed fibers.[18] The obvious counterpoint to this rural protoindustrialization was, first, the relative decline and, later, the absolute decline of the woolen industry in Leiden and the linen industry in Haarlem in the course of the eighteenth century.[19]

Though we know relatively little of the original organization of the linen production of Twente, the initiative appears to have come, in part at least, from entrepreneurs from Deventer.[20] They, along with merchants from the city of Amersfoort in the province of Utrecht, began putting out looms and materials to spinners and weavers in the impoverished countryside of Twente in the last part of the seventeenth century, and the rapid expansion of this rural production in the first half of the eighteenth century was clearly related to the rapid growth of Twente's population in the same period.[21] What this meant specifically for Deventer is not entirely clear. Surely, Deventer's long-standing commercial ties with Twente and beyond – with the growing flax and linen production of Westphalia – were strengthened in the short run, but it seems equally certain that its own modest guild-based linen industry fled the city along with the modest amounts of merchant capital that lubricated the new rural production.[22] And in the course of the eighteenth century, the entrepreneurial organization of the linen industry may gradually have shifted to Twente as well, while the commerce with the east that was associated with the linen industry gradually shifted to Zwolle, which benefited from cheaper water transport facilities. Thus, Deventer's share of the province's commercial traffic, as measured by the collection of custom duties, declined steadily in the course of the eighteenth century.[23]

These large structural shifts in Deventer's economic environment – the growth of Amsterdam's international market and the protoindustrialization of Twente – are reflected in the occupational structure of the city at the end of the eighteenth century.[24] The census of 1795, which lists the occupations of nearly 1,600 active heads of households,[25] indicates that Deventer, like so many other small provincial towns, was especially a society of shopkeepers and skilled artisans; indeed, more than half of the heads of households practiced a rich variety of specialized crafts and plied an equally diverse range of trades. The largest artisanal sectors were construction and garment-making, each employing more than 100 heads of households. Skilled carpenters, masons, and tailors alone accounted for some 11 percent of the active work force. Leatherworking and metalworking were also major pillars of the artisanal economy, employing some 55 heads of households as shoemakers and 22 as blacksmiths. Alongside these typically old-regime crafts and manufactures, there were also a large variety of people involved in the preparation and distribution of food: millers, bakers, corn chandlers and butchers together amounted to more than 5 percent of the active heads of households.

Most of these artisans undoubtedly worked in small shops which included both masters and journeymen and in many cases combined manufacturing and retailing functions. In addition, the census designates a large number of heads of households (11 percent) quite simply as *koopman* or merchant. Though the census-takers did not, for the most part, distinguish between wholesale and retail merchants, we can assume that many of these *koopmannen* worked as retail shopkeepers, like grocers, who were oriented to the local market. In one district where the census-taker did distinguish between shopkeepers (*winkeliers*) and other merchants, more than one-third of the total were shopkeepers. Extrapolating from this relatively conservative estimate, we could conclude that approximately one-third of all active heads of households were integrated into this typically old-regime world of petty-bourgeois retail commerce, secondary manufacturing, and construction.

Like its "home town" neighbors across the eastern border in the politically fragmented areas of western Germany,[26] Deventer's public life had for centuries been characterized by a variety of exclusive, corporative organizations. Especially prominent among these institutions were the guilds of artisans, tradesmen, and merchants. In an early eighteenth-century description of Deventer, Gerhard Dumbar, Sr (like his son, a distinguished Secretary of the City) listed some 27 guilds that regulated most aspects of Deventer's traditional artisanal production and commerce.[27] Many were of ancient origin, the first having been chartered in 1282, but one-third of them had been chartered in the course of the seventeenth century. Although we do not know much about the internal characteristics of Deventer's guilds in particular, the general characteristics of old-regime guilds are familiar enough.[28] Through their privileged monopolies, guilds regulated the quality and flow of goods and services as well as the supply of labor in their delimited sectors of the municipal economy, and they offered their exclusive memberships economic protection and a range of social services including pensions for the aged, the sick, and the widows of guild members. Some of the more prominent guilds – like the large *Slyters* (retail merchants) *Gilde* or the *Vier Gekroonde Gilde*, which combined the various construction trades[29] – had diverse memberships and thus had to protect a variety of economic interests. But others were clearly more homogenous, like the bakers', shoemakers', blacksmiths', and tailors' guilds.

The traditional civic and social prominence of this petty-bourgeois complex of guild-based artisans and shopkeepers was symbolized by their ancient and beautiful Gildehuis adjacent to the Weighing House on the Brink (see plate 2). Undoubtedly many people, and not just the artisans and tradesmen themselves, considered these people to be the *"burgerlijke"* backbone of an essentially stable municipality. At the same time, it is precisely in the prominence of this petty-bourgeois world that we see the residual effects of Deventer's altered position in the wider structures of the changing European economy; it is a very circumscribed economic world of small-scale trade and traditional manufacture oriented primarily to the local market. This is, of course, precisely the stodgy image of an unchanging or declining provincial town which Gerhard Dumbar, Jr, apparently wished to break away from when he emphasized Deventer's healthful and dynamic qualities in the 1780s, but there are also signs of renewal and change to be seen in the profile of Deventer's working population at the end of the eighteenth century.

In the first place, even within the traditional guild-regulated economy not everyone was oriented simply to the local market. The continued existence of small, specialized merchant guilds, like the silk merchants' (*Zijdekramers*), the wine merchants' (*Wijnverlaters*) and the woolen merchants' (*Wantsnyders*) guilds, testifies to the fact that long-distance and wholesale trade continued to be part of Deventer's role as a provincial town. In addition, the census of 1795 indicates a number of apparently new trades and manufactures which had grown up within Deventer along the protoindustrial model – that is through the multiplication of small shops outside the monopolistic control of guilds.[30] These newer manufactures or *fabrieken* included eight chair-making shops, eight basket-making shops, five tanneries, and three chamois-dressing shops, which employed on average between three and five people per shop. In addition, there were two stocking-knitting and three wool-spinning shops which appear to have employed higher concentrations of workers (ten and 21 per shop, respectively). All of these shops were developed by independent entrepreneurs who did not seek to protect their interests through the formation of guild monopolies and who depended, in turn, on unorganized wage labor, whether skilled or unskilled. Altogether they employed some 171 heads of households and thus represent a significant liberalization of the local manufacturing economy and labor market.

The knitting and spinning manufactures are especially indicative of the kind of transformation that was occurring within Deventer. The venerable linen weavers' guild, a remnant of the old guild-based textile production of the late middle ages, was by the end of the eighteenth century largely devoid of members after the wholesale shift of linen production to Twente, and the census indicates that there were only a few weavers (not likely linen weavers) left in the city.[31] But textile production had clearly not disappeared from the city; in fact, textile manufacture of all sorts still employed more than 100 heads of households, some 7.4 percent of the active working population. Now, by contrast, production had shifted to protoindustrial shops employing largely female, unskilled wage labor. If we add to the textile workers and those employed in the other *fabrieken* the large numbers of unspecialized *arbeiders* and day laborers (146 in all) listed in the occupational census, we can see that a significant and apparently growing segment of Deventer's working population lived outside the petty-bourgeois world of guild-based artisans and shopkeepers. This segment of the economy was characterized by a free labor market and was dependent on the competitiveness of entrepreneurs in markets that transcended the local community and its immediate hinterland.

Rounding out our view of the working population of Deventer we must also note a significant number of people who clearly do not fit into either the artisanal or the protoindustrial economy. In the first place, nearly 8 percent of the heads of households were involved in agriculture and fishing, much of which undoubtedly aimed at the provisioning of the city. Secondly, as a cultural and administrative center, Deventer also had a large number of households headed by liberal professionals, governmental and religious officials, and their supporting staffs. Finally, of course, there were certainly a number of *koopmannen* as well as boatmen and innkeepers who served or had close contact with both the artisanal and the protoindustrial segments of the local economy.

Indeed, there may be a danger in emphasizing such distinctions which were not readily perceived or acknowledged by well-informed contemporary observers like Gerhard Dumbar. But as we shall see in part II, the issues that arose during the course of the political conflicts of the 1780s tended, in the end, to lay bare precisely this kind of cleavage in Deventer's society.

The traditional historiography of the Dutch Republic in the eighteenth century has, of course, emphasized a quite different set of problems regarding Dutch economic development than we have been concerned with here.[32] Indeed, historians were for generations obsessed with the question of eighteenth-century economic decline, in large measure, perhaps, because contemporary writers were so concerned with the issue.[33] Much of the recent literature insists, however, that the Dutch economy declined, not in an absolute sense, but only relative to the rapid economic and demographic growth of both England and France in the course of the eighteenth century. Whatever loss of commercial functions the Dutch may have suffered was compensated for by the expansion of financial services and the resurgence of commercial agriculture on the strength of rising prices; at the same time, the obvious decline of industrial cities like Leiden and Haarlem was balanced by the growth of rural industries in the south and the east. The net result was that the Dutch Republic remained one of the most economically advanced and prosperous polities in Europe.

What does this suggest for our overall assessment of Deventer's economic performance in the eighteenth century? Certainly the qualitative shifts we have observed here had transformed Deventer into a very different, though not necessarily poorer or more backward, community than it had been before the Dutch Revolt. If, for example, we were to measure the overall welfare of the city by its assessed taxable wealth, we could point to some modest, though not spectacular, gains in the course of the eighteenth century.[34] Within those parameters, however, the economic transformation of Deventer may have resulted in a redistribution of the city's total wealth, for at the end of the eighteenth century, Deventer appears to have been characterized by greater extremes of wealth and poverty that it had known before. Thus, according to tax registers drawn up in 1767, more than one-third (37 percent) of all persons over 17 years of age were exempted from paying the minimal *hoofdgeld* (head tax), and fully 10 percent of the population was receiving some form of help from the municipal charities.[35] On the other side of the coin, the occupational census describes a considerable number of heads of households (4.8 percent of all households) as *rentenieren* – that is, retired or inactive persons living on the income from their investments. To be sure, not all of these were truly wealthy people, but there was nevertheless a broad *rentier* class from which Deventer derived its cultural and political elite. This growing cleavage between wealth and poverty by no means constituted a social crisis, the sheer dimensions of which could be said to account for the political discontent that emerged in the last quarter of the century, but this trend was obvious enough that many concerned and politically active people were convinced that *something* needed to be done to restore the city's economic fortunes.[36]

FROM REFORMATION TO ENLIGHTENMENT

If international commerce under the auspices of the Hanseatic League brought prosperity to Deventer, it was equally through its cultural leadership that Deventer gained its international renown.[37] Indeed, from the fourteenth century onward, it came to be known as one of the primary centers of religious and educational renewal in northern Europe. Under the leadership of Geert Groote, the Brethren of the Common Life not only transformed the experience of those who committed their lives wholly to religious devotion, but they were also at the forefront in the creation of new institutions of learning that reached beyond the walls of traditional cloisters.[38] In the course of the fifteenth century, moreover, Deventer's Latin School became one of the most important centers of humanist education in the Low Countries. Thus, it was also natural that Deventer quickly emerged as the most important center for the publication of printed books in the northern Netherlands – its two large publishers accounted for 40 percent of the book production in the northern Netherlands in the fifteenth century. Only in the course of the sixteenth century would Antwerp surpass Deventer in the new book trade.[39]

Renowned for its role in the late-medieval renewal of Catholic spirituality and education, Deventer was, by contrast, on the periphery of the Protestant Reformation. Relatively calm during the religious upheavals of the 1560s, Deventer was slow to join the ranks of Dutch cities committed to the Dutch Revolt in later decades, and was brought fully into the life of the Dutch Republic only after the conquest of Prince Maurice in 1591.[40] By this time, of course, the devastations of the war had done much to transform Deventer's place in not only the economic, but equally the larger cultural development of Europe. This is not to say that Deventer simply became a provincial backwater; rather, in losing its position of international pre-eminence, Deventer remained an important provincial and regional center for higher education and cultural renewal.

The general changes in Deventer's cultural environment between the sixteenth and eighteenth centuries are quite clear even though their precise impact on Deventer is not always immediately evident. To begin with, the "protestant-ization" of Deventer was the most obvious consequence of the Dutch Revolt.[41] We know, of course, that the Dutch Republic, while officially Protestant in that eventually all office holders were required to be members of the Reformed Church, remained a religiously pluralistic society, and in eastern Overijssel, in Twente, many communities remained predominantly Roman Catholic throughout the history of the Republic.[42] In Deventer, by contrast, the Reformed Church clearly gained a majority position; thus, when a national census first recorded religious adherence in 1811, approximately 75 percent of the population of Deventer were found to be Reformed, 20 percent were Catholic, while small numbers of Lutherans, Mennonites and Jews made up the remaining 5 percent.[43] The consequences of this change for a city which had made its reputation as a center of renewed Catholic spirituality and had served as an important administrative center for the Catholic Church are certainly not to be underestimated.

Still, the exigencies of war and the victory of Protestantism cannot alone be said to account for Deventer's transformation as a cultural center. With the emergence of Leiden University, founded in 1575 as an international center for humanist scholarship and Calvinist education, we can see the beginning of a broader structural shift in cultural leadership toward the increasingly more urban and commercial west. Further, during the seventeenth century, the province of Holland especially served as a haven for intellectual refugees, both Catholic and Protestant, from notably less tolerant parts of Europe. This, combined with the enormous growth of publishing, especially of classical Latin and oriental texts, served to make Holland into the premier intellectual emporium of Europe. This did not spell an immediate decline for Deventer as a cultural center; rather, as the history of the Deventer Atheneum suggests, Deventer experienced a simultaneous, albeit secondary, growth during the same period.[44]

Though no other Dutch city was in a better position at the beginning of the sixteenth century to become the site of a new university, it was not until 1630 that an Atheneum or "Illustre School" was actually created in Deventer. In the radically transformed world of the early seventeenth century – a world in which relatively fewer Dutch students were inclined to study abroad – the Deventer Atheneum was able to attract not only illustrious faculty, but a geographically diverse student body. Unlike similar schools in Harderwijk (Gelderland) and Utrecht, however, Deventer's Atheneum was, for apparently political reasons, never granted the privilege of conferring the doctoral degree, and consequently by the 1680s it had entered into a long period of stagnation extending throughout the eighteenth century. Having missed its chance to become a university, the Atheneum settled into a position of only local and regional significance for studies in theology – in which field an advanced degree was not required – and the liberal arts – as a preliminary to advanced work in medicine and law. Consequently, the social and political elite of Overijssel received their advanced degrees outside the province, demonstrating on the whole a clear preference for Leiden, though many still began their preliminary studies – the "propadeuse" following completion of the Latin School – close to home in Deventer.

At the end of the seventeenth century, the Dutch Republic received its last major wave of intellectual refugees, this time Protestants fleeing France as a result of Louis XIV's revocation of the Edict of Nantes. Unlike earlier migrants especially from the southern Netherlands, the French Huguenot intellectuals never adapted themselves fully to their new homeland; rather, as W. W. Mijnhardt has suggested, "They used the Republic above all as a sanctuary, as an employer or as a printshop," from which they hoped to lay the foundations of political and religious reform which would allow an eventual return to France.[45] Through an extended network of Huguenot refugees, the Dutch publishing industry was able to extend its influence in the European market, publishing French-language journals and distributing the ideas of the early Enlightenment. The French-oriented debates on political reform and religious tolerance spoke little to Dutch intellectuals, however; instead, a more moderate blend of Newtonian science (opposed to deism) and Cartesian philosophy was gradually grafted onto the traditional Calvinist and humanist studies within the Dutch educational system in the early part of the eighteenth century.

In the most recent studies, the Dutch Enlightenment – no longer seen simply as a hollow reflection of French, Scottish or German models – is generally portrayed as having developed a distinctively nationalist and largely introspective character in the course of the eighteenth century.[46] Many Dutch authors consciously turned their backs on the French (international) market, writing instead in Dutch about Dutch problems. In particular, an increasingly popular genre of Dutch "spectatorial" journals began to articulate to a broad reading public both a sense of anxiety about the perceived decline of the Dutch Republic and an Enlightened optimism about its prospects for moral regeneration.[47] Though this literature was largely a-political, it nevertheless served – especially in its critique of French manners as a perversion of traditional Dutch virtue – to undermine the legitimacy of the social and political elite. At the same time, the Enlightenment concern for moral improvement intensified the long-standing Calvinist concern for the reform of popular culture and the eradication of superstition, now considered not only a religious but a social disease to be cured by an all-out educational offensive.[48]

As interesting for our purposes as the specific intellectual content of the Dutch Enlightenment, is its organization, its social stratification and its pattern of dissemination. The creation of cultural societies was characteristic of the Enlightenment nearly everywhere, but in the Dutch Republic it took several distinctive forms.[49] First, there were the semi-official learned societies of Holland and Zeeland which were chartered for the expressed purpose of promoting useful knowledge, broadly defined; these recruited their members nationally and were closely identified with the social and political elite. Here we especially encounter the careful blending of Calvinist, humanist, and moderate Enlightenment ideas that generally characterized the traditional Latin culture of the learned. Secondly, there appeared a whole host of voluntary associations which were generally local in character: masonic lodges, literary societies, and reading associations. Standing outside the ranks of the learned elite, the members of the reading associations especially included many self-taught men and disproportionately large numbers of religious dissenters.[50] Here we find a special concern for general moral education and a critique of the Latin humanist scholarship still cherished by the learned societies. Finally, at the end of the century, there was a vast explosion of improving societies, most notably the so-called Economic Branch (*Economische Tak*), which was created in 1777 as a subsidiary of the Holland Society of Sciences to offer practical solutions to the problems associated with economic decline. Within the first year, 55 local departments of this organization came to include some 3,000 members from both the learned elite and the broadly literate middle class.[51]

It is striking that in all of these cases, the initiative in creating societies to promote enlightenment and national renewal seems to have come first from the urban and commercial west. Indeed, if we could draw a composite map reflecting the growth and spread of these cultural associations, Deventer and the other ancient cities on or near the IJssel River – Kampen, Zwolle, and Zutphen – would undoubtedly look like the last cultural outposts on an eastern frontier of superstition, ignorance, and backwardness. This is, in fact, the image that appears from Jeremy Popkin's analysis of Dutch print culture on the eve of the Dutch Revolution.[52] A polity characterized by some of Europe's highest levels of literacy, the Dutch Republic was well served by a large number of book publishers/sellers, some 295 in all according to a list compiled in 1778. Of these, however, all but 68 were located in Holland. In Overijssel, by contrast, only Deventer, Kampen, and Zwolle, all located on the western edge of the province, had booksellers who made the national list.

But such a Hollando-centric view is far from complete. In its provincial and regional context, Deventer was, of course, much more than an isolated outpost for the "civilizing" offensive of the Enlightenment or a buffer on the frontiers of ignorance and superstition. In the first place, one hardly needs to note, the institutions and ideas that we associate with the Enlightenment did not operate in a cultural vacuum, notwithstanding the claims of its reformers. In Overijssel, a Calvinist Christian sociability, which we still understand very little, had grown in uneasy coexistence with dissenting and especially Catholic traditions. And in the course of the eighteenth century, while many learned Calvinist pastors were being introduced to the moderate blend of humanist and enlightened ideas that characterized the educational establishment, a thrust towards pietism can be said to have renewed and extended the spirituality of the laity.[53] In its most articulated forms, the new pietism took on an institutional dimension in the formation of conventicles – small groups of Christians leading a shadowy, independent existence within the larger Calvinist churches. Unfortunately, we are in no position to draw a composite map of the growth and influence of pietism and Christian renewal, but it is clear that pietists were no less intent on cultural and social transformation than the learned reformers of the Enlightenment.[54]

Viewed from this perspective, then, Deventer's position as a cultural center looks a good deal less one-sided. A city like Deventer represented a kind of cultural crossroads – a place where one can see the interaction of elite and popular culture in all of their manifestations.[55] Just as its working population combined elements of both artisanal and protoindustrial production, so also its cultural landscape included enlightened and tolerant professors and preachers as well as pietistic Calvinists who feared secular and papist influences. In this complex cultural environment, literacy and printing are not simply to be seen as the tools of one cultural form, but as resources that were available to the enlightened and the pious alike. At the same time, it is important to realize that neither the rhetoric of enlightenment nor the language of piety was a political weapon exclusively available to one side or the other in a revolutionary situation. Rather, as we shall see, appeals for popular mobilization and concerted political action employed, on both sides, the vocabulary of Christian piety, while the learned discussions of constitutional reform – either for or against – were invariably expressed in the language of enlightenment. Here it is important to note that it was precisely in a regional cultural center like Deventer that neither enlightened nor pietistic culture was clearly dominant. Yet both strengthened the perception that *something* had to be done about the problem of moral decline.

URBAN POLITICS AND DUTCH STATE FORMATION

Though eighteenth-century Deventer seemed, in economic and cultural terms, only a shallow reflection of its medieval original, it remained a proud city. This civic pride was expressed especially in the elaborate ceremonial – by Dumbar's reckoning, the most elaborate in the entire Republic – which surrounded the annual election (*keur*) of Deventer's Burgemeesters and Sworn Councilors on February 22 (St Petri ad Cathedrum).[56] Each year in the so-called *Petrikeur*, the city's 16 Burgemeesters, its ruling magistrates who were also called *schepenen* and *raden*, were chosen by the Sworn Council (*Gezworen Gemeente*), a broad 48-member municipal council whose members were appointed for life; at the same time, the Sworn Council filled any vacancies which may have occurred in its own number by co-optation. Any Burger, that is, anyone who had either inherited or purchased the city's *burgerrechten*, was eligible for appointment to these prestigious offices, but the city's charter enjoined the electors to choose only the wisest, most virtuous, and wealthiest persons, and it was these special characteristics – what set the regents apart from the other Burgers and residents of Deventer – that the election ceremonial tended to emphasize.

For three full days beginning on February 20, the city's political elite occupied center stage. After the regents – the magistrates and councilors collectively – listened to the formal reading of the city's charter, they deliberately inspected each of the city's eight districts which, of course, involved much parading through the streets. Election day itself began with a solemn worship service in the Grote Kerk after which the regents passed in silent procession across the square to the Stadhuis (city hall) to begin the election itself. From among the 48 members of the Sworn Council, 12 were eliminated by lot in order to prevent intrigue, and having sworn the election oath before the Burgemeesters, the remaining Councilors (the electors) proceeded to the secret election. After the results were read from the steps of the Stadhuis, all the city's regents attended a large public reception and finally a private banquet at the expense of the newly elected officers. Throughout, the regents wore long black robes, and according to Burgemeester Jordens, who meticulously recorded the informal laws governing the whole process in the 1750s, any deviation from the traditional script, even in the setting of the banquet tables, could precipitate serious controversies.

The evident solemnity and inflexibility of Deventer's election ceremonial might easily suggest that the politics of the city were an unchanging holdover from the medieval past, but there were significant ways in which the city's politics had changed in the previous two centuries. Just as changes in its economic and cultural environment had altered Deventer's place in the world, so also had structural shifts in its political environment transformed the meaning and significance of Deventer's chartered independence as symbolized in the election rituals. In politics, too, Deventer had become peripheral, subject in new ways to outside influence and direction, but within its regional context, Deventer was still a central place, a city where politics could be meaningful and potent activity.

In the sixteenth century, the Revolt against Spain had set the United Provinces of the northern Netherlands on a path of political development that was decisively different from the monarchical centralization which we usually associate with early modern Europe.[57] Though resistance to Hapsburg centralization and religious intolerance was initially strongest in the southern provinces, long years of struggle and warfare resulted finally in the independence of only the northern provinces which were united in a loose confederation under the Union of Utrecht. Having formally abjured their allegiance to Philip II of Spain in 1581, the leaders of the Revolt at first tried to find a new "sovereign" who would accept the limitations they wished to impose on his authority, but by the turn of the century, they had clearly embarked on a pattern of republican state formation in which provincial "particularism" was fostered as the *sine qua non* of independence and self-government. Consequently, by the 1650s, Johan de Witt, the great Pensionary of the province of Holland, could with reasonable accuracy describe the Dutch Republic as, at bottom, a confederation of republics rather than a single sovereign state.[58]

For the province of Overijssel, the creation of institutions of self-government involved important political changes.[59] Prior to its inclusion in the Hapsburg domain in 1528, Overijssel had been subject to the Bishopric of Utrecht, under whose benign and unintrusive policies the province, or more accurately, its constituent parts – the three *hoofdsteden* plus three very diverse rural districts – enjoyed a great deal of autonomy. Under Hapsburg rule, the provincial Estates took on an increasingly important role as the provincial bargaining agent *vis-à-vis* a much more aggressive *Landsheer* or sovereign. Still, the Estates did not develop an institutional identity because government, in the sense of day-to-day responsibility for and administration of public affairs, remained essentially local. In contrast, then, to the counties of Holland and Zeeland, which were among the most sophisticated of the mini-states of northwestern Europe and the driving force of the war of independence, the province of Overijssel was ill-equipped to take on the role of "sovereign" and was further paralyzed by the almost continual warfare that kept major portions of the province under Spanish occupation from 1580 to 1597. But, as the reconquest of Prince Maurice proceeded, the Council of State, under the leadership of Johan van Oldenbarnevelt, carefully nurtured political and institutional reforms which would make provincial self-government possible (see figure 2.1).

The most important changes, which were in place by 1605, included, first of all, the creation of an Executive Committee of the Estates – the *Gedeputeerde Staaten*. The Executive Committee, which assumed important administrative and judicial functions when the Landdag (the formal meeting of the Estates) was not in session, consisted of delegates from the three *hoofdsteden* as well as the chief regional administrators – the *drosten* of Vollenhove, Salland, and Twente. At the insistence of the Council of State, the Estates also imposed a uniform system of taxation to insure that the province would be able to meet its financial obligations to the Generality. Though the cities had traditionally opposed tax reform as an instrument of Hapsburg tyranny, they could now accept it as a necessary instrument of self-government that was subject to their own control. Finally, the makers of this new Dutch state fashioned a uniform judicial and administrative system for the countryside in which district-level *schouten* or *richters* (sheriffs) and regional *drosten* were appointed by and under the control of the Estates and its Executive Committee. Thus, the province of Overijssel was able to take its place as a sovereign and self-governing "republic" under the Union of Utrecht, of equal constitutional weight with Holland even though it contributed just 3.5 percent of the Generality budget.[60]

The creation and adaptation of institutions of provincial self-government was an important step, but this in itself could not insure political stability in the Dutch Republic. At the provincial level, especially, internal disputes could occasionally paralyze the political process and thereby threaten the security of the whole Union. Perhaps anticipating such problems, the Union of Utrecht provided for voluntary mediation of internal disputes by the other provinces, but in order to insure the long-term stability of the Republic, the individual provinces had to work out their own procedures to arrive at consensus within

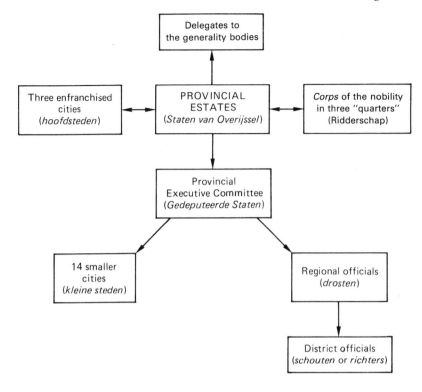

Figure 2.1 Provincial government in Overijssel.

the provincial estates.[61] In Overijssel, this entailed the development of a new political style and the acceptance of a new balance of power.

Prior to independence, the cities of Overijssel had completely dominated the provincial Estates. After meeting in a separate caucus prior to the Landdag, the cities were usually able to enforce their "majority" decisions within the Estates with the support of just one nobleman.[62] Following independence, however, the cities' unity in opposition to outside authority quickly disappeared; now they often found themselves individually unwilling to submit to "majority" decisions of which they did not approve. Thus, Deventer, resisting the combined pressures of Kampen, Zwolle and the majority of the Ridderschap (the *corps* of the provincial nobility), brought the province to the brink of civil war before the Generality was asked to mediate an internal dispute involving municipal autonomy in 1657.[63] In less extreme cases, or perhaps in order to avoid such extremities, the Estates of Overijssel came routinely to depend on a permanent Commission on Finances which, like the Executive, was composed of equal numbers of noblemen and municipal magistrates. Typically, when controversial issues came before the Landdag, they were immediately referred to the Commission on Finances, or occasionally to a special *ad hoc* commission; if compromises and consensus could not be found, then the issues simply died in committee.[64] The remarkable result of this consensual political style was that in approximately two centuries of self-government, the question of what might constitute a valid decision by majority vote (*overstemming*) within the newly sovereign Estates of Overijssel was never resolved – at least not until the Patriots forced the issue in the 1780s.[65]

Altogether then, republican independence shifted the balance of power within Overijssel, giving the nobility equal weight with the *hoofdsteden* in the provincial Estates, which under the new regime took on the added importance of sovereign authority.[66] At the same time, the Revolt transformed Deventer's position from one of municipal isolation – in which the proud trading city had kept the outside political world at arm's length – to one of political responsibility – in which it bore co-responsibility with the other constituents of the provincial Estates not only for the administration of the countryside and the smaller towns, but also for the health and welfare of the Generality as a whole. This kind of transformation entailed, of course, both opportunities and costs – opportunities in the sense that local leaders could rise to national prominence and influence in national politics; costs in the sense that local politics could be subject to outside influence.

The revolt against Spain also brought important changes in municipal politics.[67] Prior to the Dutch Revolt, Deventer's municipal affairs were controlled by a large Sworn Council (*Gezworen Gemeente*), which included 12 representatives from each of the city's eight districts, and 24 Magistrates (*Schepenen en Raden*, collectively known as Burgemeesters), who were, in rotation, the city's chief executive and judicial officers; together, the two groups legislated for the city. The members of the Sworn Council normally sat for life, while the Magistrates were elected annually for one-year terms by the Council. From the 1560s onward, however, the composition of the municipal administration began to be influenced by the varying fortunes of rebels and loyalists in the larger political struggles of the period, and by the 1580s the lines of demarcation had begun to harden. At first, Calvinists were promoted to municipal office while Catholics loyal to Spain were removed from office at the insistence of rebel leaders, but in 1587, all Calvinists were replaced by committed Catholics when the Spanish occupied the city. Then, when Prince Maurice finally lifted the Spanish occupation in 1591, an entirely new Calvinist administration was put in place, but because of an apparent shortage of qualified Calvinists, Maurice reduced the membership of the Council from 96 to 32 and the number of Magistrates from 24 to 16.

The most immediate effect of the rebel's conquest of Deventer, then, was a narrowing of the political community. Though the membership of the Council was later increased to 48, the total number of places in these exclusive political *corps* was reduced by nearly 50 percent, while Catholics were excluded from office altogether. What is more, whatever popular influence there may have been previously in the selection of the Council members was eliminated by a closed system of co-optive election. Thus, the foundations were laid in Deventer, too, for the oligarchical form of municipal government that was so characteristic of the Dutch Republic. At first there were relatively large numbers of people who served relatively short terms as Magistrates and Councilors, but gradually the range of new names narrowed as extensive family networks emerged at the center of municipal affairs.[68] By the eighteenth century, municipal politics in Deventer, as in enfranchised cities throughout the Republic, had clearly come to be dominated by a fairly narrow *rentier* elite.[69] Election to the Sworn Council made one a true "regent," a member of the elite for whom politics was an exclusive, privileged activity, but this status might be combined with a variety of economic activities or livelihoods. For those who advanced within the ranks of the elite to become a Magistrate, politics usually became a career which presupposed independent wealth and/or lucrative appointments.[70] Though new family names continued to appear in the Magistracy as old families died out, access to political power in this more restrictive sense followed clear patterns: social prominence within the community, a doctorate in law, intermarriage with established patrician families, and an apprenticeship on the Sworn Council seemed to be the most important prerequisites for political advancement.[71]

In the absence of centralized authority, decision-making on the national scale – within the Union – became an exceedingly complex process in which consensus or unanimity among the seven sovereign provinces was required on all important matters involving the Generality – taxation, the declaration of war, and the ratification of peace treaties. In practice, informal influence and persuasion were critical in the development of national policy, and leadership in foreign affairs fell to two political appointees who lacked direct decision-making authority, but led the Republic by virtue of their ability to influence others: the Council Pensionaries of Holland and the Stadhouders.[72] Holland, clearly the most populous and prosperous province, contributed 58 percent of the Generality budget, and its Pensionaries or Advocates, who served as provincial spokesmen at the Estates General, represented "Holland's interest" in the conduct of foreign affairs.[73] The Stadhouders (originally provincial governors appointed by the *Landsheer*) were appointed by the provinces severally and had no formal authority in the Estates General of the Union, but building on the military leadership provided by William the Silent and Maurice during the Revolt, the Stadhouder/Princes of Orange – as Captains-General and Admirals-General of the Union – were traditionally the most effective counter-balance to Holland's hegemony in the conduct of foreign affairs.[74]

The ebb and flow of the Stadhouders' power and influence after the

conclusion of peace with Spain in 1648 was clearly related to broader developments in international affairs and to the Republic's fortunes in land warfare in
particular. In 1650, William II's aborted attempt to force the submission of
Amsterdam in a dispute over military demobilization after the Eighty Years War
precipitated the first of two extended periods in which the position of Stadhouder was left vacant in most of the Dutch provinces. In the Grand Assembly
of 1652, moreover, the so-called States Party also definitively reaffirmed the
principle of provincial sovereignty, strengthened the direct control of individual
provinces over troops in their pay, and attempted to separate permanently the
political and military offices of the Princes of Orange.[75] During the 1650s and
1660s, the Republic proved capable of mobilizing effectively for naval warfare
under the able leadership of Pensionary Johan de Witt, but in 1672, under
intense pressure from land invasions by Louis XIV and his allies in Germany
and on the strength of widespread popular protest in the cities of Holland,
William III was appointed to the vacant position of Stadhouder of Holland. For
the first time, the position was made hereditary.[76]

Overijssel followed Holland's lead in 1650 and left the position of Stadhouder vacant, but in 1672 factional fights within the urban oligarchies led to
the province's quick capitulation to the forces of the Bishop of Munster which,
in alliance with Louis XIV, had invaded Overijssel, Gelderland, and Utrecht.
After two years of foreign occupation, Overijssel was readmitted to the Union in
1675 only on the condition that it, along with Utrecht and Gelderland, accept a
Governmental Regulation (*Regeerings Reglement*) designed by William III to
reduce the factionalism of the political elites.[77] Though the new Regulation did
not alter the institutions of government or compromise the principle of provincial sovereignty, it did alter the structure of power in that it gave the Stadhouder
the right both to approve all municipal elections and to appoint from double
lists of nominations the province's most important officials – the *drosten* and
schouten, the members of the provincial Executive, the delegates to the Estates
General, and so on.[78] By giving the Prince of Orange control over access to
municipal office and to political preferment more generally, the Regulation
effectively made him the patron of the regent elite in Overijssel.

William III's use and abuse of the patronage powers given him in the land
provinces in 1675 produced a political reaction to his sudden death (without
heir) in 1702. In the Estates of Overijssel, the Governmental Regulation was
abolished and the office of Stadhouder was again left vacant, while in Deventer,
as in several cities in Gelderland, factional struggles within the elite opened up
the opportunity for direct popular intervention.[79] In an "extraordinary" election
in 1703, the guild leaders of Deventer, who were normally excluded from the
regent elite, elected the new Magistracy and even appointed some of their own
number to the Sworn Council. The influence of the guilds did not last long,
however, as the traditional elite closed ranks and signed "contracts of correspondence" to eliminate internecine struggles over local patronage.[80] Thus, the

older patterns and methods of consensual decision-making once again came to characterize Overijssel politics in the first half of the eighteenth century.

In 1747, when French troops yet again attacked the Republic toward the end of the War of the Austrian Succession, another wave of popular protest, especially in Groningen, Friesland, and the cities of Holland, swept William IV, from the Frisian branch of the House of Orange, into an unprecedented position of strength as the first hereditary Stadhouder in all seven provinces.[81] On the strength of popular demands for political reform, William also created new Governmental Regulations for the provinces of Groningen and Friesland and executed a series of *"wetsverzettingen"* – extraordinary elections of munici-pal governments – and tax reforms in Holland. In Overijssel, by contrast, the revival of the office of Stadhouder was almost uneventful. In the absence of popular mobilization demanding change, the regents of Overijssel held out as long as they could but eventually accepted what seemed like the inevitable: they reinstated the Governmental Regulation of 1675 and appointed William IV hereditary Stadhouder as in Holland, but without an immediate shake-up in the oligarchy.

William IV's untimely death in 1750 and the subsequent regencies for his young son slowed the development of this new regime, but in 1766, William V finally took control of a republican regime that was thoroughly Orangist in the sense that his predecessors, William III and William IV, had designed the Governmental Regulations that were operative in five of the seven provinces and his patronage, and influence extended into the farthest reaches of the republican structure. That William V intended to develop the full potential of his patronage powers was especially evident in Overijssel. At the provincial level, he dispensed with the formality of selecting high officials from double nomination lists and began making the appointments directly. Similarly, in municipal elections, he began forwarding the names of his candidates for office *before* the formal elections whose outcome he had the authority to approve. Using indigenous "lieutenants" to represent his interests, the Stadhouder in effect divided the elite, whose social composition he did little to alter, into *"gunstelingen"* (favorites or clients), who gained preferment and prestige as long as they supported the Prince's policies, and the rest, who either never got anywhere or were punished for disloyal conduct by being demoted from important offices.

By the end of the eighteenth century, then, the long-range process of republican state formation had transformed Deventer from a virtually indepen-dent city-state to a provincial capital subject routinely to outside influence. To be sure, the solemnity and the strict formality of the annual municipal elections masked this political reality, but it is perhaps symptomatic of this transformation that local politicians like Burgemeester Jordens should meticulously record and argue over the particulars of this elaborate ritual precisely when it was begin-ning to lose its immediate political significance and the outcome of the elections was a foregone conclusion. The election ceremony continued as a poignant reminder, not only of days gone by, but also of what might once again be; for however tyrannical and arbitrary it might have seemed, the power of the Stadhouder's patronage remained indirect and limited. The essential fragility of the Orangist regime would become abundantly evident in the revolutionary conflicts of the 1780s, for by that time, nearly everyone was convinced that *something* had to be done to reform republican politics.

NOTES

1 *Tegenwoordige Staat van Overijssel*, vol. 3 (Amsterdam, 1781), pp. 200ff.
2 As a sovereign *Rijkstad* (imperial free city), Deventer enjoyed a great degree of independence even under the Republic, the most symbolic aspect of which may have been the fact that there was no judicial appeal to outside authorities; this sets it off, for example, from the cities of Holland which were subject to the provincial Hof van Holland.
3 Its distinctively medieval fortifications had been replaced following the liberation of Prince Maurice in 1591 by the most modern of defense-works. Compare plates 2 and 3 following p. 18 in Geoffrey Parker, *The Army of Flanders and the Spanish Road, 1567–1659* (Cambridge, 1972).
4 See J. A. Faber, et al., "Population changes and economic developments in the Netherlands: A historical survey," *A. A. G. Bijdragen*, 12 (1965), pp. 47–113.
5 A. C. F. Koch, "The Reformation at Deventer in 1579–80. Size and social structure of the Catholic section of the population during the Religious Peace," *Acta Historiae Neerlandica*, 6 (1973), p. 41.
6 The 1795 census returns for Deventer can be found in RAO, Staten Archief, 5347.
7 R. Reitsma, *Centrifugal and Centripetal Forces in the Early Dutch Republic. The States of Overijssel, 1566–1600* (Amsterdam, 1982), p. 18; B. H. Slicher van Bath, *Een samenleving onder spanning. Geschiedenis van het platteland in Overijssel* (Assen, 1957), p. 60.
8 W. Prevenier and W. Blokmans, *The Burgundian Netherlands* (Cambridge, 1986), p. 392.
9 Slicher van Bath, *Samenleving*, pp. 58–69.
10 Reitsma, *Centrifugal and Centripetal Forces*, p. 16.
11 Ibid., p. 17.
12 Slicher van Bath, *Samenleving*, pp. 69–72.
13 The *Nederlandsche Jaarboeken* and the *Nieuwe Nederlandsche Jaarboeken* reported yearly vital statistics for a number of Dutch cities in the second half of the eighteenth century. On the basis of the figures reported for Deventer in the periods listed below, I have calculated the crude birth, death, and marriage rates per 1,000 population:

	Birth Rate	Death Rate	Marriage Rate
1755–61	38.5	36.6	12.4
1769–76	39.6	35.4	12.2
1779–85	31.2	33.6	8.5

Between 1779 and 1785, the tables for Deventer were particularly elaborate, reporting not only crude numbers but also listing cause of death, age at death, and so forth.

14 See W. Jappe Alberts, *De Nederlandse Hansesteden* (Bussum, 1969).

15 On the broad outline and significance of these large structural changes, see Jan de Vries, *European Urbanization, 1500–1800* (Cambridge, Mass., 1984), Immanuel Wallerstein, *The Modern World System*, 2 vols (New York, 1974–80), and Paul M. Hohenberg and Lynn Hollen Lees, *The Making of Urban Europe, 1000–1950* (Cambridge, Mass., 1985).

16 Reitsma, *Centrifugal and Centripetal Forces*, pp. 18–20. Zwolle fared slightly better than Deventer in this respect because it benefited from trade that traveled along the Zwarte Water and Vecht waterways. Cf. Slicher van Bath, *Samenleving*, pp. 219–29.

17 The literature on protoindustrialization is by now quite large. The original statement is to be found in Franklin Mendels, "Proto-industrialization: the first phase of the industrialization process," *Journal of Economic History*, 32 (1972), pp. 241–61. For an up-to-date review of the literature, see Myron P. Gutmann, *Toward the Modern Economy. Early Industry in Europe, 1500–1800* (New York, 1988). In what follows here, I will be using the less rigorous definition of the term suggested by Charles Tilly, "Flows of capital and forms of industry in Europe, 1500–1900," *Theory and Society*, 12 (1983), pp. 123–42.

18 Z. W. Sneller, "De opkomst van de plattelandsnijverhied in Nederland in de 17e en 18e eeuw," *De economist*, 1928, pp. 691–702.

19 Cf. Johan de Vries, *De economische achteruitgang der Republiek in de achttiende eeuw* (Amsterdam, 1959).

20 Sneller, "Plattelandsnijverheid." See also Slicher van Bath, *Samenleving*, pp. 200–10.

21 Slicher van Bath, *Samenleving*.

22 By the second half of the eighteenth century the linen manufactures of Kampen and Zwolle, originally more important than in Deventer, had declined precipitously as well. Slicher van Bath, *Samenleving*, p. 210.

23 Ibid., pp. 219–29.

24 The following is based on my analysis of the results of the census of 1795. For the occupational classifications I have used see appendix I.

25 For this discussion, I have eliminated those heads of households who did not report an occupation. Thus, the total of approximately 1,600 active heads of households and the percentages based on that total differ from those used in the tables in chapters 4 and 6 where all heads of households are included.

26 See Mack Walker, *German Home Towns* (Ithaca, NY, 1971).

27 *Het Kerkelijk en Wereldlijk Deventer* (Deventer, 1732), pp. 39–51.

28 See I. H. van Eeghen, *De Gilden, theorie en praktijk* (Bussem, 1965) and C. Wiskerke, *De afschaffing der Gilden in Nederland* (Arnhem, 1938). See also Anthony Black, *Guilds and Civil Society in European Political Thought, from the Twelfth Century to the Present* (London, 1983).

29 In modern Dutch "*slijter*" usually denotes a retail merchant in alcoholic beverages, but in this case, "*slyter*" is clearly used in the more general sense of all retail merchants. The *Vier Gekroonde Gilde* included carpenters, masons, roofers, and cabinetmakers.

30 The key to the following analysis is an anonymous list of "*Fabrieken in Overijssel* –

einde 18e eeuw" which is to be found in RAO, Handschriften van de Vereeniging voor Overijsselsch Recht en Geschiedenis, 212. The list for Deventer in particular was apparently compiled in 1798 under the Batavian regime. I have corroborated this list using the occupational census of 1795. In order to arrive at a sense of the relative size of the firms listed, I simply divided the number of people listing a particular occupation by the number of firms on the list. These figures are admittedly crude, but they do at least suggest the relative levels of concentration in different kinds of manufacturing. For comparable developments in the cities Flanders and Brabant, see H. Soly, "Social Aspects of Structural Change in the Urban Industries of Eighteenth-century Brabant and Flanders," in *The Rise and Decline of Urban Industries in Italy and the Low Countries During the Late Middle Ages and Early Modern Times* (Leuven, 1988). I wish to thank the author for allowing me to see the text of this article before its publication.

31 None of the seven people who identified themselves as linen weavers on a petition in 1782 could be found back in the occupational census of 1795.

32 See Charles H. Wilson, "The economic decline of the Netherlands," *Economic History Review*, 9 (1939), pp. 111–27, Johan de Vries, *De economische achteruitgang der Republiek in de achttiende eeuw* (Amsterdam, 1959), and J. G. van Dillen, *Van rijkdom en regenten: Handboek tot de economische en sociale geschiedenis van Nederland tijdens de Republiek* (Den Haag, 1970). For more recent debates and literature, see James C. Riley, "The Dutch economy after 1650: decline or growth?" *Journal of European Economic History*, 13 (1984), pp. 521–69, and Jan de Vries, "The decline and rise of the Dutch economy, 1675–1900," *Research in Economic History*, Supplement 3 (1984), pp. 149–89.

33 On the eighteenth-century concern with the problem of decline, see W. W. Mijnhardt, "The Dutch Enlightenment: humanism, nationalism, and decline," (paper presented to the symposium "Decline, Enlightenment, and Revolution: The Dutch Republic in the Eighteenth Century," Washington, DC, March 1987), pp. 19–23.

34 For a comprehensive discussion of the statistics on wealth and poverty in the province of Overijssel, see Slicher van Bath, *Samenleving*, pp. 239–390.

35 This is calculated from the registers of the *hoofdgeld* for Deventer: RAO, Staten Archief, 2695. Slicher van Bath, *Samenleving*, argues that poverty was a growing problem in Overijssel (especially in Twente and parts of Salland) in the eighteenth century; by comparison with some other areas, then, Deventer fared relatively well.

36 As in many cities throughout the Republic, the growing strain of poor relief led in Deventer to proposals for the formation of an *armenfabriek* in which the dependent poor would be put to work. See GA Deventer, Republiek I, 351: "Antwoorden op een door stedelijk bestuur uitgeschreven prijsvraag naar 'het beste plan van een fabriek van wollen stoffen of anderen arrd, waardoor arme luiden en kinderen aan den arbeid kunnen geholpen worden' . . ." See also GA Deventer, Republiek I, 297: "Stukken betreffende de onderhandelingen tussen het stedelijk bestuur en Gautier Zindel . . . 1777."

37 A. G. Jongkees, "De Nederlandse laat-middeleeuwse cultuur in Europese samenhang," *AGN*, vol. 4 (Haarlem, 1980), pp. 372–6; see also pp. 377–438 more generally for the importance of Deventer as a cultural and religious center.

38 M. A. Nauwelaerts, "Scholen en onderwijs," *AGN*, vol. 4, pp. 363–5.

39 P. F. J. Obbema and A. Derolez, "De productie en verspreiding van het boek, 1300–1500," *AGN*, vol. 4, pp. 360–2.

40 Reitsema, *Centrifugal and Centripetal Forces*.
41 Koch, "The Reformation at Deventer."
42 Slicher van Bath, *Samenleving*, pp. 104–8.
43 Algemeen Rijksarchief, Binnelandsche Zaken, 1013–1014.
44 Willem Frijhoff, "Deventer en zijn gemiste universiteit. Het Atheneum in de sociaal-culturele geschiedenis van Overijssel," *Overijsselse historische bijdragen*, 97 (1982), pp. 45–79.
45 Mijnhardt, "The Dutch Enlightenment," p. 5.
46 See Mijnhardt, "The Dutch Enlightenment," and Mijnhardt, "De Nederlandse Verlichting: een terreinverkenning," *Kleio*, 19 (1978), pp. 245–63; also L. H. M. Wessels, "Tussen Ratio en Revelatio. De Nederlandse Verlichting beoordeeld: enkele historiographische notities betreffende cultuur, mentaliteit en religie in de achttiende eeuw," in *De Periferie in het centrum. Opstellen aangeboden aan M. G. Spiertz* (Nijmegen, 1986).
47 Mijnhardt, "The Dutch Enlightenment," pp. 13–19, and the extensive literature cited there.
48 Willem Frijhoff, "Dutch Enlightenment in front of popular belief and practice: an interpretation" (paper presented to the Symposium "Decline, Enlightenment, and Revolution: The Dutch Republic in the Eighteenth Century," Washington, DC, March 1987).
49 Mijnhardt, "The Dutch Enlightenment," pp. 29–39.
50 Cf. P. J. Buijnsters, "Nederlandse leesgezelschappen uit de 18e eeuw," in *Nederlandse literatuur van de achttiende eeuw* (Utrecht, 1984), p. 198.
51 Mijnhardt, "The Dutch Enlightenment," p. 35.
52 Jeremy Popkin, "Print culture in the Netherlands on the eve of the revolution" (paper presented to the Symposium "Decline, Enlightenment, and Revolution: The Dutch Republic in the Eighteenth Century," Washington, DC, March 1987).
53 See F. Ernst Stoffler, *The Rise of Evangelical Pietism* (Leiden, 1965), P. N. Holtrop, *Tussen Pietism en Reveil. Het "Deutsche Christentumsgesellschaft" in Nederland, 1784–1833* (Amsterdam, 1975), and Lambert A. Mulder, *De Revolte der Fijnen. De Afscheiding van 1834 als sociaal conflict en sociale beweging* (Meppel, 1973).
54 Cf. Rhys Isaac, "Preachers and Patriots: popular culture and the revolution in Virginia," in *The American Revolution. Explorations in the History of American Radicalism*, ed. Alfred F. Young (DeKalb, Ill., 1976).
55 Cf. Buijnsters, "Nederlandse leesgezelschappen," pp. 187–8.
56 Dumbar, *Tegenwoordige Staat*, p. 127. For the description that follows I have depended on J. I. van Doorninck, "Oude regeeringsgebruiken te Deventer," *Bijdragen tot de Geschiedenis van Overijssel*, 2 (1875), pp. 226–40, 300–21, and 3 (1876), pp. 249–57.
57 The standard works on the history and structure of the Dutch republican state are Robert Fruin, *Geschiedenis der Staatsinstellingen in Nederland tot den val der Republiek*, 2nd edn ('s-Gravenhage, 1922), and S. J. Fockema Andreae, *De Nederlandsche staat onder de Republiek*, 2nd edn (Amsterdam, 1962). For a refreshing new approach to the making of the Dutch state, See M. 't Hart, "Cities and statemaking in the Dutch Republic, 1580–1680," *Theory and Society* (forthcoming).
58 G. de Bruin, "De souvereiniteit in de republiek: een machtsprobleem," *BMGN*, 94 (1979), pp. 110–21.
59 Reitsema, *Centrifugal and Centripetal Forces*. For a comparative perspective on state

formation in Overijssel, see W. Ph. te Brake, "Provincial histories and national revolution: the Dutch Republic in the 1780s" (paper presented to the Symposium "Decline, Enlightenment, and Revolution: The Dutch Republic in the Eighteenth Century," Washington, DC, March, 1987).

60 Provincial contributions to the Generality budget were fixed by a quota system fairly early on; see Fruin, *Staatsinstelligen*, pp. 192–4.

61 G. de Bruin, "Geschiedschrijing over de Gouden Eeuw," in *Kantelend Geschiedbeeld*, ed. W. W. Mijnhardt (Utrecht/Antwerpen, 1983).

62 Reitsma, *Centrifugal and Centripetal Forces*, pp. 10–11.

63 C. H. T. Bussemaker, *Geschiedenis van Overijssel gedurende het Eerste Stdhouderloze Tijdperk* ('s-Gravenhage, 1888).

64 G. J. ter Kuile, "Rechtspraak en bestuur in Overijssel ten tijde van de Republiek der Vereenigde Nederlanden," *VMORG*, 67 (1952), pp. 141–68, and 68 (1953), pp. 69–97.

65 On the fascinating problem of voting in the Estates, see M. de Jong, *Joan Derk van der Capellen, Staatkundig levensbeeld uit de wordings tijd van der moderne democratie* (Groningen/Den Haag, 1922).

66 There is no study of the nobility (*Ridderschap*) in Overijssel; see more generally, Sherrin Marshall, *The Dutch Gentry, 1500–1650. Family, Faith and Fortune* (New York, 1987).

67 See Dumbar, *Tegenwoordige Staat*, and Reitsma, *Centrifugal and Centripetal Forces*.

68 H. Kronenberg, "In en om de Deventer Magistraat, 1591–1795," *VMORG*, 44 (1927), pp. 73–92, and *Kronenberg*, "Verhouding tussen adel en patriciaat in Deventer," *VMORG*, 65 (1950), pp. 84–9.

69 Kronenberg, "Deventer Magistraat;" cf. D. J. Roorda, "Het onderzoek naar het stedelijk patriciaat in Nederland," in *Kantelend Geschiedbeeld*, pp. 118–42.

70 Besides being eligible for appointment to important offices, local regents also disposed of large numbers of local offices as patronage; cf. "Ampten, Beneficiën, Officien, Tractementen, enz. door de regeering van Zwolle begeven," *Bijdragen tot de Geschiedenis en Oudheidkunde*, 1 (1874), pp. 49–71, 134–68, 269–78.

71 Using the lists of Magistrates and Sworn Councilors (printed in Dumbar, *Deventer*) and genealogies available for many leading families, it would be possible to chart the interlocking networks of kin relations among the regents of Deventer. Even a quick check of the family names of office holders in 1780 reveals that the two families (Jordens and Van Suchtelen) had five representatives apiece in government. The Hagedoorn family held four seats on the Council; the Dapper and Jacobson families three each; and so on. In all, 11 families filled 39 of the 64 regent offices in Deventer.

72 See De Bruin, "Gouden eeuw."

73 Cf. H. Wansink, "Holland and Six Allies: the Republic of the Seven United Provinces," in *Britain and the Netherlands*, vol. 4, ed. J. S. Bromley and E. H. Kossman (The Hague, 1971).

74 On the history of the office and of the individual Stadhouders, see H. H. Rowen, "Neither fish nor fowl: the Stadholderate in the Dutch Republic," in *Political Ideas and Institutions in the Dutch Republic* (Los Angeles, 1985), and Rowen, *The Princes of Orange. The Stadholders in the Dutch Republic* (Cambridge, 1988).

75 Fruin, *Staatsinstellingen*, pp. 270–83.

76 D. J. Roorda, *Partij en Factie. De oproeren van 1672 in de steden van Holland en Zeeland, een krachtmeting tussen partijen en facties* (Groningen, 1978).

77 Fruin, *Staatsinstellingen*, pp. 288–92. Cf. D. J. Roorda, "William III and the Utrecht 'Government-Regulation:' background, events and problems," *Low Countries History Yearbook*, 12 (1979), pp. 85–109.

78 Though the Regulation stipulated that the Stadhouder was to make appointments from lists of nominations, the nominations were eventually dispensed with and the appointments made directly by the Prince; cf. De Jong, *Capellen*, pp. 228ff.

79 W. F. Werthiem and A. H. Wertheim-Gijse Weenink, *Burgers in verzet tegen regenten-heerschappij. Onrust in Sticht en Oversticht, 1703–1706* (Amsterdam 1976), A. H. Wertheim-Gijse Weenink, *Democratische Bewegingen in Gelderland 1672–1795* (Amsterdam, 1973) and W. Th. Keune, "Gebeurtenissen rondom de verkiezing van Schepenen en Raad en de Gzworen Gemeente van Deventer in 1703," *VMORG*, 81 (1966), pp. 119–29.

80 J. I. van Doorninck, "Deventer Contracten van coorespondentie (1709–1710)," *VMORG*, 13 (1883), pp. 48–55.

81 J. A. F. de Jongste, *Onrust aan her Spaarne. Haarlem in de jaren 1747–1751* (Amsterdam, 1984); P. Geyl, *Revolutiedagen te Amsterdam* ('s-Gravenhage, 1936); C. J. Guibal, *Democratie en Oligarchie in Friesland tijdens de Republiek* (Assen, 1934).

3
Deventer in a Revolutionary World

Historians of Europe are generally agreed that in the last third of the eighteenth century, "Europe as a whole, but the west in particular, had moved into an age of crisis whose repercussions are apparent in almost every aspect of government and social and economic life."[1] At the material level, the resurgence of population growth threatened to outstrip established lines of food supply. Governments were necessarily involved in the provisioning of cities and armies, but food riots nevertheless became a regular feature of the political landscape, especially in England and France. On a very different plane, the Seven Years War, though costly for combatants and non-combatants alike, did little to resolve outstanding problems in international relations; if anything, the competition for empire between England and France became more bitter, this despite the immense strain that international conflict placed on government finance. In addition, from the "Wilkes and Liberty" movement in England to Maupeou's "revolution" in France, there was abundant evidence of serious political strife that threatened to undermine established regimes of whatever stripe.

Meanwhile, there was a new sort of trouble brewing on the other side of the Atlantic in England's North American colonies. Beginning with the crisis precipitated by the Stamp Act in 1765, through the resistance to the so-called Intolerable Acts, and culminating in the First Continental Congress in 1774, a loosely organized protest movement developed into a substantial political force willing and able to challenge Europe's greatest imperial power. When overt hostilities between colonial militias and British troops began in 1775, the shots are often said by Americans to have been "heard 'round the world." Even if we discount the obvious nationalist hyperbole of such a claim, it is nevertheless true that the American War of Independence inaugurated a new era in the history of the North Atlantic World – what R. R. Palmer called "the age of the democratic revolution."

As this new era of political crisis and revolutionary upheaval began, the Dutch found themselves in a particularly delicate position. Having undergone fundamental shifts in economy and society since the Golden Age of the seventeenth century, the Dutch Republic was faced with unattractive choices in international affairs. Indeed, defense and foreign policy issues were hotly debated throughout the 1770s.[2] Since the Treaty of Utrecht ended the last of Louis XIV's wars with the Dutch in 1713, the Republic had pursued a policy of strict neutrality in European affairs, but now commercial interests in the maritime provinces, especially the city of Amsterdam, demanded protection for Dutch shipping which was being harassed by English privateers. The Stadhouder, Prince William V of Orange, who was commander of both the army and the navy, condemned the proposals for rebuilding the sagging navy as hostile to the sea-faring English whom he considered a "natural" Dutch ally. For his part, the Prince demanded that any increases in the navy be balanced by augmentation of the Republic's standing army as a defense against Catholic France. To do both, however, seemed financially impossible for the haggard Republic; so there the issue stalemated.

After 1775, this traditional sparring between officials of the province of Holland and the city of Amsterdam, on the one hand, and the Stadhouder and his clients, on the other, was greatly exacerbated by the growing conflict in North America. The Prince, responding to a formal British request, supported loaning the so-called Scottish Regiment (in Dutch service since 1592) to England for use against the rebellious American colonies. When the secret request was publicized, however, the furor was great enough that the opposition prevailed and the British had to look elsewhere for auxiliary troops. To many people in mercantile Holland, like Pieter van Blieswijk, the Grand Pensionary, England seemed to be the enemy. The American colonies, he wrote, were doing precisely what the Dutch had done in the Eighty Years War, and the Dutch were obliged to help them rather than the English.[3] What he did not state publicly was that Dutch traders clearly stood to profit both from their smuggling trade with North America through the Caribbean and from the hoped-for dissolution of the British imperial system. Still, nothing was done to bolster Dutch defenses.

The situation became critical for the Dutch Republic in 1778 when France and Spain joined the Revolutionary War on the side of the American colonies. The British, invoking a 100-year-old treaty, demanded military support from the Republic, but the Estates General reaffirmed the Republic's long-standing policy of strict neutrality, thereby refusing to help. In addition, England charged that Dutch merchants were shipping naval stores to France and began seizing Dutch ships in the Channel. As the Dutch maritime interests, assuming in pamphlets the title of "Patriots," clamored for unlimited convoy to protect Dutch ships against "tyrannical" and "rapacious" England, pro-British "Orangists" accused Holland's merchants of sacrificing the nation for small profits.[4]

Meanwhile, representatives of the city of Amsterdam began secretly negotiating a commercial treaty with the United States which was intended to take effect only when the rebels won their independence. When a draft of this treaty was accidentally captured by the British at sea, it precipitated a British declaration of war on December 20, 1780.

FROM WAR TO REVOLUTION

Thus, the once-mighty Dutch Republic was dragged willy-nilly into the Fourth English War (1780–4), a naval war with the undisputed masters of the sea. For some Dutch Anglophobes, this indirect involvement in the War of the American Revolution seemed like a long-awaited chance to participate in the dismemberment of the British Empire. But the opportunity to rehabilitate the navy had been squandered for nearly a decade, and it was, after all, William V, pro-British to the core, who was to direct the war effort. As it happened, then, the disastrous course of the war was not surprising. The British immediately seized important Dutch trading posts in Asia and the Caribbean and effectively blockaded Dutch shipping to Amsterdam for several years. In the few actual battles that were fought before the cease-fire of 1783, the Dutch navy was generally humiliated, though a naval skirmish at Doggers Bank, which ended in a virtual draw, did briefly revive Dutch spirits and reawaken memories of the naval heroes of the previous century.

The outcome of the Fourth English War was equally disastrous, even though the Dutch were technically on the winning side. In the negotiations leading to the formal signing of the Treaty of Paris in May 1784, the Dutch were isolated from their French and American allies, and in order to secure the return of St Eustatius, its important smuggling station in the Caribbean, the Republic had to give up Negapatum in Ceylon and important trading monopolies in the Far East. The traditional Dutch policy of neutrality was also effectively ended, and henceforth the Dutch Republic was doomed to be caught up in the competition of her more powerful neighbors. But perhaps most seriously, the war proved to be the *coup de grâce* for the Dutch economy. As Charles Wilson suggests,

It is probably true that with her rapidly increasing volume of industrial exports, England was bound to replace Holland as the world market *par excellence*, but the change came more suddenly than anyone anticipated. . . . In the war of 1780 to 1783, the Dutch were hopelessly beaten, their commerce reduced to nothing, the Bank of Amsterdam ruined, and Dutch capital lured away by French propaganda from the safest investments in Europe.[5]

In terms of international politics and economics, then, involvement in the American Revolutionary War had a dramatic impact on the Dutch Republic, though the full range of its effects would not have been immediately apparent to contemporaries. In domestic politics, by contrast, the impact of the war was immediately obvious and thus even more dramatic. While exhausting the meager resources of the Dutch state, the war served to divide the Dutch people as never before. This development can be seen in the voluminous pamphlet literature of the years 1781 to 1783.

The number of pamphlets published annually tripled during the war years while the declining number of pamphlets dealing with foreign affairs indicates that the war itself was a dying issue.[6] Whereas before the war foreign aggressors loomed large in the pamphlets as the greatest threat to the independence of the Republic, during the war the tyrants and ogres of Dutch publicists turned out to be their fellow citizens: the real enemy seemed to be subversion from within. This internalization of the conflict began in 1781 with various efforts to blame the war on antagonistic political factions. The Orangists accused the regents of Amsterdam of reckless and treasonous activity in unilaterally negotiating a commercial treaty with the United States. The Patriots defended the "far-sighted" and "well-intentioned" policy of Amsterdam and blamed the Prince and his advisors for the disastrous course of the war. This more or less predictable pattern of mutual recrimination was broken in September 1781, however, with the publication of a remarkable pamphlet entitled *Aan het Volk van Nederland* (To the People of the Netherlands).[7]

Aan het Volk, an uncharacteristically long pamphlet, was a relentless attack on the Prince of Orange, in which the message was clear from the beginning:

My esteemed fellow-citizens! It is not just since yesterday or the day before that you are deceived and maltreated; no, for almost two centuries now, not to mention earlier times, you have been the plaything of all sorts of imperious people who, under the guise of caring for your interests and liberty . . . have aimed at absolutely nothing else than laying a hereditary yoke upon your free shoulders.[8]

The case against the Prince was simple: following in the footsteps of his ancestors, William V had arrogated so much power to himself through the abuse of his patronage powers and his control of the military that he alone was responsible for the woes of the Republic. Not only was the Prince responsible for the disastrous course of the war, but he also persecuted any regent who dared to oppose his policies. Even the alleged excesses of his personal life exposed his hypocrisy: "Yes, Prince William, it is all your fault."

"We are on the edge of destruction," the pamphlet concluded, and with time running out, anything undertaken to save the dear Fatherland from destruction would be useless as long as the people remained passive spectators. Thus, *Aan het Volk* ended with an agenda for popular political action:

Assemble, all of you, in your cities and in your villages in the countryside. Meet peaceably, and choose from your midst a moderate number of courageous, virtuous, and pious men; choose good patriots whom you can trust. Send them as your delegates to the places where the Estates of the several provinces meet, and charge them to . . . undertake in the name and on the authority of this nation, together with and alongside the Estates of each province, a careful investigation into the reasons for the far-reaching inertia and faint-heartedness with which the defense against a formidable and above all active enemy is being undertaken. Charge them also . . . to choose a council of advisors for His Highness [the Prince] . . . and as soon as possible to devise and initiate whatever measures that might be considered useful to save the Fatherland in its desperate plight.

Have your delegates report to you their activities from time to time, openly and in public by means of the public press. Provide for the freedom of the press, because it is the only support of your national liberty . . .

Take up arms, all of you, choose yourselves those who must command you, and proceed with modesty and composure just like the people of America where not a single drop of blood was shed before the English attacked them, and Jehovah, the God of Liberty, who led the Israelites out of the house of bondage and made them a free people will also surely support our good cause.[9]

Aan het Volk van Nederland was easily among the most influential and successful pamphlets of its time. Although it was banned and a reward was offered for the identity of its author, it went through four clandestine printings in 1781 and was translated into French, English, and German. Like Tom Paine's *Common Sense* had done in America in 1776, it crystallized the terms of the political debate at a critical moment and permanently expanded and politicized the meaning of "patriotism." Undoubtedly many factors account for the success of this pamphlet – not least of them its passion – but two in particular may have recommended it to its Dutch audience. Unlike many other pamphleteers, the author of *Aan het Volk* provided a single, plausible explanation – the megalomania of the Prince of Orange – for a variety of problems that might have seemed completely unrelated to the Fourth English War. Perhaps more importantly, however, he offered his readers a plan of action that was designed to reduce the overarching influence of the Prince and his "fawning lot of grandees."

To be sure, this was not the only voice heard in the fall of 1781 and during the rest of the war years. Orangist writers generally continued to attack the regents of Amsterdam and those who defended their actions; they extolled the virtues of the House of Orange and emphasized the necessity of an "eminent head" to guide the Republic. Orangist pamphlets were, however, far outnumbered by a diffuse opposition literature. Many pamphlets followed the pattern of *Aan het Volk*, using "history" to attack the Prince or applying arguments about ancient liberties and natural rights to subjects as diverse as freedom of the press and the hunting rights, citizen militias and military justice. But Patriot writers did not agree on all points. Some writers were convinced that the fundamental problem was not an evil Prince but evil advisors, and for a time it was Duke

Louis of Brunswick-Wolfenböttel, William's closest advisor, who bore the brunt of the attack. Others, discarding the traditional historical framework of Dutch political debate, stressed natural law as the basis for liberty. A large proportion of the political writing, however, was neither carefully reasoned nor intended to be intellectually persuasive. Take, for example, the following epitaph for R. M. van Goens, outspoken Orangist from Utrecht:

> To the honor of him, who for his punishment must never rest in the grave:
>
> A Councilman's son, enslaved to honor and reputation, PROFESSOR, ALDERMAN, and REGENT by virtue of his birth, who was first a debaucher, and later a traitor, in wantonness of superior spirit, an English Patriot, and full of personal glory. The wicked author of a seditious treatise, the vomit of society and a pest in everyone's eyes, VAN GOENS is suspended here by his legs for the ravens and vultures.[10]

One did not have to be acquainted with natural law theory or the history of the Republic to understand the author's point.

The cacophony of the pamphlet literature – the emotional outbursts perhaps more clearly than the reasoned arguments – illustrates the depth of the social and political crisis that was precipitated by the Fourth English War. The situation was fluid because ideologies and political programs were not yet a matter of habit or convention, but it is clear that the international crisis that gave birth to the American republic and bankrupted the French crown ignited in the Dutch Republic a massive explosion of controversy and conflict that culminated in Patriot revolution and Orangist counter-revolution in 1787. In the absence of centralized political institutions, the actual struggle for power between Patriots and Orangists took on a disjointed and piecemeal quality because each province offered revolutionaries different opportunities and challenges. In the account that follows, we will focus on developments in Overijssel which, as a sovereign province, provided the immediate context for Deventer's municipal revolution, but we will relate these events as much as possible to their broader context.

"NOTRE WILKES"

Each Dutch province experienced the Patriot Revolution differently because their distinctive histories had prepared the ground in different ways. In Overijssel, the revolutionary conflicts of the 1780s clearly grew out of conflicts within the ruling oligarchy in the 1770s, and in order to survey that history, we will do well to begin with J. D. van der Capellen. Even before the outbreak of war, Van der Capellen's unconventional politics had exposed the cracks within the Orangist regime in Overijssel and had fostered both public scrutiny of the ruling oligarchy and popular protest to change its policies.

In the spring of 1770, Joan Derk Baron van der Capellen, a young nobleman from Gelderland, applied for admission to the Estates of Overijssel as a member of the Ridderschap.[11] He had previously applied for admission to the Ridderschap of Gelderland, but his application was denied on technical grounds. Not wishing to have his political ambitions so easily denied, Van der Capellen, who was married to a noblewoman from Overijssel, took up part-time residence in Zwolle and acquired nominal ownership of a noble estate (*have-zate*) in Overijssel where he could meet the less stringent requirements for admission. His application was supported by the three enfranchised cities – the *hoofdsteden* – but it was steadfastly opposed by the leadership of the nobility. According to Van der Capellen's biographer, his application elicited opposition especially because he was an outsider; at stake was the issue of whether the Ridderschap could choose it own membership.[12] After more than two years of waiting, Van der Capellen finally received the support of William V as Stadhouder, who broke the deadlock between the cities and the nobility in order to assert his own influence in the province. In October, 1772, Van der Capellen attended his first Landdag.

It is ironic that Van der Capellen should have relied on the Stadhouder's influence to launch his political career because he quickly became one of the Prince's most implacable enemies. Van der Capellen was apparently convinced that "the free institutions of the Republic were being threatened by a tendency toward absolutism," and the Republic's standing army, he thought, was an instrument of tyranny in the hands of the Stadhouders. A free press and a citizens' militia were, conversely, the best means to defend liberty. Thus, as early as 1773, Van der Capellen spoke out forcefully against the Stadhouder's proposals to augment the army, and in 1775, it was he who blocked the loan of the Scottish Regiment to the British for use in North America. Again, Van der Capellen frustrated William's efforts to augment the army in 1778, this time by threatening to exercize the peculiar Dutch version of the *liberum veto*.[13] Because the issue required unanimous decision at both the provincial and national level, one dissenting vote in the Ridderschap of Overijssel could subvert the whole project. Such actions gained Van der Capellen national attention, and in his private correspondence, the Stadhouder began calling Van der Capellen "notre Wilkes."[14]

Van der Capellen also focused on reform issues within Overijssel. In a published speech to the Landdag in 1777, he attacked the manner in which provincial appointments were being made by the Stadhouder. According to the provisions of the Governmental Regulation, the deputations to the Estates General, the provincial Executive Committee, and other provincial officers were to be chosen by the Stadhouder from lists of nominations by the Estates, but as we have seen, the nominations were dropped in favor of direct appointments by the Prince. In his speech, which demanded strict adherence to the Regulation, Van der Capellen argued that "failure to live up to the Constitution, which draws the line between the authority of the Estates and the authority of the Stadhouder, and upon which the liberty and security of the Nation rest, must have the most serious consequences."[15] Admitting that the nomination procedure was almost entirely ceremonial (the Stadhouder had the prerogative to ignore the nominations), Van der Capellen insisted that the ceremony was important to demonstrate "that in this land, which fought for its independence, government is operated not arbitrarily but according to the rules of holy, unalterable constitutional laws."[16]

Van der Capellen's speech had no practical effect because it was sent to committee for further study. Nevertheless, as a statement of principles, its implications were not lost on the Stadhouder and his allies within the Estates. The Count of Heiden Hompesch, Drost of Twente, wrote immediately to the Prince to say that "the implications of his reasoning are startling." He went on to chide the Prince for ever having supported Van der Capellen's admission to the Ridderschap, and the Prince readily agreed it had been a mistake.[17] But Van der Capellen had done more than trouble the normally placid waters of aristocratic government; he had opened up government to public exposure by publishing his speeches and related documents. He had also translated Richard Price's *Observations on the nature of civil liberty*, a radical-Whig tract that became an instant success in the Netherlands. Still, his political battles did not begin in earnest until he addressed the issue of the *drostendiensten* and thereby attacked the power of the *drosten*.

The *drostendiensten* were periods of mandatory labor service demanded twice-yearly of all inhabitants of the countryside for the personal benefit of the *drosten*, the province's powerful regional administrators. Although the origin of the services is not clear, the available evidence suggests that they originated as a "bureaucratic usurpation . . . a sort of official extortion against which nothing could be done."[18] As early as 1759, a group of peasants (*boeren*) and cotters from the district of Haaksbergen sent petitions to the Estates asking to be exempted from the *drostendiensten*, but it was not until 1776 that the Estates approved a monetary substitution for the actual services. The city of Zwolle protested this decision (to no avail) on the grounds of archival evidence that suggested the services had been formally abolished in 1631. Meanwhile, in the spring of 1777, a petition from the district of Enschede complained of worsening conditions: with the possibility of new revenue from the monetary substitution, the Drost of Twente was apparently enforcing the obligations more strictly than ever.[19]

Van der Capellen finally spoke out on the matter in the spring of 1778 when he declared that "these services are, by their nature, a form of slavery; and . . . *None* of our *Inhabitants* is obliged to perform them." He also expressed his indignation at "the impudence, the criminal audacity of those who did not scruple after the year 1631 . . . to subject our inhabitants once more to the humiliating yoke of servitude."[20] As usual, Van der Capellen's speech was published, this time before it was delivered at the Landdag. Obviously aimed at a broader audience than the regents in the Estates, the pamphlet was distributed free throughout the province. Many members of the Ridderschap were indignant and demanded an *ad hoc* committee to examine the speech's allegations. Meanwhile, petitioners throughout the province implored both the Estates and the Stadhouder for release from the "slavery of the *drostendiensten*," and Van der Capellen's friend F. A. van der Kemp, a radical Mennonite preacher from Leiden, began writing a series of pamphlets to publicize the issue nationally. For his part, Van der Capellen armed himself with testimony from old men in Kamperveen whose recollections supported his claim that in parts of the province, as least, the *drostendiensten* had only recently been revived.

In the fall of 1778, Van der Capellen defended his attack on the *drosten* who were responsible for the *drostendiensten*, but the Estates reaffirmed by majority vote its earlier decision regarding monetary substitution. They also issued a public proclamation denouncing the petitioners whose requests "were not made with the spirit of submission that loyal residents and subjects owe their lawful sovereign;" the proclamation also condemned those who had incited such "improper and punishable conduct." But most importantly, the Estates ordered the state's attorney (*advocaat-fiscaal*) to prosecute Van der Capellen for libeling former members of the Estates and for publishing documents still under consideration by the assembly. Pending the outcome of the legal proceedings, Van der Capellen was suspended from his seat in the Ridderschap.[21]

For Van der Capellen, public condemnation of his actions and suspension from the Ridderschap were an unexpected personal calamity. Believing in his rectitude, yet fearing the humiliation of a trial before his peers, he vacillated between demanding a speedy trial and seeking accommodation through the mediation of the Stadhouder. But matters were beyond his control. In 1779, the three cities supported by five members of the Ridderschap attempted to seek accommodation by sending the matter back to committee, but the majority of the Ridderschap was vigorously opposed. There the case stalemated on the technical problem of *overstemming* – the unresolved question of what constituted a valid majority decision within the Estates. While the towns and the nobility exchanged legal briefs on this more restricted issue, Van der Capellen's case was all but forgotten. Writing from his patrimonial estate in Gelderland in May, 1780, Van der Capellen was despondent: "I am definitely convinced that we have been sold and betrayed – and almost delivered [into their hands]. . . . Outside the protection of the law, I have no more interest in this cursed Land, where brute force sits upon the throne."[22]

Van der Capellen's despair of being able to accomplish anything through legal channels was certainly justified. For four years he was excluded from the political arena, and his case never did come to trial. The problem was that his opposition politics had finally evoked a fundamental and apparently irreconcilable split within the regent elite of Overijssel: on the one side, he had earned the enmity of the Stadhouder and the majority of the Ridderschap who were the

Prince's most faithful allies; on the other side, he had gained the support of the three enfranchised cities and a few of his noble colleagues. As it happened, this enduring division within the ruling oligarchy opened up a unique opportunity for popular intervention into Overijssel politics, and when Van der Capellen finally regained his seat in the Estates of Overijssel, it was as the political symbol of a newly activated force in Dutch politics: *het Volk.*

What clearly changed the situation for Van der Capellen was the Fourth English War and its political fallout. The war was his kind of issue, and though it remained a closely held secret for nearly a century, Van der Capellen was, in fact, the anonymous author of *Aan het Volk van Nederland.* With this pamphlet he attempted to re-enter politics, but in a new way. *Aan het Volk* was just one of many pamphlets that decried the "injustice" of Van der Capellen's suspension from the Ridderschap and publicized local issues, like the *drostendiensten,* with which he was associated. Thus Overijssel's conflicts became national issues, and Van der Capellen became a Patriot hero. Meanwhile, in Overijssel, earlier and more forcefully than elsewhere, large doses of inflammatory rhetoric and popular political action backed up specific Patriot demands. Indeed, in the Patriot-dominated press, Overijssel was often seen as a model of political action and organization.

Van der Capellen's stirring call to political action in *Aan het Volk* evoked its first response in the spring of 1782. The Republic faced a fundamental choice: whether to recognize the United States envoy, John Adams, and negotiate a defense treaty with the United States or perhaps France, or whether to accept preliminary peace offers from Britain. Adams had been propagandizing the American cause and soliciting financial support privately for some time, but his success in the capital markets of Amsterdam hinged on official recognition which did not seem to be forthcoming. For Patriot strategists like Van der Capellen, recognition of Adams as the representative of a sovereign state and eventual alliance with the United States offered a sure means of avoiding what they considered a premature and humiliating peace. In March, then, petitions addressed to various levels of government and demanding recognition of Adams were circulated in a number of cities throughout the Republic, in- cluding Deventer, Kampen, and Zwolle.[23]

The Overijssel petitions did not address the strategic advantages of alliance with the American republic so much as its anticipated economic benefits. The Deventer petition, for example, pointed out that for some time, and especially since the outbreak of the war, the commerce and industry of the Republic had been declining with the most serious consequences for Overijssel in particular. Chair-making, woolspinning, stocking- and hat-making – all these manufac- tures in Deventer alone were suffering severely from the economic crisis. In Kampen, the petitioners dwelled on the crisis in the local woolen industry which, they claimed, had declined to one-eight its previous size. The Deventer petition also mentioned the special plight of textile merchants in Twente whose business had fallen off dramatically, of *boeren* who depended in part on the sale of raw wool and flax, and even of landlords whose tenants could not afford to pay their rents. The economy of Overijssel was suffering, and a commercial treaty with the United States seemed like the first step toward economic recovery. "[If] we enter into an Alliance with America, then the petitioners dare to say unconditionally, with hearts full of love for the Fatherland, that they have the surest expectation of seeing the old prosperity of our Fatherland completely restored."[24] The petitioners predicted further that America was too agricultural to develop its own industries, that Americans would gladly exchange raw materials from the new world for Overijssel's manufactured products.

Given that Deventer's petition, for example, had just 66 signatures, the campaign on behalf of John Adams did not represent the kind of broad mobilization that Van der Capellen had called for, but it was a beginning that demonstrated the potential of popular collective action. The Burgemeesters in all three cities immediately forgot their previous hesitations and charged their delegates to the next Landdag to press for recognition of John Adams as US ambassador. The Estates of Overijssel resolved to recognize Adams on April 15, 1782, and the Estates General, in turn, accepted his credentials and officially recognized the United States four days later. Within six months, the Republic had already concluded a treaty of friendship and commerce with North America.[25] Thus, the first modest effort of the Patriots in the cities of Overijssel was a resounding success by comparison with the petitions of the *boeren* against the *drostendiensten* in 1778.

With recognition of the United States, issues of foreign policy and national defense receded temporarily into the background in Overijssel. The well-informed *Nieuwe Nederlandsche Jaarboeken* reported, nevertheless, that there was considerable agitation throughout the province over a number of local issues: the *drostendiensten*; Van der Capellen's readmission to the Ridderschap; the problem of *overstemming* in the Estates; the election of municipal magistrates; the hunting rights of *burgers* (city folk); and the jurisdiction of military courts. The list is remarkably eclectic and, with the exception of the election of Burgemeesters, suggests an almost non-political thrust. Yet examined more closely, the list can be seen to display a remarkable coherence.[26]

Van der Capellen and the *drostendiensten* had already become familiar Patriot causes, and in conjunction with them, the technical question of *overstemming* took on special significance because it seemed to block their resolution. The first three issues, then, pitted the Patriots against the nobility and, by extension, the Stadhouder, their patron and ally. Further down the list, the election of Burgemeesters, hunting rights, and the jurisdiction of courts martial were all long-standing problems, dating from the re-introduction of the Governmental Regulation in 1748. To object to the Stadhouder's "recommendations" and to demand "free" election of magistrates by the Sworn Councils was to challenge the Prince and his local allies on yet another front. Similarly, the issues of hunting rights and military jurisdiction were related to the power and prestige of the Stadhouder and the nobility: at the same time as the Governmental Regulation had been revived, the Estates had approved regulations that made game hunting a noble prerogative and expanded the jurisdiction of courts martial (under the Stadhouder's control) to include all civil and criminal cases involving military personnel. *Aan het Volk van Nederland* had publicized these developments as instances of Orangist tyranny, as attempts to disarm the public and to increase the Stadhouder's control over the military at the expense of the civilian population. Thus, demands for hunting rights and the restriction of courts martial shared the common element in the Patriots' list of demands in Overijssel: they challenged the Stadhouder and his noble allies.

The Patriots in the three cities organized new and larger petition drives around the primary Patriot issues in advance of the October 1782 Landdag: abolition of the *drostendiensten*, reinstatement of Van der Capellen, and resolution of the *overstemming* issue. These petitions, much more than those on behalf of Adams, demonstrated the degree of politicization of the urban population and the potential of their mobilization for political action. One Patriot journal reported that the request garnered more than 2,000 signatures in Zwolle; the Deventer petition had 1,460 names; and in Kampen it was reported to have had the support of "the majority of Burgers and Residents."[27] In all three cities, petitions were addressed to both the Magistracy and the Sworn Councils, and in each case, the Council, which generally supported Van der Capellen, pressured the Magistracy to take firm positions in favor of the Patriot demands.[28]

Expectations and tensions were so high that the Drost of Twente, fearing the worst, suggested to the Stadhouder that he strengthen the garrison in Zwolle where the Landdag was to meet.[29] Van der Capellen reported, "The situation here [in Zwolle] is such that one has difficulty keeping the people calm. In Deventer it is even worse, and I have it on good authority that if the Landdag where presently there, it would not be advisable for me to enter the city since the citizens would simply carry me into the Assembly."[30] When the Landdag began, the problem of *overstemming* once again thwarted the cities' hopes for abolition of the *drostendiensten*, but both Van der Capellen and the Ridderschap seemed willing to compromise on the issue of his readmission. After several days of negotiation, he signed a vague declaration that proclaimed his innocence yet could be construed as an apology to the Ridderschap. Thus, on November 1, 1782, just before the Landdag adjourned, Van der Capellen made a triumphal return to the Assembly amid shouts of "Vivat Capellen!" from crowds along his way.

The reinstatement of Van der Capellen was celebrated as a major Patriot victory. The news occasioned public rejoicing in cities throughout the Republic, and Patriot journals and broadsides printed countless poems in praise of the "brave" Van der Capellen. Even students at Lingen, across the border in

Germany, demonstrated their approval of the Patriots in Overijssel.[31] Though the other Patriot issues remained unresolved, the readmission of Van der Capellen deserved the celebrations because it symbolized the power of a newly activated political force – *het Volk* – and the vulnerability of aristocratic government to public pressure. After all, "the voice of the People" had accomplished with relative ease what Van der Capellen and a modest number of aristocratic allies had not been able to achieve in four years of legal maneuvering. Now William V's nickname for Van der Capellen – "notre Wilkes" – seemed more apt than ever.

THE PERIPHERY AT THE CENTER

If political initiative and leadership in the Dutch Republic normally came from the urban and commercial west, then the surest confirmation that these were extraordinary times may be the fact that land provinces in general and the city of Deventer in particular led the way in mobilizing ordinary people for collective political action. It was not immediately clear, however, whether the Patriots would be able to maintain their temporary advantage and capitalize on their victories. Van der Capellen was, of course, pleased with the new lease on his political life, but he was also concerned about the unresolved issues. Writing to his cousin R. J. van der Capellen, a Patriot leader in the Ridderschap of Gelderland, he underscored the necessity of maintaining popular mobilization, and to him petitioning seemed the ideal method.

This is my plan . . . to keep the Burgerij in hand so that they themselves by signing petitions take action on their own, that is, the public's, affairs. In that case . . . there is still a good chance to save the Republic. These address are, in effect, the same as *het Volk* having representatives or even assembling in person, while they have none of the turbulence of a public meeting.[32]

Soon it would be apparent that the October petitions were not merely a flash in the pan, for in the next few months the Patriots in Deventer led a flurry of activity that left little doubt about the persistence of the movement.

At the beginning of December 1782, "a great number of respectable Burgers and Residents" of Deventer signed a formal "Act of Appointment" for 12 representatives of the Burgerij.[33] The first of its kind in the Dutch Republic, this new "Burgercommittee" may have been modeled after the American committees of correspondence, for it was charged not only with the task of organizing local action but was intended to communicate with Patriots elsewhere. In any case, the first fruit of the committee's work was a petition circulated at the end of December and signed by "a considerable number of persons."[34] The petition complained of attempts by the *drosten* to control the election of Burgemeesters and Sworn Councilors by influencing the recommendations of the Stadhouder; it asked, therefore, that the Council ignore the Prince's recommendations and choose only the *"Vroomste, Beste en Welgegoedste"* (most pious, excellent, and wealthy) citizens in accordance with their oath of office and at the same time restore to their rightful positions of authority within their corps two Magistrates who had recently been demoted by the Prince.

In January 1783, the Burgercommittee helped to create a similar committee in Zwolle, and in the following month the two committees coordinated a petition campaign in advance of the next Landdag.[35] Among other things, the petitions demanded an official proclamation against the *drostendiensten* and urged that the Estates look into possible criminal prosecution of the Drost of Twente for abuse of his office. The petitions also supported the rights of the *kleine steden* – the smaller chartered towns that were not represented in the Estates. Although they stood outside the mainstream of political life in Overijssel, many of the 14 *kleine steden* became important centers of Patriot activity. At the urging of their citizens, representatives of the small towns in Twente especially were seeking to free themselves from the influence of the *drosten*, who encroached on their judicial independence and interfered in their municipal elections.[36] Thus, while supporting the common Patriot cause, the Patriots in the small towns were striking out on their own as well.

In the spring of 1783, Patriot mobilization took on an important new dimension. In Deventer, a group of approximately 100 men organized a *"vrije burger compagnie"* (free burger company) and petitioned the municipal administration for official sanction.[37] Before long, there were similar attempts in Hardenberg, Ommen, Enschede, Ootmarsum, Delden, Oldenzaal, Zwolle, and Kampen. These voluntary *exercitie genootschappen* (exercise associations), or *vrijcorpsen* (free corps) as they were often called, approximated the kind of citizens militia Van der Capellen envisioned as important means of defending "liberty" against the "tyranny of Princes." Standing in many cases alongside existing civic guards (*schutterijen*) which were controlled by the regents, the *vrijcorpsen* had an unmistakable political thrust. The prologue to the regulations of the Deventer Vrijcorps, for example, cited "the duty of every properly disposed Burger to preserve, to the best of his ability, the liberty, security and tranquillity of his Fatherland in general and his city of residence in particular"; at the same time, it noted the machinations of unspecified malevolent persons (*kwaadwilligen*) who would extinguish the courage of their fellow citizens.[38]

The militias were, in a sense, experiments in popular government; they were organized, as Van der Capellen asserted in a speech to the Zwolle Vrijcorps, with the greatest possible influence accorded to the members themselves.[39] Although the officers were usually required to pledge their allegiance to the local authorities, they were elected directly by the members, each of whom had one vote. Moreover, the regulations of the Deventer Vrijcorps stated explicitly that "distinctions of status [*staat*], rank or religion" would not be taken into consideration.[40] The militias drilled regularly and sometimes ostentatiously in public – in summer typically in an open field close to the center of the town, in winter often inside a church after the Sunday services with the pews shoved to one side. As a measure of the militias' popularity, the *Nieuwe Nederlandsche Jaarboeken* reported that in the small town of Oldenzaal, a collection for the local *vrijcorps* took in 1,400 guilders; the town's maidens were said to have sewed appropriate banners for the volunteers. In Almelo, the militia took in nearly 3,000 guilders.[41]

These new activities were accompanied by more Patriot victories, the most dramatic of which occurred in the annual municipal election in Deventer.[42] On February 22, 1783, the Sworn Council held by popular demand a "free" election: they removed from office an outspoken Orangist Burgemeester, Everhard Herman Putman; they elected also two new Burgemeesters and filled four vacancies on the Council without regard to the Prince's recommendations; finally they restored to positions of leadership the two Burgemeesters whom the Prince had demoted. After an uncharacteristically long and suspenseful delay, the Stadhouder accepted the removal of Putman and approved the Council's choice of Magistrates, but he asserted his "prerogative" by replacing two of the men chosen for the Sworn Council. On March 17, amid a large demonstration of popular support, the Council decided to stick with its original election, persuaded the Prince's candidates to renounce their positions, and notified William that he could disapprove of local elections only when there was evidence of corruption and intrigue. The Stadhouder had little choice but to back down, albeit under protest, and the skirmish left little doubt about the strength of the Patriot movement in Deventer. In subsequent elections, the Councils of Kampen and Zwolle easily followed Deventer's example, thereby ending the Stadhouder's important patronage in the cities of Overijssel.[43]

In the provincial Estates, the Patriots' victories were equally important. In February 1783, the Estates finally approved a public proclamation abolishing the *drostendiensten*. In recognition of Van der Capellen's important role in bringing about that decision, representatives of the *boeren* of Twente presented him with a ceremonial gold medallion commemorating their liberation from the "yoke of servitude."[44] Before the year was out, several other popular demands had been satisfied as well. For example, the jurisdiction of military courts, which the Patriots saw as symbolic of the Stadhouder's "tyranny," was severely restricted within the province, and a committee of the Estates began a special investigation of the alleged corruption of the Drost of Twente, the Stad-houder's trusted friend in the Ridderschap.[45] In short, the Patriots were steadily eroding the authority and prestige of the Prince and his most important allies. Still, the technical issue of *overstemming* remained unsolved, and at the end of 1783, the Ridderschap's determined resistance on this issue temporarily halted the Patriots' string of easy victories and brought on the most serious constitutional crisis in Overijssel since the middle of the seventeenth century. When, at the December 1783 Landdag, the delegates of the three cities supported by just two noblemen attempted to abolish the nobility's exclusive hunting privileges by majority vote (*overstemming*), the majority of the Ridderschap flatly refused to recognize the decision. After a long shouting match resolved nothing, the delegates of the cities walked out of the assembly, refusing to reconvene the Estates until the Ridderschap gave in.[46] With that the sovereign government of Overijssel simply ceased to function. The spring of 1784 brought serious flooding along the IJssel River, and in Deventer the highest water in memory flooded all but a few streets. But the provincial authorities were powerless to aid the victims, for as Van der Capellen described the situation in March, "Our province is at present in a state of perfect anarchy."[47] In April, the cities and the Ridderschap narrowly avoided fiscal disaster by separately approving the year's taxation. Ironically, the only time the Estates convened in 1784 was in May when the Drost of Vollenhove finally persuaded the warring factions to hold a special session for the sole purpose of ratifying the peace treaty ending the Fourth English War.[48]

The hardened positions of the opposing sides left little room for negotiation or compromise, and in order to break the deadlock, both sides eventually agreed to submit the case to an ad hoc commission from the other six provinces as provided for in the Union of Utrecht. On March 5, 1785, well over a year after the Estates had dissolved, the commission finally decided in favor of the cities, declaring that their votes plus the vote of a single nobleman constituted a valid majority.[49] Though the *overstemming* decision was not an occasion for popular Patriot celebrations, it represented an extraordinary victory for the Patriots. Having successfully challenged and discredited the consensual political practices of the past, they had legitimated instead the politics of majority rule under terms very advantageous to them. Henceforth, the Ridderschap, the corporative base of the Stadhouder's most faithful allies, could no longer be considered an equal partner in provincial government, and as a result, the Patriots had only to control the (*hoofdsteden*) in order to control the whole province.

During the long period of political paralysis, however, there was much uncertainty about where this new political enthusiasm and agitation would lead. The untimely death in June 1784 of J. D. van der Capellen, the movement's only universally recognized leader, further increased the uncertainty about the future. To be sure, by this time the Patriot movement was substantial enough to survive the loss with no apparent difficulty, but no one emerged to replace him as the movement's chief spokesman. Their political success nevertheless forced the Patriots to face a new political issue that was not easily resolved: who would fill the void left by a much-diminished Stadhouder? At first the Patriots in Overijssel, following Van der Capellen, had insisted on strict adherence to the Governmental Regulation; as recently as 1783, the influential *Post van den*

Neder-Rhyn, for example, had defended the Regulation as the constitutional basis of government in Overijssel: "If one takes away this foundation; if one breaks this oath [to the Regulation]; that is, if one tacitly separates oneself from this sworn precept, then one destroys, in fact, the whole existence of the Government, and one reduces the State to absolute Anarchy."[50] But as the Prince and his allies ever more insistently defended the status quo, which was rooted in the same Regulation, there was a gradual, but decisive, shift in the tenor of the pamphleteers and publicists who popularized and defended the Patriots' cause.

An anonymous pamphlet entitled *Brief aan een Vriend* signaled the change when it attacked the Governmental Regulation itself, judging the interests of the Fatherland to outweigh the interests of the Stadhouder. To justify his attack, the writer offered what he considered "long established Truths:" "that sovereignty rests in *het Volk*; that *het Volk* cannot give up its liberty with the consequence that it cannot get it back; that *het Volk* can choose whatever form of government it understands to be consistent with its own interest."[51] Besides, he continued, the Orangists simply cannot have it both ways: either the Regulation could be changed legally at the present time, or else the Regulation (which itself replaced earlier agreements) could not have been introduced legally in 1672 and 1748. Having thus destroyed the basis of the Stadhouder's power in theory, if not in fact, the Patriots, like the author of this *Brief*, began discussing ways of institutionalizing their own influence in Overijssel politics.

In demanding constitutional changes to create a political space for *het Volk*, the Patriots also quietly dropped their original claim to be restoring a golden past and imagined themselves instead to be creating a new future purged of the mistakes of the past. An editorial in the *Blaadje zonder titel voor burger en boer in Overijssel*, a local Patriot journal, argued, for example, that *Vrijheid* (Liberty, Freedom) had never been properly understood or realized in the history of the Republic.[52] That the rebels against Spain had not understood or realized the meaning of the word is evident in the fact that they looked in vain for another monarch: "The obscurity of the middle ages was still not cleared up enough and the people were still not enlightened enough to form ideas of republican government." Surveying the history of the Republic, he wrote: "In 1675 William III, and in 1747 William IV restored Liberty, and in 1702 people thought they had found Liberty because William III had died. But when were they right? Certainly not in any of these cases because they never attached the right meaning to the word 'Vrijheid' . . ." *Vrijheid*, the author concluded, must mean Liberty for all people, not just a group or faction of politicians.

Another pamphleteer, declaring that "a Revolution is at hand," expressed the excitement and optimism of many Patriot writers as they set about designing a new political future for Overijssel.

It is true that we can have a more favorable idea of the imminent transformation [as compared to previous Revolutions]; – it is happening not with undue haste, but with composure; – not by means of an ignorant and agitated Commons, but by means of the most knowledgeable and excellent part of the People . . .[53]

Het Volk now understands, he continued, that in the past faulty methods were used to restore Liberty; these were "unlimited influence of the Stadhouder" and "Aristocratic domination." In the future, the ambition of both the Stadhouder and the regents would have to be restricted by constitutional laws; both would have to be made dependent on *het Volk*. To that end, the regents would have to be chosen by the people.

That much the Patriots could generally agree on: the new constitution would have to provide for some form of representative democracy (*representatieve volksregeering*). Although Van der Capellen never renounced his allegiance to the existing Regulation, he anticipated this new consensus in a letter to a friend shortly before his death. "I am no friend of pure democracy, nor of large redresses or changes; but do not hide the fact that I will never lend a hand to set up the aristocracy on the ruins of the *Stadhouderschap*."[54] Even "Wandelaar Zwaarhoofd" (the wandering pessimist), who professed to being pessimistic about the ability of the people to choose its representatives wisely, assumed that the people should have a role in the administration of public affairs.[55] In all, the greatest problem for most writers seemed to be to steer a middle course between the equally unattractive alternatives of aristocracy or "family government" and anarchy or "complete government by the people." And consistent with this new emphasis, the Patriots augmented their list of enemies: "aristocrats" now took their place alongside the partisans of the Stadhouder and the English.

FROM REVOLUTION BACK TO WAR

As the Patriots in Overijssel organized a broad popular movement and demanded a role for ordinary people in public affairs, they were certainly not alone. Indeed, throughout the Republic, there were Patriots who seemed to be moving in precisely the same direction, though not always at the same time or with the same success.[56] Here we have examined the developments in Overijssel in considerable detail, not because they were unique or exceptional in some striking way, but in order to show how it was that the Patriots came to follow the path that they did. The point is that at every step the Patriots seemed to be experimenting, to be groping their way along an uncertain road toward revolution. The leaders of this movement do not appear to have been brilliant strategists or great theoreticians; rather in the context of a humiliating and disastrous war, they developed their organizations and their political programs in response to ever-changing circumstances in their communities and in their province. At times they appear to have been inspired and emboldened by the example of the Americans whose cause they observed and supported from a considerable distance, but soon the Patriots in Overijssel would have another inspiring example much closer to home.

In the ancient city of Utrecht, in another of the land provinces, the Dutch Patriots first learned how to engineer a municipal revolution, and the pattern of conflict there helped to condition expectations elsewhere in the Republic.[57] The struggle for control of Utrecht really began in 1784 when, in response to popular agitation, the government invited the citizenry to register their grievances against the existing Governmental Regulation. Among the responses was a specific Patriot proposal to democratize the Municipal Council by replacing co-optation with a complicated electoral system. In the primary stage all Burgers, except those on poor relief, would be enfranchised. When the Patriots' proposal was rejected, there followed a series of confrontations between the Municipal Council and large crowds of Patriots who regularly assembled outside the Stadhuis to press their demands. On several occasions, a Burger-committee supported by large petitions and noisy demonstrations, wrenched concessions away from the Council only to see the promises recanted later. In March, August, and December of 1785 and again in March of 1786, the Patriots appeared to make only incremental gains until finally the Council accepted the electoral principle and removed from office those Magistrates who objected to the changes. On August 2, 1786, then, Utrecht's first elected regents were sworn into office amid a great popular festival on the large public square called the Neude.

Among those who witnessed this remarkable event was John Adams, now serving as American envoy in London. A month later he wrote to Thomas Jefferson: "We were present at Utrecht at the August Ceremony of Swearing in their new Magistrates. In no instance, of ancient or modern History, have the People ever asserted more unequivocally their own inherent and unalienable Sovereignty."[58] While Adams was especially impressed with the assertion of popular sovereignty, in this case, we might also take note of the immense patience both sides seemed to display as the drama played itself out. The regents ultimately had no choice but to submit unless, of course, they wished to call on the Prince to send troops to defend them. The popular movement, on the other hand, seemed to be slow to discover its numerical advantage when it assembled thousands of people outside the Stadhuis, and at times the Patriots were incredulous when confronted with the duplicity of the local authorities. Still, they never wavered from their goal of electoral representation, and in the end they prevailed. In sum, once they overcame their inhibitions, the Patriots found that making revolution in the municipal setting was a fairly easy and straightforward task, and as time went on they became not only wiser but considerably less patient.

The problem with the municipal revolution at Utrecht, however, was that it was inconclusive. The provincial Estates of Utrecht, dominated by Orangist clients, refused to recognize the legitimacy of the popular elections and packed up for a safer haven in Amersfoort. In response, the revolutionary government of Utrecht convened its own rump version of the provincial Estates and effectively divided the sovereignty of the province. Meanwhile, in the fall of 1786, as a clear token of the Orangist regime's resolve to defend itself, the provincial Estates of Gelderland authorized the Prince of Orange to use regular army troops to subdue two small Patriot-dominated towns – Elburg and Hattem – which refused to accept the Prince's interference in municipal elections.[59] Hundreds of Patriot militiamen from as far as away as Oldenzaal in Twente had steamed to Gelderland to defend the rebellious cities, but when the first shots were fired, they fled in disarray across the IJssel River to Kampen and Zwolle. In the aftermath, hundreds of Patriots' houses were sacked and plundered by the invading forces.

Both inspired and sobered by these events, the Patriots in Overijssel soon led the way in establishing revolutionary control of a whole province, aided of course by the recent decision on *overstemming*.[60] In August 1785, massive petitions in the three *hoofdsteden* demanded that the Governmental Regulation be abolished; that all citizens have the opportunity to voice their grievances against local and provincial government; that the Sworn Councils continue the election of Magistrates, but that the Burgerij elect the members of the Councils; and finally that the people be given the right to remove representatives from office. Though this package of demands was considerably more radical that previous requests, it still met with a favorable response. The citizens of Deventer, Kampen, and Zwolle were invited to voice their grievances in the autumn of 1785, and in each city Burgercommittee reports on these grievances were published in January 1786. In the spring and summer of 1786, special constitutional commissions, soliciting public comment and criticism, distributed draft constitutions for municipal government which, in each case, provided for the election of the Sworn Councils by the enfranchised Burgerij.

But just when they seemed ready to usher in a new political era with hardly a fight, the Patriots' coalition in Overijssel began to exhibit signs of strain and to encounter resistance that threatened to halt the progress of reform altogether. Leaders of the smaller chartered cities, where the Patriots enjoyed enormous popular support, complained loudly and bitterly that the interests of the small cities were being ignored, even sacrificed by the Patriots in the *hoofdsteden*,[61] and in Zwolle, an increasingly belligerent Magistracy finally drew the line and refused to accede to the Patriots' demand for electoral reform and abolition of the Governmental Regulation. Meanwhile, in Deventer, the *"generale ouderlieden"* (general elders) of the guilds complained that the Burgercommittee had ignored their grievances and that the new draft constitution, as a result, threatened their corporate interests as well as the interests of "true religion." When their demands for a halt to the constitution-writing process were rejected by the municipal administration, the guild leaders created a new Burgercommittee that openly allied itself with Orangist regents like Everhard Putman, whom the Patriots had earlier demoted from Burgemeester to Councilor.

In the first few months of 1787, the Patriots finally moved decisively to capture key governmental institutions in Overijssel and began to reshape these institutions in order to consolidate their power. The crucial series of events began in Zwolle at the end of January when, under intense popular pressure, the votes of the Magistracy split evenly and the Sworn Council unilaterally abolished the Governmental Regulation. On the day of the annual municipal election (January 25), the Council agreed to accept as guidelines a series of 24 articles published earlier by the Burgercommittee and to remove from office any Burgemeester who would not endorse the Patriots' program. After uncharacteristically long hours of deliberation, the results of the election were finally announced by torch light from the steps of the Stadhuis: only seven men, previously the supporters of Patriot reforms, were returned to the Magistracy, while nine new faces appeared on the list. When these new Burgemeesters were sworn in without the Stadhouder's approval, the city was firmly in Patriot hands.

To the editors of the *Nieuwe Nederlandsche Jaarboeken*, a normally objective chronicle of events in the Republic, the actions of Zwolle's Sworn Council seemed blatantly illegal – the Council simply did not have the authority to abolish the Governmental Regulation, and by majority vote at that. For their part, however, the Patriots seemed to content with only the marginal appearance of legality, for their legitimacy was rooted in the "will of the People." In Deventer, successive resolutions at the beginning of February condemned the opposition's demand to halt deliberations on the new constitution, forbade all political activity by the guilds, and established stiff penalties for unauthorized meetings and activities. As the *Jaarboeken* summed up the situation, "No means were spared in order to smother this *volksstem* [voice of the people] which was so displeasing." On the eve of the annual municipal election, a large Patriot petition urged the Sworn Council to follow Zwolle's example in abolishing the Governmental Regulation for the city and required all Burgemeesters to pledge their support for constitutional reform. Accordingly, on February 22, the Council abolished the Regulation and five Burgemeesters who refused to support constitutional reform were replaced by five well-known Patriots.

At the provincial level, Zwolle's bloodless *coup* finally cleared the way for the abolition of the provincial Regulation by the Estates on January 30, 1787, by the majority vote of the delegates of the three cities supported by eight noblemen. Though the majority of the Ridderschap protested this action as "unconstitutional," Overijssel became thereby the Patriots' first revolutionary province. At the Landdag in March the Patriots began deliberating the provisions of a new provincial constitution, but it was not until a special session in May that they took specific steps to institutionalize their control. They freed the smaller towns to elect their own governments without outside interference, approved new rules for internal control of appointments to provincial offices, and proceeded to make new appointments to all vacant offices, including the provincial Executive Committee and the deputation to the Estates General. Finally, in June, the Patriots eliminated the last vestige of the Stadhouder's power in Overijssel by relieving him of his post as Captain-General.

Once in power, however, the Patriots found that they had to bolster their position with more than petition campaigns, demonstrations, and governmental resolutions; indeed, armed defense quickly became the new regime's greatest preoccupation. Despite legislation against public disorders, the *Jaarboeken* reported, "dissensions and acts of violence are erupting on all sides." Thus, perhaps the most important work of the revolutionary Estates was the creation in May of a special Defense Commission to coordinate the province's military preparedness. When the Council of State in The Hague refused to send supplies to relieve a severe shortage of ammunition, the Defense Commission dispatched a contingent of Vrijcorps volunteers to capture the army's garrison and supply depot at Ommerschans. Later, militiamen from Vollenhove were sent to help their beleaguered comrades at nearby Blokzijl, and when the Patriots learned that the staunchly Orangist government of Hasselt had secretly requested a garrison of Orangist troops, the Defense Commission occupied the city, prevented the creation of an Orangist garrison just in the nick of time, and helped to set up a Patriot government and militia there. During the summer months, at the urging of the provincial association of the Patriot militias, the Commission also began to make plans for a volunteer army to defend the province, especially from Orangist troops in the province of Gelderland.

As the Patriots consolidated their control in Overijssel, conflicts were heating up in other provinces as well. Revolutionary conflict was slower to develop in maritime Holland than in the land provinces, but when it did, the popular movement seized power with remarkable speed.[62] One of the problems was that most of the municipal governments in Holland had always been Patriot in the original anti-Orange sense. In Amsterdam, especially, the moderate Patriot regency maintained a firm control of the Civic Guard throughout 1786, but in the first five months of 1787, the clamor of more radical voices grew louder. A steady stream of petitions combined with frequent appearances at meetings of the Municipal Council by the most aggressive junior officers of the Vrijcorps made a moderate course less and less tenable. Finally a petition with 16,000 signatures and a massive demonstration on the Dam tipped the scales, and Amsterdam, too, was purged of Magistrates who would not accept democratic reforms. Patriot *coups* quickly followed in Rotterdam, Schiedam, and Gorinchem, but the Patriot's conquest of Holland was not complete until the so-called Flying Legion – a small militia contingent commanded by a Vrijcorps officer from Delft – precipitated *coups* in Delft and seven other cities during the summer.

In the northern province of Groningen, Patriot control of the city of Groningen assured Patriot domination of the province's delegation to the Estates General, but this could not disguise deep divisions between the city and the surrounding Ommelanden which together made up the provincial Estates.[63] In Friesland, by contrast, militant Patriots, having been consistently frustrated in their attempts to deflect the reactionary policies of the provincial Landdag in Leeuwarden, convened a rival Landdag in Franeker and began preparing for a military confrontation with their Orangist enemies.[64] For their part, Orangists managed to maintain their dominant and apparently unassailable position in the Estates of Zeeland, while they consolidated their control of the provincial government of Gelderland by executing purges of the magistracies of Zutphen and Arnhem accompanied by violent crowd action against the leaders of the Patriot movement there.[65]

The result of all this was the essential paralysis of Dutch politics at the national level. By a simple tally of the provinces in the summer of 1787, it might be said the Patriots were ahead of the game – Holland, Groningen and Overijssel were controlled by Patriots, Zeeland and Gelderland by Orangists, with Utrecht and Friesland divided between rival Estates. In fact, depending on which of the rival delegations from various provinces were recognized as official, either one side or the other might assemble a bare majority of the provincial votes in the Estates General. But even in more tranquil times, simple majorities could not prevail on matters of substance in Dutch republican politics. Thus, as long as the constituent provinces were so deeply divided, the United Provinces of the Netherlands effectively ceased to function as a collectivity. And given the apparent unwillingness of either side to compromise, everyone expected the Republic to be engulfed by civil war.

Working with French advisors and army officers, the Patriots of Holland established a military "cordon" around their province, while the Prince of Orange amassed whatever troops remained loyal to him in Gelderland and eastern Utrecht to threaten both Overijssel and the city of Utrecht. Despite these domestic preparations, however, it was the force of international arms and money that finally broke the political deadlock that gripped the Dutch Republic. A large influx of British secret service funds during the course of 1787 was intended to lay the foundations of an indigenous Orangist counter-revolution, but in the end, King Frederick William of Prussia used the pretext of an alleged insult to his sister, Princess Wilhelmina of Orange, to invade the Republic in September and to tip the delicate political balance in favor of the Orangists.[66] Though the city of Amsterdam held out until October 10, the Patriots, in general, offered little military resistance to the Prussian legions, and in some parts of the country violent Orangist crowds sent thousands of Patriots into exile in the Austrian Netherlands and France. Before the year was out, the Orangist "restoration" was complete.

Since the Patriots in Overijssel expected to be attacked by Orangist troops across the IJssel River from Deventer, they were not prepared for an invasion from the east. Part of a much larger force, nearly 900 Prussian hussars crossed Overijssel's eastern frontier on September 13, arriving first at Ootmarsum; from there they fanned out in smaller units to the other cities of Twente, moving gradually westward across the province and arriving finally at Zwolle on September 24. Meanwhile, a small contingent of Prussian horsemen came from Wageningen via Zutphen to Deventer on September 20. The deeply divided and demoralized city fell easily to the Prussian patrol despite the large number of Patriot volunteers stationed there. Though the Prussians professed only to want to pass through the province en route to Holland, they disarmed the Patriots' militias wherever they went. In Deventer, however, the "rejoicing" of the triumphant Orangists "quickly turned into indulgent wantonness and revenge." The houses of a number of leading Patriots were plundered and many prominent Patriots fled the city for their personal safety before the Prussian commander finally called for reinforcements to restrain the Orangist crowds (see plate 3). At the same time, the whole Magistracy and most of the members of the Sworn Council were removed from office at the insistence of the "Representatives of the Burgerij and Guilds." In the following weeks and months, moreover, many of the city's clerks, teachers, ministers, and even members of the Reformed Church Council were removed from their posts because of their Patriot sympathies. Thus, Deventer, once the Patriot city *par excellence*, became the scene of the province's most thoroughgoing Orangist counter-revolution.

THE PROBLEM OF DEVENTER

In retrospect, 1787 stands out as an especially critical year in the developing political crisis of the West. In the same autumn as the Dutch Patriot Revolution was aborted by foreign intervention, representatives of the United States of America were drafting a new Federal Constitution, motivated in part by the escalating pattern of domestic conflict that climaxed in Shays's Rebellion. At the same time, Joseph II of Austria's autocratic reforms were galvanizing a diverse opposition coalition that would soon drive him from his Belgian territories. And further to the south, the bankruptcy of the French crown led to the meeting of the Assembly of Notables and opened up the first, aristocratic phase of the French Revolution. The age of the democratic revolution was entering a new phase. From this point on, France occupied center stage, and soon even the common meaning of the term "revolution" would be transformed by the violent and protracted struggles there.

Compared to the drama of the French Revolution of 1789, the Dutch Patriot Crisis of the 1780s seems like a long crescendo within which *piano* only gradually shades into *forte*. The climax, the Patriot Revolution itself, was not a sudden or dramatic break with previous developments; rather, it seems to have been a logical extension of earlier events, commitments and claims, consistent in many ways with the routine forms of republican political conflict. To be sure, there were important transitions within this larger political process, such as when a broad coalition of political challengers first emerged or when these challengers first made exclusive claims to governmental control in the name of *het Volk*. But the critical break came when the challengers finally decided to enforce their claims at the expense of committing illegal acts and the established regime was simultaneously unwilling or unable to resist those claims. Still, the old regime refused to die, and for several months both republican sovereignty and the loyalty of the Dutch people were thoroughly divided. Though quite unlike the French Revolution of 1789, this situation was revolutionary in a peculiarly Dutch sense that obviously mirrored the fragmented structures of the decentralized Republic.

Having situated Deventer within the broad chronology and geography of long-term structural change and democratic revolution in the Dutch Republic, we can finally begin to analyze the internal dynamics of Deventer's municipal revolution. Like so many other eighteenth-century cities, Deventer provided a space where ordinary people could become political, where they could begin to make politics their routine and on-going concern. And like their counterparts in North America, the Patriots of Deventer began to develop constitutional mechanisms to insure that theirs would be a continuing political presence. In this way, Deventer's revolution fits squarely within the broader patterns of democratic revolution in the West. Yet Deventer's revolution was in many ways special. In the early days of the Patriot Crisis, many people in Deventer gladly chipped away at the legitimacy and authority of the old-regime elite, but by the time the Patriots actually seized power in 1787, they were sharply divided by the project of constitutional reform. In this small provincial town at the core of Europe's international economy, then, we can see with exceptional clarity how *democratic* revolution could awaken deep divisions among the very same people who had earlier been united in opposition to the "tyranny" of the old regime. In short, the history of the Patriot Revolution in Deventer shows us what was divisive and thus, in a profound sense, *revolutionary* about democratic revolution.

NOTES

1 Olwen Hufton, *Europe: Privilege and Protest, 1730–1789* (London, 1980), p. 348.
2 A. C. Carter, *Neutrality or Commitment: the Evolution of Dutch Foreign Policy 1667–1795* (London, 1975) and J. S. Bartstra, *Vlootherstel en Legeraugmentqatie. 1770–1780* (Assen, 1952).
3 J. W. Schulte Nordholt, *Voorbeld in de Verte. De Invloed van de Amerikaanse revolutie in Nederland* (Baarn, 1979), pp. 65–7.

4 See, for example, *Brief van een oprechten Fries aan den heer Z. D. H.* (1779), *Antwoord van een jong orderdaan* (1779), and *Brief van een heer te Utrecht, aan zijn vriend te Amsterdam* (1779).

5 C. H. Wilson, "The economic decline of the Netherlands," *Economic History Review*, 9 (1939), p. 126.

6 This judgment is based on the size of the collection of pamphlets for each year at the Koninklijke Bibliotheek in The Hague; see W. Knuttel (ed.), *Catalagus van de Pamphletten-verzameling berustende in de Koninklijke Bibliotheek*, vol. 5 (The Hague, 1905). In his recent research on the popular press in the 1780s, N. C. F. Van Sas has argued for the importance of new "spectator"-style political journals over against the traditional pamphlet as a vehicle for political debate. While this is ubdoubtedly true for the decade as a whole, it does not hold for the war years under discussion here. Cf. N. C. F. van Sas, "The Patriot Revolution: New Perspectives" (paper presented to "Decline, Enlightenment, and Revolution: The Dutch Republic in the Eighteenth Century," Washington, DC, March, 1987).

7 *Aan het Volk van Nederland* (Ostende, 1781). On the authorship and publication history of this pamphlet, see M. De Jong, *Joan Derk van der Capellen. Staatkundig levensbeeld uit de wordings tijd van de moderne democratie* (Groningen/Den Haag, 1922), pp. 381–416.

8 *Aan het Volk van Nederland* (modern commemorative edn, Weesp, 1981), p. 63.

9 Ibid., pp. 142–3.

10 *De wensch van de Utrechts-burgery, vernietigt door een raadsman van Willem den vyfden . . .* (Utrecht, 1781).

11 In the following sketch of Van der Capellen's politics, I am dependent throughout on De Jong, *Capellen*.

12 De Jong, *Capellen*, p. 106.

13 Certain fundamental issues (called *punten van bezwaar*), like the declaration of war, granting of privileges, creation of new taxes, etc., always required unanimity in Overijssel. William V was painfully aware of the similarity of this system to the famous Polish *liberum veto*: "it is certainly to be desired that, the sooner the better, another plan for deciding matters [at the Estates] be devised to replace the cursed Polish system of the *liberum veto* which is responsible for the partition of that kingdom by its neighbors not even ten years ago" (quoted in De Jong, *Capellen*, p. 228).

14 The Prince was, of course, referring to the notorious John Wilkes who had created a great stir in Britain just a few years earlier; cf. G. Rudé, *Wilkes and Liberty* (Oxford, 1962).

15 *NNJ*, 1777, p. 791.

16 Ibid.

17 De Jong, *Capellen*, pp. 236–7.

18 Ibid., p. 269.

19 Most of the official documents relating to the *drostendiensten* were published at one time or another; I have used the reports in *NNJ*, 1779, pp. 311–66, 621–71, 812–48, 1423–59; 1780, pp. 1101– 23; 1781, pp. 710–2, 1137–54, 1273–1319.

20 *NNJ*, 1779, pp. 327–41.

21 De Jong, *Capellen*, 229–306.

22 W. de Beaufort (ed.), *Brieven van en aan Joan Derck van der Capellen van de Poll*

(Utrecht, 1897), p. 178. The allusion here to Christ's betrayal is unmistakable, though Van der Capellen is often accused of having more than a "savior complex." Following M. de Jong, Van der Capellen's biographer, many authors insist that Van der Capellen's politics betray a kind of personality split that was irreconcilable. Prof. and Mrs W. F. Wertheim have defended him against such charges in their introduction to the modern edition of his pamphlet, *Aan het Volk van Nederland.*

23   De Jong, *Capellen*, pp. 462–7.

24   *Egte stukken betreffende het voorgevallene te Deventer* (Deventer, 1783), p. 5.

25   De Jong, *Capellen*, p. 273; *NNJ*, 1782, 458–9, 1611–80.

26   *NNJ*, 1782, pp. 1264–5. This view is in sharp contrast to that of I. Vijlbrief. Like many modern historians, Vijlbrief has a hard time taking the Patriots' concerns seriously: "The spectacle that the Patriots present to us is definitely not absorbing or compelling. Alongside the great questions that the war raised, insubstantial expedients were used to fight over unimportant matters: hunting rights, *drostendiensten*, admissions and readmissions, endowment of the scantiest offices – these are the things that excite the burgers and move them to action. The pamphlets and newspapers were full of a language that tickles our funny bones", *AGN*, vol. 8 (Utrecht/Antwerpen, 1955), p. 142.

27   De Jong, *Capellen*, p. 492; *Egte stukken*, pp. 10–16; *NNJ*, 1782, p. 1278.

28   De Jong, *Capellen*, pp. 491–3.

29   Ibid., p. 494.

30   De Beaufort, *Brieven*, p. 352.

31   De Jong, *Capellen*, p. 513.

32   De Beaufort, *Brieven*, pp. 400–1.

33   *Egte stukken*, pp. 24–30.

34   Ibid., pp. 31–4.

35   *NNJ*, 1783, pp. 663–73; *Egte stukken*, pp. 35–40; *Requesten en adressen van de burgery der stad Zwolle* (Zwolle, 1784), pp. 19–36.

36   De Jong, *Capellen*, pp. 542–52.

37   *Egte stukken*, pp. 78–9.

38   *NNJ*, 1783, pp. 1449–56.

39   *De Post van de Neder-Rhyn*, no. 221, pp. 591ff.

40   *NNJ*, 1783, p. 1451.

41   Ibid.; *Geschiedenis van het exercitie-genootschap der stad Almelo . . .* (n.d., n.p.).

42   *Egte stukken*, pp. 46–77; *NNJ*, 1783, pp. 1799–1835.

43   *NNJ*, 1783, pp. 1262–3; De Jong, *Capellen*, p. 646.

44   *NNJ*, 1783, pp. 1264–6, 1784, pp. 894–7.

45   Ibid., p. 1780.

46   *Antwoord op de missive J. V. Z. bevattende een verslag van het merkwaardigste bijzonderheden op den jongst afgelopen Overysselschen Landdag voorgevallen* (Amsterdam, 1784).

47   De Jong, *Capellen*, p. 682; De Beaufort, *Brieven*, p. 783.

48   *NNJ*, 1784, pp. 1172–3.

49   *NNJ*, 1785, pp. 520–5.

50   *De Post van de Neder-Rhyn*, no. 151, pp. 347–54.

51   *Brief aan een vriend, over de noodzakelykheid van de verandering van het Regeeringsreglement in Overyssel* (Dord, 1785).

52   *Blaadje zonder titel voor burger en boer in Overijssel*, no. 4, pp. 25–32.

53 *Antwoord aan een Burger to Campen, over de bezwaren die in de hoofdsteden geoppert worden, tegen het Regeerings-reglement in Overijssel, door een burger te Zwolle* (Zwolle, 1785).

54 De Beaufort, *Brieven*, p. 764.

55 *Blaadje zonder titel*, no. 7, pp. 54–6.

56 A reasonable survey of Patriot mobilization in general can be found in Simon Schama, *Patriots and Liberators. Revolution in the Netherlands, 1780–1813* (New York, 1977).

57 I. Vijlbrief, *Van anti-aristocratie tot democratie* (Amsterdam, 1950), A. van Hulzen, *Utrecht in de Patriottentijd* (Zaltbommel, 1966), and Schama, *Patriots and Liberators*, pp. 88–100.

58 J. Boyd (ed.), *Works of Thomas Jefferson*, vol. 10 (Princeton, NJ, 1954), p. 348.

59 H. A. Westrate, *Gelderland in de Patriottentijd* (Arnhem, 1903).

60 The following account is based broadly on the extensive reports in the *Nieuwe Nederlandsche Jaarboeken*, supplemented in some areas by pamphlets which will be cited and discussed more fully in Part II below.

61 See *Blaadje zonder titel*, pp. 161–8, 217–23, 369–76.

62 P. Geyl, *De patriottenbeweging* (Amsterdam, 1947), pp. 96ff; Schama, *Patriots and Liberators*, pp. 110–21.

63 K. Hildebrand, "De Patriottentijd in Stad en Lande, 1780–1787," *Groningse volksalmanak*, 1950, pp. 1–71.

64 W. W. van der Meulen, *Coert Lambertus van Beijma. Een bijdrage tot de kennis van Frieslands geschiedenis tijdens den patriottentijd* (Leeuwarden, 1894).

65 C. H. E. de Wit, *De Nederlandse Revolutie van de achttiende eeuw* (Oirsbeek, 1974), pp. 110–13.

66 Alfred Cobban, *Ambassadors and Secret Agents. The Diplomacy of the First Earl of Malmesbury at The Hague* (London, 1954).

PART II

The Dynamics of Municipal Revolution

4

The People Enter Politics

There was something truly remarkable, even spectacular, about the rise of the Patriot movement in Deventer. The very first signs of organized political action, following the outbreak of war with England and Van der Capellen's stirring call to arms in "*Aan het Volk*," came in April 1782, when 66 merchants, manufacturers, artisans, and boatmen signed a petition in support of John Adams and recognition of the United States. By the time a Treaty of Friendship and Commerce with the United States had been ratified in October, there was a new petition drive underway in Deventer which, by comparison with the first, represented a tidal wave of popular political activity: more than 1,460 signatures, representing more than two-thirds of the adult male population,[1] supported the standard list of Patriot demands regarding the upcoming provincial Landdag. Then, in rapid succession, the Patriots elected a Burgercommittee at the beginning of December, circulated two more large-scale petitions at the end of December and the beginning of February 1783, and created a voluntary militia in mid-March. Success followed success as Patriot demands were, with very few exceptions, satisfied by local and provincial authorities: chiefly, the *drostendiensten* were abolished, Van der Capellen was readmitted to the Ridderschap, and the Sworn Council held a "free" election of Burgemeesters. A pamphlet which recounted these events in the summer of 1783 bubbled with enthusiasm and confidence:

To free the oppressed Countryman from illegal exactions, to restore persecuted Virtue to her throne, to preseve Liberties and Privileges unviolated, to burst the shackles of servility, to support and secure against tyranny the delicate Freedom of City and Fatherland – these were, in recent days, the unanimous undertakings of DEVENTER'S Burgerij and Government.[2]

It is entirely typical of the nascent political movements at the end of the eighteenth century that the Patriots of Deventer should fancy themselves setting out on a task of restoration and preservation (rather than creation) at the same time as they were building an unprecedented popular force in Dutch politics. The collective action and popular politics of cities like London, Boston, Charleston, Brussels, and Paris exhibited a similar blending of old and new traits.[3] Indeed, throughout the Atlantic world popular movements adapted what was old and practiced in the vocabulary of protest and collective action to new and changing political objectives and realities. How the old and new were blended in Deventer can be seen clearly in the series of petition campaigns which proved so remarkably successful in 1782 and 1783.

Petitioning for redress of grievances was an old and venerable tradition in communities like Deventer. Ordinary people, either individually or more likely in groups such as guilds, regularly asked their Magistrates to uphold what they considered their legal rights and privileges, to relieve them of particularly irksome burdens or to grant them some kind of special dispensation or support in time of crisis. The large collections of such documents in many old-regime municipal archives suggest not only that the citizenry saw petitioning as an effective means of communication but also that the authorities tacitly accepted the obligation to receive and to act favorably on reasonable requests. In the 1780s this old tradition of humble petition was politicized and made a good deal more aggressive. The leader of the Patriot movement in its early phase, Van der Capellen, saw petitioning as a self-consciously political act; he thought, perhaps a bit overdramatically, it was the functional equivalent of having representatives or public meetings to influence policy decisions.[4] As it happened, in the course of 1782 and 1783 petitions quickly became the routine and preferred mechanism by which the new political movement could express approval or disapproval of local officials, argue for action on important demands, or even demand a general "redress of abuses in the constitution."[5]

But it was not simply the content that changed to make the petitions into political tools. The scale of the undertaking was of unquestionable importance to the political effectiveness of the petition campaigns. The largest petition, that of October 1782, had just three pages of text but no less than 30 pages of signatures.[6] Clearly the petition was intended to be a show of force. The arguments for abolition of the *drostendiensten* and reinstatement of Van der Capellen in the Ridderschap were, in any case, familiar to those on the receiving end of the petition. The real message here was that if the Magistrates rejected the argument, or simply failed to act, they risked the condemnation of the overwhelming majority of the population. To be sure, not all petitions had the signatures of the clear majority of the population, but each time the Patriots were able to demonstrate the support of "a great number of the most respectable Burgers and Residents" of the city.[7] Thus even the smallest petition, the hastily organized campaign of December 1782, still represented nearly 20 percent of the adult males of the community and was, in fact, sufficient to the task of convincing the Sworn Council to reject the Stadhouder's recommendations in the upcoming municipal elections.[8] In any event, even a relatively small petition provided the Patriots with the opportunity to demonstrate their political muscle by assembling an imposing crowd of people in the Grote Kerkhof outside the Stadhuis for the formal presentation of the petition (see plate 4).

Thus, in the 1780s humble entreaties were transformed into aggressive ultimatums, and the Patriots, like their counterparts in North America and England, proved that old wineskins could hold new wine at least for a while. Well-organized, broadly based petition drives proved especially effective in the Dutch context for two complementary reasons. On the one hand, municipal governments generally did not command the repressive capability to resist the clearly expressed "will of the people."[9] On the other hand, a well-timed petition could strengthen the hand of local authorities in dealing with the Stadhouder or the other members of the provincial Estates. In either case, large-scale petitions gave the black-robed Burgemeesters and Sworn Councilors of a city like Deventer enough of a push to transform sober hesitancy into firm action.

AN OCCUPATIONAL PROFILE

Since petitioning represented the main thrust of popular politics in Deventer during the Fourth English War, the petitions themselves provide us with an invaluable measure of the strength and character of the early Patriot movement. Although the first, small petition demanding recognition of the United States has been lost, copies of the three larger petitions have been preserved with signatures intact. Not all signatures on the petitions are legible, but it is possible to identify approximately half as heads of households in the census of 1795.[10] Since the petitions varied significantly in both size and content, there emerges from this research a remarkably vivid and dynamic view of the social composition and institutional background of an urban revolutionary movement-in-the-making.

During the first large-scale petition campaign in October 1782, the Patriots demonstrated the immense potential of a concerted effort to bring large numbers of people into the political arena. Building on the success of their earlier effort on behalf of John Adams, the Patriots now launched a frontal attack on the nobility by demanding readmission of Van der Capellen to the Estates, immediate abolition of the *drostendiensten*, and resolution of the *overstemming* problem in favor of the *hoofdsteden*.[11] Obviously determined to guarantee the success of their efforts, they flushed out every possible source of support. Even if we discount those who apparently signed more than once, it is clear that the October petition represents the Patriot movement at its strongest

Table 4.1   Occupational profile of Patriot signatories, October 1782

Occupation	Census 1795 (%)	Petition Oct.1782 (%)	Index census= 100
Manufacturing	38.6	53.8	139
Trade and transportation	16.9	23.0	136
Social services	5.3	6.0	113
Agriculture and fishing	6.4	4.6	72
Unskilled labor	8.4	3.2	38
Miscellaneous	6.7	3.2	48
Inactive	17.6	6.1	35
Total	100.0 (n=1,929)	99.9 (n=526)	

with at least 1,300 supporters. Using the census of 1795, I have been able to identify the occupations of 526 or approximately 40 percent of the total. Table 4.1 groups the identifiable signatories according to broad occupational categories and, as a benchmark for interpreting the data, expresses the overall size of each occupational group as a percentage of all heads of households in 1795.[12] With all due allowance for the uncertainties of nominal data linkage, we can see in table 4.1 the profile of the Patriot movement of Deventer as it burst onto the political stage in October 1782.

In broadest outline, the image of the Patriot movement seems to conform reasonably well to what we have come to expect of popular political movements in eighteenth-century cities. Foremost on the list, of course, is the full array of skilled artisans and tradesmen that was so characteristic of pre-industrial cities in northwestern Europe. Within the large category of manufacturing, we find the tailors, bakers, shoemakers, carpenters, weavers, and blacksmiths we would expect to find active in the sections of Paris as well as the crowds of London and Boston.[13] Alongside these we see a broad assortment of shopkeepers, merchants, innkeepers, boatmen, and carters who are grouped into the category of trade and transportation; with the possible exception of the ubiquitous Dutch boatman (*schipper*), these, too, could be expected to figure as prominently in political movements throughout the North Atlantic region. Together, those active in manufacturing and trade and transportation accounted for fully three-quarters of the people who signed the first Patriot petition. Further down the list we find a passel of lawyers, doctors, teachers, and students as well as a few market gardeners, day laborers, and disabled or retired people – all of these groups clearly less numerous but not to be ignored among the artisans and shopkeepers.

As broadly as the Patriots cast their net in search of support for this important petition, it is none the less clear that they did not pull in an entirely representative group of people. In order to measure the representative quality of the signatories, I have calculated what we might call an index of mobilization which expresses the rate of over- or under-representation of the various occupational groups relative to the size of the same groups in the census of 1795.[14] It is immediately obvious, then, that the two largest occupational groups were decidedly over-represented in the Patriot movement while the smaller, more marginal occupational groups were, with one exception, significantly under-represented. The exception here is, of course, the collection of professionals – lawyers, doctors, ministers, teachers – politicians, and public employees whom I have grouped together in the category of "social services." Though these people were the smallest occupational group in the total population, they were the third largest group among the Patriot signatories in October 1782. Still, this is not greatly surprising. We would generally expect educated professionals to be over-represented and day laborers to be under-represented among activists in eighteenth-century political movements.

On November 1, 1782, three weeks after this variegated assortment of Patriots presented the regents of Deventer with their "humble petitions," J. D. van der Capellen, whom William V had astutely dubbed "notre Wilkes," was readmitted to the provincial Estates. Though he was a member of the Estates by virtue of his noble ancestry, his new lease on political life was symbolic of the power of popular political activism. Spurred on by this highly visible triumph, the Patriots of Deventer began, at the beginning of December, to circulate a new petition that took aim at the prerogatives of the Stadhouder and urged the Sworn Council to hold a free election of Burgemeesters – free, that is, of the Prince's recommendations.[15] Partly because they were addressing an obviously receptive audience, partly because they were pressed for time, the Patriots devoted less effort to drumming up support this time around. Still, they managed to produce a petition with nearly 400 signatures before the month was out. Of this number, I could identify 210 (more than half of all signatories) whose occupational profile is presented in table 4.2. In contrast with the October petition which reflected the Patriot movement at its broadest extent, this petition can be said to reflect the most easily mobilized group of Patriot supporters.

The most interesting feature of the Patriot coalition as we see it in table 4.2 is the fact that although all groups have dropped in absolute numbers there is a clear shift toward the very groups which were proportionally over-represented on the first petition. In order to measure this shift, I have calculated the percentage of increase or decrease since the October petition in each group's share of the total number of signatories.[16] It is clear, then, that while the two largest groups remained relatively over-represented, only one, trade and transportation, actually increased its proportion of the total – and this by a

Table 4.2   Occupational profile of Patriot signatories, December 1782

Occupation	Census 1795 (%)	Petition Dec.1782 (%)	Index census= 100	Change since October
Manufacturing	38.6	54.2	140	+1%
Trade and transportation	16.9	32.9	194	+43%
Social services	5.3	4.8	90	−20%
Agriculture and fishing	6.4	1.4	22	−70%
Unskilled labor	8.4	1.0	12	−69%
Miscellaneous	6.7	1.4	21	−52%
Inactive	17.6	4.3	24	−30%
Total	100.0 (n=1,929)	100.0 (n=210)		

remarkable 43 percent. The result was that the three largest groups now accounted for more than 90 percent of the total in this scaled-down version of the Patriot's coalition. Conversely, the four smallest groups now constituted just 8 percent of all signatories. The most precipitous decline was registered by the agricultural and unskilled workers; the unskilled laborers also became the most under-represented occupational group, with an index of only 12.

This differential and fluctuating image of the Patriot coalition is reinforced by the last of the three petitions. Following the Sworn Council's decision to grant the Patriots' demand for free elections of Magistrates, the Patriots mounted yet another petition drive in February 1783.[17] Once again they attacked the influence and prerogatives of the nobility and their patron, the Stadhouder, demanding among other things legal prohibition of "vexatious prosecutions" such as Van der Capellen had endured, support for the rights of the smaller chartered towns, and abolition of the special military court system controlled by the Stadhouder as Captain-General of the Army. This time the Patriots made a more concerted effort to drum up support for the petition, perhaps because it was addressed to the Burgemeesters who represented a more cautious audience. But the result − 714 signatures − did not match the production of the previous October. Thus, in the February petition we still see a somewhat select group of Patriots, of whom I could identify 349 or just under half of the total (table 4.3).

As the Patriots again drew in larger numbers of people, they reversed the trend that was so noticeable in the occupational profile of the signatories in December. The share of the four most marginal groups jumped from 8 to 14 percent, with two of these categories more than doubling their share of the total. Still, all of these groups remained substantially under-represented and their collective share of all signatories remained slightly below that of October 1782. Conversely, the two largest occupational groups declined to 81 percent of

Table 4.3   Occupational profile of Patriot signatories, February 1783

Occupation	Census 1795 (%)	Petition Feb.1783 (%)	Index census= 100	Change since December
Manufacturing	38.6	51.9	134	−4%
Trade and transportation	16.9	28.7	170	−13%
Social services	5.3	5.2	98	+8%
Agriculture and fishing	6.4	3.2	50	+129%
Unskilled labor	8.4	1.7	20	+41%
Miscellaneous	6.7	3.7	52	+164%
Inactive	17.6	5.7	32	+32%
Total	100.0 (n=1,929)	100.0 (n=349)		

the total with the largest drop among those active in trade and transportation, the only group to increase in December. By comparison with the more marginal groups, however, the largest occupational groups remained substantially over-represented within the overall configuration of the Patriot movement.

In order to summarize the basic outline of the Patriot movement over time, we can graph the indices of mobilization for each occupational group on each of the petitions. Figure 4.1 illustrates, then, how the fluctuations in the size and profile of the Patriot movement, however drastic they may have been, did not alter the basic pattern of over- and under-representation that was apparent in the first petition. The fact is that the commercial, skilled artisanal, and pro-fessional segments of Deventer's population – what the Patriot pamphleteers liked to refer to as the "most respectable Burgers and Residents" – formed the basis of the new political movement. Although there is nothing particularly surprising about this pattern of Patriot mobilization, the Deventer petitions themselves give us an exceptionally clear indication of why this pattern was so consistent and firm.

GUILDSMEN AND OTHERS

On the petitions of December 1782 and February 1783, the members of many craft and merchant guilds proudly signed together under the name of their guild, with the officers of the guild usually signing first. Thus, in December 1782, 234 of the 384 signatories (61 percent) identified themselves as members of a dozen guilds. Likewise in February 1783, 296 or 41 percent of the 714 signatories identified themselves as guild members. These lists of signatures can by no means be considered exhaustive guild membership directories, but for our present purpose they are interesting precisely because they include only

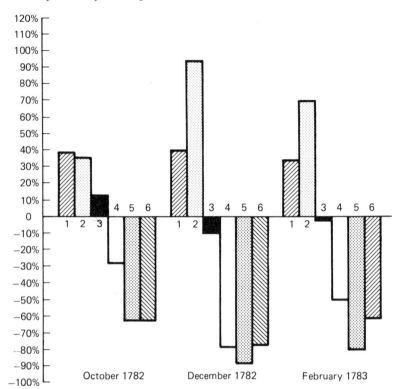

1 Manufacturing
2 Trade and transportation
3 Social services
4 Agriculture and fishing
5 Unskilled labour
6 Other

Figure 4.1   Over- and under-representation of occupational groups.

those members who consciously identified themselves with their guild – those who were actively participating in the political activity of the guild. If we focus on the political record of those guild members who can also be identified in the occupational census,[18] we can see clearly how the Patriots depended on these old-regime corporations as they put together a popular political movement in Deventer.

On the large petition of October 1782, 140 men who later identified themselves as guild members were among the 526 people I could identify in the 1795 census; they accounted for approximately one-quarter of the identifiable signatories. Although they did not specify their guild affiliation at this point, it is clear that many were becoming involved through their guild organizations. A large number of shoemakers, for example, signed together on page 11, a number of coopers on page seven, and many of the blacksmiths on page ten, all of which suggests that their signatures were solicited when the guild was assembled. Still, not all guilds were involved in this organized way in October: the signatures of the members of the large retail merchants guild (*Slyters Gilde*) were scattered throughout the some 30 pages of the petition.

With the petition of December 1782, the role of the guilds became both dominant and explicit. Following the signatures of the newly elected Burger-committee on the top of the first page, the guilds filled the first 12 pages of the petition. Signatures of non-guildsmen did not appear until the last three pages, which were identified specifically as *particulieren* (individuals, private persons). In all, guild members accounted for more than three-fifths of the signatures even though in absolute numbers their participation had actually declined slightly from 140 to 134. Thus, it seems that when the Patriots' Burgercom-mittee quickly organized a petition drive in the waning days of 1782, they could depend on the organizational base of the guilds to gather a respectable number of signatures. In February 1783, the guilds again dominated the first ten pages of the petition, but this time the pages of signatures including *particulieren* increased. As a result, the guild members constituted only by 46 percent of the identifiable signatories, even though more guild members signed this petition than had the previous two.

Summarizing these fluctuations, figure 4.2 illustrates graphically the role that guildsmen played in the early months of the Patriot movement. Whether they were merchants or craftsmen, blacksmiths or pastry bakers, those who iden-tified with their guilds were the solid, reliable core around which the movement was built. Meanwhile, those who stood outside the guild structures – the so-called *particulieren* – accounted for nearly all the variation in the size of the Patriots' petitions; their numbers among those whose occupations could be identified fluctuated wildly from 386 down to 73 and back up to 188. Since it was precisely in the commercial and industrial sectors of the economy that' guilds were predominant, it is easy to see why the corresponding occupational groups were consistently over-represented in the Patriots' coalition and es-pecially when less effort was devoted to the petition drives.

The importance of politically active guilds can be seen even more clearly if we focus on the most faithful petition-signers. In all, I have been able to identify 622 people who signed at least one of the first three major petitions; of these, 173 (28 percent) were identified as members of guilds. By contrast, there were just 152 people who signed all three petitions, and of those 68 percent were guild members. As table 4.4 indicates, nearly 90 percent of these most faithful petition-signers were from the two largest occupational groups, but within those groups there were large variations in the level of mobilization. Textile workers, who appear to have had no active guilds, were not represented at all, while metalworking, woodworking, leatherworking, and the garment and food

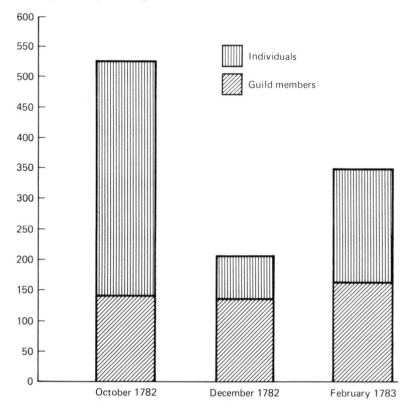

Figure 4.2   Active Patriots: the role of guilds, 1782–3.

trades had indices of over 200. Indeed these groups provided more than half of the core supporters of the Patriot movement though they constituted less than one-quarter of the working population. Merchants and shopkeepers were not as over-represented, but they still constituted another 22 percent of the Patriot core. On the whole, it was precisely those occupational groups in which an above-average percentage of all petition-signers were guildsmen that were over-represented among the Patriot faithful.

Clearly those merchants and craftsmen who were organized in guilds and in the habit of meeting regularly in the pursuit of collective interests could be recruited easily and reliably as groups. Conversely, *particulieren* were proportionally under-represented in the Patriot movement because, lacking corporate status and internal organizations, they had presumably to be recruited one-by-one. But to emphasize the important distinction – suggested by the Patriots themselves – between guildsmen and *particulieren* is also to underscore the sense in which the Patriots in Deventer represented not a single, monolithic

Table 4.4   The core of Patriot support, 1782–3

Occupation	Census 1795 (%)	Patriot core (%)	Index census= 100	Guild members[a] (%)
Manufacturing				
Construction	5.8	5.9	102	15
Metalworking	2.2	7.2	327	38
Woodworking	3.2	6.6	206	41
Leatherworking	5.4	11.8	218	41
Textiles	6.1	0.0	0	0
Garments	6.0	14.5	241	48
Food	5.7	11.8	207	40
Miscellaneous	4.5	3.3	73	24
Subtotal	38.6	61.2	159	33
Trade and transportation				
Commerce	12.1	22.4	185	40
Transportation	4.8	5.9	122	39
Subtotal	16.9	28.3	167	39
Other	44.5	10.5	24	5
Total	100.0 (n=1,929)	100.0 (n=152)		28

[a]Guild members = guildsmen as a percentage of all signatories in category.

movement, but a broad coalition of very different types of people. In the context of a humiliating and economically disastrous war, *rentiers* and common laborers, wholesale merchants and small shopkeepers, guild masters and journeymen, preachers and professors could all unite in opposition to the Stadhouder and the provincial nobility and in defense of "the delicate Freedom of City and Fatherland." Later, when the war was over and these people set about the far more difficult task of restructuring their own community, they would discover their differences. But for the moment, it may actually have seemed as if their "undertakings" were "unanimous."

A QUESTION OF LEADERSHIP

To mobilize so quickly large numbers of people who were broadly, if not equally or consistently, representative of the various segments of Deventer's working population was no mean achievement for the Patriots. Even as straight-forward an activity as a large petition drive required organizational resources and leadership abilities that not all Patriot sympathizers possessed in equal abundance. Given the prominence of guildsmen among the rank and file of the Patriot movement, it should come as no surprise to find that guildsmen were also prominent among the leadership of the Patriot movement. But just as the act of petitioning combined old and new traits, so also the organization and leadership of this new political force combined traditional and innovative qualities to make it successful.

It is unclear who put together Deventer's very first petition demanding recognition of the United States. The reports that merchants, craftsmen, and boatmen were the most prominent signatories suggest that the guilds may have been involved.[19] Still, it was the members of the Deventer chapter of the *Economische Tak*, one of several new reforming societies founded in the 1770s, who immediately wrote to thank Deventer's Magistrates for their efforts when John Adams's credentials had finally been accepted.[20] It may, in fact, have been groups like the *Economische Tak* or the larger *Maatschappij tot Nut van het Algemeen* which stood behind the nation-wide petition campaign. In any case, it is clear that when the Patriots addressed themselves to local and provincial problems, they turned to the corporative institutions of the old regime to get the job done. The *generale ouderlieden*, the elders or senior officers of the guilds, and the two senior officers of the Civic Guard, the largely ceremonial and ineffective municipal watch, drafted and circulated the petition of October 1782.[21] Surely the unprecedented size of this petition is eloquent testimony to the political effectiveness of these ostensibly a-political organizations.

On December 1, 1782, however, the ad hoc leadership of the guilds and the Civic Guard was superseded by a formally commissioned Burgercommittee, the first specifically political organization created by the Dutch Patriots during the 1780s.[22] It is very easily possible that in establishing this Burgercommittee, the Patriots of Deventer were imitating the committees of correspondence that were central to the American revolutionary movement, since *Aan het Volk* had specifically enjoined the Dutch to follow the example of the Americans. In any case, Deventer's nationally publicized and imitated "Act of Appointment," signed by "a great number of respectable Burgers and Residents," commissioned 12 representatives to draw up and circulate petitions on behalf of the Burgerij, to watch over the actions of local government, to correspond with Patriots elsewhere, and in general, to act as public advocates and spokesmen for the Burgerij. Though the Burgercommittee was typical of the new, voluntary, special-purpose associations that became prevalent at the end of the eighteenth century, it was specifically intended to formalize and strengthen the ad hoc leadership of the guilds and the Civic Guard by adding eight at-large representatives to their number. Thus, the new committee was intentionally built around an old-regime corporative frame. The new committee members included two merchants, the owner of a sugar refinery, a baker, and a shopkeeper. Of the 12, at least three can be identified as guild members, and in accordance with the explicit policy of allowing representation of religious dissenters, three of the committeemen were Mennonites.[23]

The Burgercommittee was obviously designed to effect a more-or-less permanent coalition between guildsmen and *particulieren*, and it immediately set about its task with a good deal of energy. It drafted and circulated the petition of December 1782, and in January aided in establishing a similar committee in Zwolle. Then, in cooperation with the Zwolle committee, it drafted and circulated the petition of February 1783. Later in that month, the members of the Committee were also integrally involved in the city's challenge to the Stadhouder's "recommendations" in municipal elections; when the Prince tried to install his own people, the Committee used its influence to persuade the Prince's candidates to decline their positions in favor of the Sworn Council's candidates. Thereafter, secure in the support of the broader community, the Committee began to pursue a more independent course of action. Thus, it frequently submitted petitions and requests in its own name and depended less often on massive petition drives.[24]

It is probably not coincidental that the Burgercommittee's enthusiasm in organizing massive petition drives declined at about the same time as the Patriots created the second of their new political organizations: the Vrijcorps. Initial plans for a Patriot militia had been discussed as early as December 1782, shortly after the creation of the Burgercommittee, but a final decision to go ahead with the organization and approve its regulations waited until March 3, 1783. The Vrijcorps' elected officers then petitioned the Magistrates for official sanction on March 23, and by the end of the month the new militia was in business.[25] The Vrijcorps reportedly began in 1783 with approximately 100 members, but by the end of 1784 its ranks had swelled to 300.[26]

We know very little about the Vrijcorps' early activities, except that the troops exercized regularly in public places when the weather permitted. Beginning in 1784, various officers actively participated in the meetings of provincial and national Vrijcorps federations, and in the fall of 1786, volunteers were sent to defend the rebel cities of Elburg and Hattem, across the border in Gelderland, from attack by the Prince of Orange. The importance of the Vrijcorps was, however, as much political as it was military. Patriot petitions signed by hundreds of local residents might be persuasive, but more than 300 men under arms constituted a force that municipal authorities could scarcely resist – unless, of course, they wished to ask the Stadhouder, as Captain-General of the Army, to garrison and deploy regular troops in the city. The Vrijcorps was obviously the strong arm of the Patriot movement in Deventer, and it obviated the need of frequent petition campaigns to demonstrate the Patriots' political muscle.

Unfortunately, we do not have a membership list for the new Vrijcorps, but the eight officers who signed their names to the petition requesting official sanction from the Magistrates suggest another way in which the Vrijcorps was important to the Patriot coalition in Deventer.[27] If the membership of the Burgercommittee can be said to reflect the social diversity of the Patriot movement, quite the opposite is true of those who were elected officers of the

Vrijcorps. From the Colonel Commandant on down, the officers were drawn from the elite of Deventer society. Only one of the eight was active in either trade or industry: Hendrik Budde was a prominent merchant. Four others – A. G. Besier, G. J. Jacobson, W. G. Lemker, and Lambert Bannier – were lawyers, while Georg van Hemert and J. J. Schmaus were *rentiers*. W. G. Storm van 's Gravesande was born in British Guyana and became a Burger of Deventer in 1776; he, too, may have been a *rentier*. In any case, the political connections of these men were even more impressive. Almost all were from prominent patrician families, and Van Hemert and Lemker had been members of the Sworn Council since 1759 and 1773, respectively. Budde, Besier, Jacobson, and Bannier were all elected to the Council in the controversial election of 1783 – at the same time as they were drawing up plans for the Vrijcorps. Storm van 's Gravesande was elected the following year. Thus, seven of the eight original officers were members of the Sworn Council by 1784.

This evidence suggests, then, that through the officers of the militia, the Patriot movement was able to forge an alliance with an important element of the regent elite. The Patriot movement, in fact, had much to offer disaffected members of the Sworn Council. For more than 30 years the Council's most important function – the annual election of the Magistracy – had been thoroughly compromised by the patronage system of the Stadhouders. Moreover, in relation to the Magistracy, the Council had lost much of its initiative in legislative matters with the result that by the end of the eighteenth century, Deventer was run for all practical purposes by resolutions enacted by the Burgemeesters alone rather than by the *Concordaaten* of the Council and the Magistracy acting in concert. All of this changed during the Patriot Crisis, however. The Sworn Council, spurred on by the popular movement, easily reasserted its authority in the "free" elections of Burgemeesters that began in 1783. At the same time, the Book of Concordaaten swelled with an unprecedented number of "Contributions" (*Inbrengens*) from the Council.[28] For those on the Council who supported these initiatives, the coalition with the Patriot movement, effected through the militia, was an invaluable political asset.

For the vast majority of Patriots who stood outside the ruling oligarchy, the alliance with the Council was equally important. The Vrijcorps officers who sat in the Council provided the movement with valuable political experience and institutional connections that the members of the Burgercommittee, standing completely outside the municipal government, simply could not offer. More importantly, these men were living proof of how divided and vulnerable the oligarchy was. By electing dissident members of the Sworn Council as their officers, the Patriots not only strengthened their movement but weakened the municipal government's ability to resist Patriot demands.

As the various pieces of the Patriot coalition came together and the alliances were formalized by the Burgercommittee and the Vrijcorps, the new political movement in Deventer seemed virtually invincible. For example, by March

1783, both the Magistracy and the Sworn Council had accepted *all* of the demands the Patriots had made in their February petition. Another petition relating to defense policies got similar positive results in December. By February 1784, the annual municipal elections had, in effect, been transformed into a kind of Patriot festival. Large crowds of people turned out to watch the Vrijcorps perform its drills and to cheer the election of three more Patriots to Council vacancies.[29]

Even so, the Patriots had some tense moments along the way. In the spring of 1784, for example, the Burgercommittee caused something of a flap when it demanded that 25 years be established as the minimum age limit for Sworn Councilors.[30] A majority of the Council objected not only to the substance of the proposal, but to the tone in which it was written, and they voted it down. When the Burgercommittee and the Patriot minority on the Council nevertheless continued to press the issue, outside observers as diverse as Van der Capellen and the editors of the *Nieuwe Nederlandsche Jaarboeken* condemned their actions as an illegitimate attempt to force through a minority view. It was, thus, a serious threat to municipal harmony. Despite the public slap from Van der Capellen, the Burgercommittee organized a petition campaign in the fall to give added weight to their demands. Although a skeptical municipal government claimed that irregularities flawed the petition – for example, some of the signatories were found to be minors – they nevertheless gave in to the Patriots' pressure and approved the age limitation at the beginning of 1785.

Another ironic wrinkle emerged in the Patriots' coalition in the course of 1784. A. F. Ruckersfelder, Professor of Theology at the Deventer Atheneum, warned his friend Van der Capellen that he suspected "a certain ex-Burgemeester," by which he surely meant E. H. Putman whom the Sworn Council had removed from office in 1783, was attempting to sow discord in the Patriot movement by encouraging some of the guilds to make unrealistic demands for direct popular election of Sworn Councilors. According to Ruckersfelder, who opposed the idea because it was divisive, the guildsmen thought that "if they were to enjoy freedom, they would have to elect the Sworn Councilors themselves."[31] The issue proved to be only a minor irritation at the time and was quickly eclipsed by the crisis in the provincial Estates over the question of *overstemming*. But only a year later, direct election of Sworn Councilors would no longer be the suspiciously unrealistic dream of a few guildsmen; it would stand as one of the primary demands of the Patriot movement as a whole.

The resolution of the *overstemming* controversy in favor of the *hoofdsteden* represented a major turning point in the Patriot Crisis in Overijssel. With that victory in March 1785, the long-standing struggle to reduce the power of the Stadhouder and the nobility was essentially over; all of the Patriots' original demands had been satisfied. The Patriots now moved the conflict to a new plane by demanding basic constitutional reforms to institutionalize popular sovereignty. Thus, in August 1785, a large petition demanded abolition of the Governmental Regulation, creation of a municipal commission to examine the ancient rights and privileges of the Burgerij, and popular elections of Sworn Councilors.[32] Unfortunately, this petition has not survived intact. It is possible, however, that 29 pages of signatures were separated from the text and improperly inventoried in the Deventer Archive as a "protocol of signatures of the members of the guilds of Deventer."[33] If this hunch is correct, then it appears as if the demand for constitutional reform received the support of more than 850 signatories in Deventer. The block support of many of the guilds on the first pages of the petition suggests, moreover, that the Patriot coalition had been mobilized in much the same way as in 1782 and 1783, with the guilds serving as the foundation upon which the edifice of a much broader movement could be built.

A COMPARATIVE PERSPECTIVE

Thus far I have repeatedly emphasize the typically eighteenth-century features of the popular movement in Deventer: the ubiquity of petty-bourgeois artisans and shopkeepers, or the thoroughgoing mixture of traditional and innovative traits in both the movement's demands and the actions undertaken to promote them. By way of conclusion, however, a brief comparison of Deventer with her sister-cities, Kampen and Zwolle, will serve the very useful function of highlighting some of Deventer's special qualities and thus of bringing us back down from the world of vague similarities to a reality where even slight variations can be significant.

From a distance, it would seem as if these three cities followed roughly the same political trajectory. In all three cities, politicization was rapid and extensive during the war, and by 1784 each of the municipal governments, following Deventer's lead and backed by expressions of popular support, had defied the recommendations of the Stadhouder in municipal elections. Then, in August 1785, Patriots in all three cities signed petitions demanding abolition of the Governmental Regulation and popular election of the Sworn Council. Underneath this basic outline, however, there lies a great diversity of experience.

In Zwolle, the largest of the enfranchised cities,[34] the Patriots put together a popular movement that rivaled or surpassed Deventer's in sheer numbers and range of activities. For example, the petition of October 1782, regarding Van der Capellen and the *drostendiensten*, reportedly had more than 2,000 signatures affixed to it,[35] and though the Zwolle Vrijcorps was formed later than Deventer's, it had 425 men under arms by the end of 1784.[36] In August 1785, the Zwollenaars clearly outdid their allies in Deventer when they mobilized fully 50 percent of the heads of households for the petition demanding basic constitutional reform and popular elections. The signatories to that petition indicate, moreover, that the Patriots in Zwolle had been able to draw support from all segments of the working population, but with a preponderance of petty-bourgeois artisans and shopkeepers.[37]

As was the case in Deventer, beneath this pattern of mobilization there stood the bedrock of the corporative guild structure. Van der Capellen, who otherwise looked on guilds as archaic economic institutions, strongly advocated using them as the basis for popular mobilization in Zwolle in particular. To work through the guilds, he argued, was to mobilize immediately at least half of the population of this city; conversely, without their support he thought little could be accomplished.[38] Thus, having organized the first massive petition drive, the Presidents and Vice-Presidents of the guilds were also the prime movers behind the creation of the Burgercommittee in Zwolle. The formal "Act of Qualification" was endorsed by 20 of the city's 22 guilds, as corps, and established a 16-member committee comprised of equal numbers of guildsmen and *particulieren*.[39]

The chief difference between the developments in Deventer and Zwolle is the evident tension between the popular movement and Zwolle's municipal government. The pamphlet writer from Deventer was undoubtedly exaggerating when he suggested that municipal politics in Deventer were always characterized by unanimity of purpose among the government and the people. Still, it is striking that when Van der Capellen and others were attempting to form a Patriot Vrijcorps in Zwolle, they encountered all sorts of roadblocks and had finally to invoke the considerable clout of the guilds in order to overcome the determined opposition of Zwolle's Magistracy.[40] The available evidence does not indicate whether or not the Patriots had established close ties with disgruntled members of Zwolle's Sworn Council, though M. van Heusen-Bruggeman's research on the petition of August 1785 suggests that in Zwolle the Patriots enjoyed relatively less support from the intellectual and political elite than they did in Deventer.[41] In any case, it seems to be true that Zwolle's Sworn Council enjoyed very little institutional independence and thus little leverage over the Magistracy.[42] The result was that whereas Deventer's Patriots could effectively exploit divisions within the ruling oligarchy, Zwolle's popular movement had to go it alone against a solidly conservative Magistracy led by Burgemeester L. Rouse, who was one of William V's closest allies in Overijssel. After 1785, that division between the Orangist Magistracy and the popular Patriot movement in Zwolle became increasingly serious and important.

By comparison with Zwolle, the overwhelming impression one has of Kampen, the smallest of the *hoofdsteden*,[43] is that it was extremely peaceful during the political crisis. One writer summed up the situation in 1785 as follows:

Our Burgerij is peaceful and obedient to the orders of their regents. Is there another city where regent and Burger agree more fully in the redress of political abuses? Where else can you find a Burgercommittee like ours which is completely accepted by the government?[44]

The apparent tranquility in Kampen was, however, predicated on circumstances remarkably different from those which assured "unanimity" in Deventer. In the first place, popular political action, though occasionally visible, was weak and sporadic. M. de Jong notes, for example, that the important petition of October 1782 was signed by only 128 persons in Kampen.[45] The largest petition, dating from 1787, had only 463 signatures.[46] The Patriots of Kampen were, moreover, slow to create independent organizations to facilitate popular mobilization, and when they did, the influence of the local oligarchy was clearly evident. The local Vrijcorps, the last to be formed in the *hoofdsteden*, was overshadowed and outnumbered more than two to one by the active Civic Guard which had as its commander Abraham Vestrinck, the oldest and most powerful member of the corps of Burgemeesters who was often known as the "Prince of Kampen."[47] And the Burgercommittee, elected finally in October 1785, was scarcely the spontaneous creation of an activist Burgerij; it was created at the behest and under the watchful eye of the government for the limited purpose of receiving the grievances of the citizenry following the petition in August 1785.[48] In short, the peacefulness of the city obscures, as W. A. Fasel suggests, the essential weakness of the popular Patriot movement in Kampen.

It is possible, I suppose, that in Kampen there was no real *need* to mount massive petition campaigns or to elect a Burgercommittee to enforce Patriot demands. After all, Kampen's Magistracy under the leadership of Burgemeester Vestrinck was generally united in opposition to the Stadhouder and the nobility without that kind of push from below. And when they occasionally hesitated to endorse Patriot demands, the Patriot-dominated Sworn Council, which in the absence of a local Burgercommittee corresponded with the Burgercommittees of Zwolle and Deventer, was able to prod the Burgemeesters into action. More fundamentally, however, the virtual absence of a popular movement in Kampen reflects the essential weakness of the guilds there. In both Deventer and Zwolle, the corporative independence and *esprit de corps* of the guilds made them a powerful force – the most easily mobilized and reliable core of the Patriot coalition. In Kampen, however, the guilds lacked that kind of independence and spirit; most significantly, they could not even meet without the expressed permission of the Magistracy.[49] Thus, the guilds were incapable of organizing popular political action independently, and in the absence of an organizational base either in the corporative guilds or specifically political institutions like the Burgercommittees of Deventer and Zwolle, the Patriot movement remained the stepchild of the partician elite.

On the whole, then, we might conclude that Deventer deserved its reputation as a model of both popular mobilization and internal harmony during the early years of the Patriot Crisis. Certainly it is hard to imagine that any other city in the Dutch Republic was in a better position to usher in the revolutionary new age of representative democracy when tyranny would be checked and liberty preserved by creating a government subject only to the will of the people. As is so characteristic of revolutionary movements, however, the unity of purpose that was easily achieved in the work of attacking the old regime proved elusive in the work of creating a new one to replace it.

NOTES

1 This calculation is based on the assumption that approximately one-quarter of the population of 8,200 was adult and male. Cf. B. H. Slicher van Bath, *Een samenleving onder spanning* (Assen, 1957).
2 *Egte stukken betreffende het voorgevallen te Deventer* (Deventer, 1783), p. 3.
3 Cf. Charles Tilly, "The web of contention in eighteenth-century cities," in *Class Conflict and Collective Action*, ed. Louise A. and Charles Tilly (Beverly Hills,Ca/London, 1981).
4 W. H. de Beaufort (ed.), *Brieven van en aan Joan Derk van der Capellen van de Poll* (Utrecht, 1879), pp. 400–1.
5 For the broader significance of this kind of collective action in the Patriot Revolution, see W. P. te Brake, "Popular politics and the Dutch Patriot Revolution," *Theory and Society*, 14 (1985), pp. 199–222.
6 GA Deventer, Republiek II, 133.
7 This is almost a cliché in the voluminous Patriot literature; see, for example, *Egte stukken, passim*.
8 This petition had a total of 384 signatures; see GA Deventer, Republiek II, 133.
9 R. M. Dekker, *Holland in beroering* (Baarn, 1982), pp. 95–109, emphasizes the potent repressive capabilities of the regents of cities in Holland, but that picture seems to assume a unity of purpose or at least a reasonable working relationship between local magistrates, provincial authorities, and the commanders of the army – conditions that were noticeably absent in the 1780s.
10 See appendix II for a discussion of the procedures and guidelines used in this research.
11 GA Deventer, Republiek II, 133: "Request der Burgerij aan de Gezworen Gemeente." This is actually a duplicate of the petition, complete with signatures, that was sent to the Sworn Council; it asked the Council to support the petition to the Magistrates. I have not been able to find the copy of the petition that was presented to the Magistrates.
12 Note that the percentages and totals for the census of 1795 differ from those used in chapter 2 because in this context I have included all heads of households, whether active or inactive.
13 Compare, for example, Gwyn A. Williams, *Artisans and Sans-Culottes. Popular Movements in France and Britain during the French Revolution* (New York, 1969), and Dirk Hoerder, *Crowd Action in Revolutionary Massachusetts, 1765–1780* (New York, 1977) as well as the many pioneering studies of George Rudé.
14 This index of mobilization is calculated as follows: the percentage of signatories on the petition in each category is divided by the percentage of heads of households in the census for the same category; the quotient is, in turn, multiplied by 100.

15　GA Deventer, Republiek II, 133: "Request aan de Gezworen Gemeente tot het doen van eene vrije keur, enz."

16　This figure is calculated as follows: the percentage of signatories in each category on the earlier petition is subtracted from the percentage of signatories in the same category on the later petition; the difference is divided by the percentage in this category on the earlier petition; and the quotient is multiplied by 100.

17　GA Deventer, Republiek II, 133: "Dank-adress en nader request aan de Gezworen Gemeente."

18　Though one could presumably infer a person's occupation from his guild membership, I did not do so in order not to inflate artificially the importance of guild members in the identifiable signatory totals. Only those who appear in the 1795 census were included in the larger data base; cf. appendix II.

19　*Egte stukken*, pp. 1–6.

20　Ibid., pp. 8–9.

21　Ibid., pp. 24–30.

22　Ibid., and M. de Jong, *Joan Derk van der Capellen* (Groningen/Den Haag, 1921).

23　The names of Mennonites were identified using the index in the Deventer Archive of names associated with the local Mennonite congregation.

24　*Egte stukken*, pp. 50–77, and *NNJ*, 1783, pp. 1799–835.

25　*NNJ*, 1783, pp. 1449–56, and *Egte stukken*, pp. 78–80; see also the "wetten" or regulations of the militia printed on pp. 81–9.

26　GA Zwolle, Oud Archief, A-75: "Stukken (w. o. gedrukte notulen) betreffende diverse Overijsselse exercitie genootschappen, 1784–1787."

27　These names were printed in *Egte stukken*, pp. 78–80. In order to learn more about the political leadership of Deventer, I have consulted, whenever possible, the genealogies of leading Deventer families that are indexed and collected in the Deventer Archives. Genealogies often list occupations and educational experience of family members. In addition, the annual *Naamregister van alle Heeren leden der Regeering in de Provintie Overijssel* noted the special titles – for example, M. D. (medical doctor) or Mr. (master of law) – of provincial or municipal officials. These sources will not be cited separately below.

28　GA Deventer, Republiek I, 6: "Register van Resolutien van Schepenen en Raad en Gezworen Gemeente ('Concordaaten')."

29　*NNJ*, 1784, pp. 462–5.

30　De Jong, *Capellen*, pp. 692–706, and *NNJ*, 1785, pp. 877–83.

31　De Beaufort, *Brieven*, p. 836.

32　*NNJ*, 1785, pp. 1483–6.

33　This strong suspicion is based on two internal characteristics of the document: it follows the standard format of the Patriot's earlier petitions, with members of the Burgercommittee, for example, signing first; it can be dated after August 1785 because the names of the committee members are those elected then, not those elected in 1782. There were no other large-scale petition drives in Deventer until 1787. On the composition of the new committee and the 1787 petition drive, see chapters 5 and 6 below.

34　The population of Zwolle in 1795 was 12,220.

35　De Jong, *Capellen*, p. 492.

36 GA Zwolle, Oud Archief, A-75.
37 M. van Heuven-Bruggeman, "Een rekest in Zwolle in de nazomer van 1795," *VMORG*, 91 (1976), pp. 70–95.
38 W. W. van der Meulen (ed.), "Brieven van J. D. van der Capellen tot den Pol", *Bijdragen en Mededelingen van het Historisch Genootschap*, 28 (1907), p. 194; cf. De Jong, *Capellen*, p. 673.
39 *Requesten en adressen van de burgerye der Stad Zwolle* (Zwolle, 1784); cf. De Jong, *Capellen*, pp. 537–9.
40 Van der Meulen (ed.), *Brieven*, p. 247; De Jong, *Capellen*, p. 673.
41 "Een rekest in Zwolle," pp. 83–9.
42 For a comparison of the municipal governments in Deventer, Kampen, and Zwolle, see De Jong, *Capellen*, pp. 476–81. In relation to the Magistracy, the Sworn Council of Zwolle enjoyed relatively little independence. It had, for example, no separate book of resolutions, and it met only at specific times of the year unless it was convened by the presiding Burgemeesters who apparently set the agenda.
43 The population of Kampen was 6,214 in 1795.
44 Quoted in W. A. Fasel, "De Democratisch-Patriottisch woelingen te Kampen," *VMORG*, 74 (1959), p. 97.
45 De Jong, *Capellen*, p. 492. In Deventer, 1,460 signatures represented approximately 71 percent of the adult male population (see note 1 above); in Zwolle, 2,000 signatures represented approximately 65 percent; and in Kampen, 128 signatures represented approximately 8 percent of adult males.
46 M. van Dam, "Kampen," in *Herstel, Hervorming of Behoud? Tien Overijsselse steden in de Patriottentijd, 1780–1787* (Zwolle, 1985), p. 89.
47 Fasel, "Democratisch-Patriottish woelingen," p. 94.
48 Ibid., p. 97. An earlier attempt to create a Burgercommittee in Kampen came to nothing; cf. De Jong, *Capellen*, pp. 539–40, 645–6.
49 De Jong, *Capellen*, p. 589. The weakness of the guilds is perhaps a reflection of the fact that Kampen was more of a commercial than a manufacturing center by comparison with Deventer and Zwolle.

5
Toward a Democratic Future

From the outset, the Patriot movement held as one of its fundamental tenets an unrelenting opposition to the political power of the Prince of Orange. His pro-English foreign policy was seen as the reason for the disasters of the Fourth English War; his patronage was regarded as the source of political corruption at home; and his command of the Republic's mercenary army seemed to threaten traditional liberty. Backed by overwhelming expressions of popular support, the government of Deventer gladly chipped away at the Stadhouder's influence in local affairs, and after the first "free" election of Magistrates and Sworn Councilors in 1783, the annual *Petrikeur* on February 22 became a sort of Patriot festival to celebrate the diminution of the Stadhouder's power locally. This anti-Orange phase of the Patriot movement finally reached a climax during the *Petrikeur* of 1786.

The day began with the traditional religious service in the Grote Kerk. Choosing as his text Ecclesiastes 10: 16–17, the Reverend W. Suermond launched into a long-winded sermon on the characteristics of good government which was a thinly veiled attack on the Prince himself. He urged the Sworn Council to elect a government that, among other things, is "dependent only on our general interests and not on courtly favors."[1] Later, as the Councilors assembled in the Stadhuis to begin the complex lottery and election, they were pointedly reminded of their enemy's former influence by a large portrait of Stadhouder/King William III, the man who had first imposed the hated Governmental Regulation on the city in 1675. The portrait, painted by no less a master than Gerard ter Borch, occupied a place of honor above the mantel in the Raadzaal and was surrounded by the coats of arms of leading patrician families. On this special day several members of the Sworn Council, dressed in their black robes and apparently filled with Patriotic fervor, tore the portrait from its mounting, paraded it through the various rooms of the Stadhuis, beheaded the painted figure of William III, and finally destroyed the painting entirely.[2]

With this act of symbolic regicide (or tyrannicide as the Patriots would no doubt have insisted), the Patriots would seem to have demonstrated their command of the rhetorical and symbolic field of battle. Any thought of making peace with the Stadhouder and the old regime he represented seemed to be out of the question. Meanwhile, the Patriots had already begun the far more difficult task of setting their own agenda for the political future of the city. In August 1785, another massive petition had demanded the immediate abolition of the Governmental Regulation, asserted the right of the Burgerij to elect and remove from office the members of the Sworn Council, and asked that all citizens be given the opportunity to express their grievances against local and provincial government.[3] In September, all the citizens of Deventer, either individually or as groups, were invited to submit their grievances to the members of the Patriot's Burgercommittee, and by January 6, 1786, the Burgercommittee had sifted through the grievances and submitted its report to a special municipal commission charged with the task of writing a new constitution.[4] In March, the Municipal Commission issued its first report concerning the reform of provincial government,[5] and in August, it published a second report on the reform of municipal government to which was appended a *Concept Reglement* or Draft Regulation.[6] Thus, within a year, the first stage of the constitution-making process had been completed.

This was a heady time for all Patriots, but during this new stage in the movement, the majority of the people once again receded from the center of municipal politics. Petition drives and public demonstrations gave way to learned constitutional discussions, for it seemed only natural that the rank and file should be spectators while their leaders were entrusted with the critical task of drafting plans for the city's future. The Commission's second report did, nevertheless, outline a scenario for deliberations leading to the formal adoption of the new constitution – public deliberations that would once again include the citizenry at large. After a brief period to give individual regents an opportunity to examine and comment on the document, the Sworn Council and the Magistracy would meet as corps to present their respective considerations and to adopt changes in the draft as necessary. The revised constitution would then be submitted for ratification by a majority of the city's enfranchised voters.

What this scenario did not anticipate was the fiery opposition that the *Concept Reglement* would evoke. The first signs of opposition appeared almost immediately after the Commission's report was published in August, and by November a second Burgercommittee, opposed to the first, had been formed.[7] This new Burgercommittee protested further consideration of the Draft Regulation, and when its requests were denied or ignored, it threatened violence. The Municipal Commission argued consistently, if not convincingly, that in due course all citizens would be allowed to express their judgment and to accept or reject the new constitution.[8] Despite the opposition, the government circulated a revised edition of the Draft Regulation on February 10, 1787, but the ratification procedure was stalled by internal conflicts before it was cut short by counter-revolution in September.

Thus, in the course of 1786, while the grievances of the Burgerij were being translated into proposals for constitutional reform, the apparent harmony of the early years of the Patriot movement gave way to dissension. Clearly something had been lost in the translation. In order to understand what was at stake in this developing struggle, we will examine first the citizens' grievances and the way they were handled by the Burgercommittee; secondly what, in responding to these grievances, the Municipal Commission proposed to change in the municipal constitution; and finally what the opposition found so objectionable in the Draft Regulation.

FROM GRIEVANCES TO LAWS

As if to underscore the importance of this new phase of the political struggle, the Patriots had chosen, in the summer of 1785, a new Burgercommittee which was charged with the task of receiving and reporting on the grievances of the citizenry.[9] Of the original committee, only one member was re-elected: Hendrik Brilman, a baker. For the rest, the new committee consisted of two more bakers, a brewer, four merchants, the Rector of the Latin School, a Professor at the Atheneum, and two others whose occupations I could not identify. Like the first committee, six of the 12 were guild members, and again at least one was a Mennonite.

The most prominent and influential member of the new Burgercommittee was Frederick Adolf van der Marck, Professor of Law at the Atheneum.[10] In 1773, Van der Marck had been expelled from the Groningen Academy for teaching "liberal ideas" – for emphasizing natural law and the concept of the political sovereignty of the people. At the time, King Frederick (the Great) of Prussia had befriended him and provided a post at Lingen. In 1783, however, at the insistence of his friend and admirer, J. D. van der Capellen, a special chair had been created for him at Deventer. The goal was, as Van der Capellen expressed it, to make Atheneum into a "training school for Patriots," and to that end Van der Marck gave weekly public lectures in Dutch rather than the customary Latin for the benefit of the general public.[11] Van der Marck, along with Herman Bosscha of the Latin School, served as spokesman for the committee and undoubtedly guided its deliberations.

In total, this new Burgercommittee received 13 sets of written grievances which, taken as a whole, were so diffuse as to defy easy generalization.[12] As with the French *cahiers* in 1789, political, social, economic and religious issues were often inextricably entwined. At the same time, there was a thorough blending of the language of Calvinist renewal and enlightened reform. Some grievances expressed individual complaints while others represented the collective wisdom of a group of Burgers or a guild. In most cases, however, the authors preferred to remain anonymous. If nothing else, the grievances reflect with unusual candor the wide range of issues that agitated Deventer's population in the 1780s and the many sources of discontent that underlay the revolutionary conflict. The members of the Burgercommittee must have been impressed by the diversity in the interests that they were expected to represent to the authorities.

An elaborate set of grievances submitted by "a group of seven Burgers" illustrates the breadth of concerns expressed by those who responded to the government's invitation. First, a series of seven points attacked official corruption and fiscal mismanagement. The Burgers urged, for example, that all intrigue, bribery, and solicitation for public office be prohibited; that the functions of public office be executed by the appointee himself; that public financial records be regularly audited; that the administration of municipal properties be reformed; and that the Sworn Council conduct a general investigation into the reasons for the decay of municipal finances. On a different plane, these "seven Burgers" complained about the inequitable distribution of the pews (*zitplaatsen*) in the city's churches and suggested specific measures to curb the arbitrariness of the Kerkmeesters in this matter. Finally, these same Burgers demanded that nobles be specifically excluded from municipal office, that 25 be established as the minimum age for appointment to municipal office, and that Roman Catholics be allowed the same privileges (*voorregten*) as Mennonites who at the beginning of the eighteenth century had been granted access to *burgerrechten* (burger-rights) and guild membership but were nevertheless excluded from holding political office.[13]

Not all of the petitions were so lengthy or comprehensive. A request by 250 Roman Catholics, for example, simply reaffirmed an earlier petition to the Magistrates asking that they be allowed to purchase *burgerrechten*.[14] Others demanded various forms of economic reform or protection in the local marketplace. The bakers' guild, for instance, complained that heavy municipal excises gave bakers in the surrounding countryside unfair competitive advantages and asked, therefore, that taxes be equalized as soon as possible.[15] Another grievance urged that municipal fairs, at which outsiders sold their wares freely, be abolished because they "tended to the disadvantage of Commercial [*Handeldryvende*] Burgers and the corruption of morals;" it went on to request that manufacturers be allowed to sell their goods only through local retail merchants.[16] Still another complained of frequent misconduct by attorneys and solicitors and asked that all judicial processes be expedited.[17]

Altogether these assorted complaints, accusations, and requests suggest a general political and social malaise. Meddling of outsiders in municipal affairs, corruption and secrecy in government, mismanagement of public finances, inequitable taxation, arbitrary and slow justice – all of these recurring themes express a pervasive distrust of established authority. Concern for the city's declining economy was expressed in a number of demands for improvement of navigable waterways, for various forms of economic protection, and for reform in the management of municipal charities and communal resources – meadows, woods, and wastelands. Collectively, the inhabitants of Deventer found ample reason for dissatisfaction with the status quo. But for the Burgercommittee, which seemed to be primarily interested in constitutional issues, the bulk of the grievances offered little practical advice. Most of the petitions suggested only minor policy adjustments to eliminate inequities or to curb abuse of power.

In its final report, the Burgercommittee published all of the grievances it received, but from the mass of complaints it distilled what it considered the 22 most justified criticisms of municipal and provincial government. These "well-founded" grievances, the Committee argued, deserved special consideration, while all others would have to be set aside until the constitutional issues were satisfactorily resolved. Still, in the last part of its report, the Committee endorsed a few of the "lesser" grievances as being especially justified and added some of its own complaints to the list. In the end, then, the Committee's recommendations are as interesting for what they ignored as for what they endorsed.

Only one group of 22 Burgers had submitted what might be considered a coherent package of demands relating to *constitutional* reform,[18] and it is telling that 11 of what the Burgercommittee considered the 15 most important criticisms of municipal government were derived from the arguments of these Burgers. In the Burgercommittee's final list, the first series of points attacked the exclusiveness and insularity of corporative government. In particular, the Committee complained that Sworn Councilors were selected by co-optation and not elected by the Burgerij; that Sworn Councilors were appointed for life and deliberated in secret; that close kinship relations among governing officials were not sufficiently limited by law; and that the Burgercommittee itself was not officially recognized and was still denied access to municipal financial records. At the same time as it attacked the exclusiveness of corporative government, however, the Committee wished to reinforce the corporate identity of the city itself. The report argued, for example, that Burgers should not be subject to the jurisdiction of the provincial Executive in cases involving provincial taxation; that nobles – those eligible to sit in the Ridderschap – should be excluded from holding municipal office; that municipal employment should not be given to outsiders (*vreemdelingen*) who were not yet Burgers of the city. On a more hesitant note, the Committee suggested that legislation enacted by majority vote should also be repealed by majority vote (unanimity was presently required). It urged, furthermore, that the Municipal Commission consider the very difficult constitutional question of how to ensure that executive and legislative power be sufficiently separated in municipal government. Finally, the Committee complained that unrestricted freedom of the press had not yet been guaranteed in law.

To distill this particular set of grievances from the mass of complaints and accusations was a bold and important step for the Burgercommittee to take. To do so, it had to set aside the bulk of the grievances, no matter how urgently expressed or how easily resolved, in favor of a few demands expressed by a small number of respondents. Thus, it rejected what it considered minor policy adjustments, such as the various demands for protection of guild interests, in favor of proposals for a significant reorientation of political institutions on the unstated assumption, so common to eighteenth-century democrats, that constitutional reform must necessarily precede the resolution of "lesser" social, political, or economic problems. On one controversial issue, however, the Committee was forced to choose between two clear and mutually exclusive alternatives. Three petitions had advocated *burgerrechten* for Roman Catholics, but another anonymous set of grievances, besides urging protection of the rights and privileges of the guilds, specifically demanded "that no one must enjoy the *Burger-Recht* unless he is an advocate of the Reformed Christian Religion."[19]

The idea of allowing Roman Catholics to become Burgers of the city was not a new one: in 1781 the Magistracy had proposed to the Sworn Council that they establish a joint commission to investigate the possibility of offering *burgerrechten* to Roman Catholics "in order to expand the Commerce and Welfare of the City."[20] The precedent for such a proposal was the extension of *burgerrechten* to the tiny Mennonite minority in Deventer at the beginning of the eighteenth century. Since then, many enterprising Mennonites had migrated to Deventer, and in the 1780s prosperous Mennonite entrepreneurs – proprietors of proto-industrial *fabrieken* – like Gerrit Bolte, Jan van Calcar, and Hendrik Busse-maker, emerged as Patriot leaders. By comparison with the small Mennonite community, however, Roman Catholics constituted a sizeable minority (20 percent) of the local population, and those who championed their civil rights probably hoped for even greater economic benefits for Deventer.

In the context of enlightened thinking about religious toleration, the notion of granting Burger status to Catholics seems natural and straightforward enough. But the opposition to it was not to be taken lightly. As we have already seen, guild-based artisans and shopkeepers were the backbone of the Patriots' popular mobilization, but now their demands for the protection of guild privileges and economic interests were coupled with the idea of excluding religious dissenters from the status of Burger. In an apparent effort to compromise the issue, the Burgercommittee included among its lesser recommendations the vague suggestion that Catholics might be granted *burgerrechten* without prejudice to the rights of the guilds. But Professor van der Marck had nevertheless addressed the issue of religious toleration in his public lectures, openly ridiculing the guilds for excluding Catholics,[21] and in the end, this issue especially would come back to haunt the Patriots.

DRAFTING THE CONSTITUTION

The Burgercommittee's published report was well received by the Municipal Commission charged with acting on the grievances. The Commission was made up of four Burgemeesters (G. D. Jordens, A. J. Weerts, J. W. Tichler, and W. H. Cost) and four Sworn Councilors (L. Bannier, M. van Doorninck, A. G. Besier, and G. J. Jacobson) assisted by Gerhard Dumbar, as City Secretary. This was a distinguished group: all of them held university degrees in law and Dumbar was a well-known legal scholar and historian. All had good Patriot credentials, and the four Sworn Councilors were high-ranking officers in the Vrijcorps.

With no apparent points of disagreement between the two groups, the Commission easily incorporated the Burgercommittee's recommendations into its second report and the "Draft Regulation [*Concept Reglement*] for the government of Deventer" which was appended to it. The Commissioners especially endorsed the notion that constitutional reform deserved primary consideration. As they saw it, the Draft Regulation in the end would have to be approved by the Burgerij, but decisions concerning lesser complaints would not. To submit all grievances to the judgment of the Burgerij would be to favor "complete democracy" (*volstrekte volksregeering*) which, the report averred, was equivalent to anarchy. Instead, the Commission proposed the system of "democracy by representation" (*volksregeering bij representatie*) in which the representatives of the people, not the people themselves, would decide matters of policy. With a heavy dose of typically eighteenth-century optimism, the Commissioners assured their readers that

one can reasonably expect that, once the Form of Government is arranged to the general satisfaction of the Burgerij and the Regents, that is, absolved of all dependence except on the people, then the subsequent decisions of the Government will be received with greater satisfaction.[22]

To the members of the Commission as to the Burgercommittee, then, "democracy by representation" seemed to be the ultimate solution to *all* of the city's problems.

The Draft Regulation which followed the report was a complex, 52-page document consisting of 284 articles divided into five major sections. The first 18 articles defined the "Rights and Obligations of the Burgerij." Then a very long and complex series of articles outlined procedures for the election of Burgemeesters by the Sworn Council (Art. 19–92) and the Sworn Councilors by the Burgerij (Art. 93–164). Another long section carefully defined the authority and prerogatives of the Magistracy and the Sworn Council with particular attention to the powers of the Sworn Council (Art. 165–229). The fourth section (Art. 230–277) dealt with miscellaneous subjects including appointment procedures for City Secretaries and voting procedures in the Council. Finally, the last section (Art. 278–284) provided for regular revision of the Regulation, the first time after three years and thereafter every 12 years.[23]

The first 18 articles dealing with the rights and obligations of the Burgerij were probably the most important, and they certainly proved to be the most controversial. In a style so characteristic of eighteenth-century constitutions, the document began with general propositions – strikingly similar, in fact, to the Pennsylvania Constitution of 1776.[24]

I   All men are born equally free and independent and all government or authority in Civil Society originates in the will of the People.

II All Government should serve to promote the general welfare of the People and not to promote the special interest of particular persons or of corps [*Kollegien*] that include only a segment of the People.

III The Burgerij of this City has the right to govern itself and to regulate its internal affairs without the assistance or approval of anybody outside it.

IV Consequently, the Burgerij also has the right at all times, whenever it judges that the Form of Government of the City does not conform to the broad objectives of Government, to change it or to abolish it entirely and replace it with another Form of Government.[25]

Thus, the document moved quickly from the general principle of equality to the sovereignty and right of self-government of the people of Deventer. To assert municipal sovereignty was nothing new, but to do so without immediate allusion to ancient rights and privileges was. To deny, moreover, the legitimacy of special interests and exclusive corps was, in theory, to wipe the political slate clean and to define municipal politics anew.[26]

Continuing, the introductory articles postulated, in order, the right of revolution against arbitrary authority, the right of majority rule, the illegality of the Stadhouder's influence in local government,[27] the "inalienable" right of freedom of expression and the press, the right to petition for redress of grievances, the right of free and open debate and deliberation in government, the right of the Burgerij to remove unworthy regents, and so on. A few articles attempted to adjust the traditional sense of rights to the new political world. Thus, Article XV stipulated that Roman Catholics would henceforth be granted *burgerrechten* on an equal footing with Mennonites, while nobles would be excluded, in specific circumstances, from holding municipal offices (Art. XVI–XVIII). In all, the first 18 articles of the Draft Regulation asserted many more rights than obligations for the citizens of Deventer. Besides being obliged to address their government peacefully and respectfully, the Burgers were required to bear arms to defend the city against both external aggression and internal oppression.

Whether the remaining sections of the Draft Regulation, once in place, would have lived up to these lofty principles or actually instituted "representa-tive democracy," as the Municipal Commission claimed, is not immediately apparent. One thing is, however, quite certain: if the authors of the Draft Regulation were sincere about their democratic principles, they were equally determined not to appear to break too sharply with the past. As they expressed it in their report, the Commissioners were "delighted" to find that "the govern-ment of this City is fortunately constructed in such a way that [our] objective could be achieved with very few changes."[28] Though twentieth-century his-torians are generally inclined to think, with the French Jacobins, that democ-racy can only be implemented and preserved nationally, these Dutch constitution-makers were, like the Americans earlier, naturally inclined to adapt their democratic principles to the more fragmented political structure they inherited.[29] And given this natural point of departure, the Commissioners' argument was essentially correct. It was, for example, a fairly simple and straightforward matter to make the Sworn Council into a representative body by replacing co-optation with popular election, or to shift the balance of power with the municipal structure by defining explicitly the legislative prerogatives and authority of the Sworn Council over against the executive functions of the Magistracy. In these and many other ways, the Draft Regulation resuscitated old-regime institutions and political practices and integrated them into a theoretically new political system.[30]

In some ways, however, the Commissioners, all members of the current municipal administration, were willing to sacrifice principle for their own political interest. Although they advanced the right of the Burgerij to remove unworthy representatives and also established procedures for the popular election of the Council, they exempted from those arrangements all, including of course themselves, who had been appointed to the Council for life. Only new Councilors would be subject to recall, and, as in the past, Burgemeesters who were not re-elected would regain their original seats in the Council. The Draft Regulation provided, furthermore, that unless recalled by an elaborate and cumbersome process, Sworn Councilors would automatically be returned to office each year – a provision designed, it would seem, with the interests of the established regent rather than a politically active populace in mind. In order to compensate for the slow implementation of direct representation by popular election, the Commission proposed that until two-thirds of the Council had been elected by the Burgerij, the Burgercommittee should continue to rep-resent the interests of the Burgerij. Obviously, those already in power were careful to preserve their own positions.

In the final analysis, then, the Draft Regulation must be considered a relatively modest proposal for political change. In theory, of course, it was radically revolutionary, rooting political authority in the "sovereignty of the people" rather than the "privileges" of exclusive, old-regime corporations. But in practice, the Draft Regulation would have occasioned little immediate change in the personnel of government. It might, in fact, have strengthened the hand of the patrician oligarchy in the short run by legitimating the *de facto* break with the Stadhouder's patronage without immediately imposing new formal restraints on those in power. The Draft Regulation was, in short, a controversial document that represented a narrow, constitutionalist vision of the political future and at the same time satisfied only a small fraction of the grievances of the citizenry.

Naturally the publication of the Draft Regulation in the summer of 1786 provoked a good deal of discussion, some of which was reflected in the political press. Several members of the Sworn Council, for example, published lengthy critiques that they presented to the Council for its deliberations. Although all of them approved of the spirit of the document, they offered a variety of criticisms and suggestions for improvement. Hendrik Hagedoorn[31] and Georg van Hemert[32] thought that the Burgercommittee should become a permanent institution because it would facilitate good relations and communications between the government and the people. W. H. van Hoevell[33] argued that "complete democracy" (*volstrekte volksregering*) was not as bad as the Commission's report implied; both he and van Hemert proposed, in fact, that all new legislation be subject to the approval of the Burgerij! Otto Westenink[34] argued for a simpler electoral system and a clearer separation of the legislative, executive, and judicial powers of government. Westenink, Van Hemert and Van Hoevell all suggested that every Sworn Councilor be immediately subject to recall, even those who had been appointed for life. All of these commentators approved of complete freedom of the press and praised the proposal to give *burgerrechten* to Roman Catholics. All urged, moreover, that only Sworn Councilors be considered eligible for election as Burgemeester. Without this important perquisite, they argued, it would be difficult to attract talented men to serve in the Council.

The published criticism of these Sworn Councilors was incisive, but sympathetic and obviously directed toward strengthening the constitutionalist vision of political reform embodied in the Draft Regulation. Only Otto Westenink commented more broadly on the grievances of the Burgerij, but he was exceptional in his apparent willingness to admit economic and social problems to the discussion before the resolution of the constitutional issues. In the end, some of these criticisms were translated into minor technical adjustments incorporated into the revised edition of the Draft Regulation. But for the most part this essentially reasoned and reasonable debate was drowned out by the shriller voices of critics who stood outside the patrician oligarchy and who launched a clearly unsympathetic attack on the whole Draft Regulation.

AN OPPOSITION EMERGES

The Patriot Burgercommittee and the Patriot-dominated Municipal Commission, in preparing the Draft Regulation, made two bold decisions on behalf of the people of Deventer. First, the Burgercommittee had established the priorities of the reform movement, ruling that fundamental constitutional change must necessarily take precedence over "lesser" political and social problems. Secondly, the Municipal Commission radically redefined municipal politics; it declared that political sovereignty rested in the people, that representative democracy was the proper way to recognize that sovereignty, and that the enfranchised Burgerij should include Roman Catholics as well as Protestants. As we shall see, the "Opposition" objected both to the Burgercommittee's priorities and to the Commission's redefinition of municipal politics. They argued that the Burgercommittee had perverted the intentions of the people in its Report and that the Municipal Commission had actually compromised the rights of the Burgerij in its Draft Regulation.

What precisely did the opposition find objectionable in the proposed constitution? The answer to this important question is by no means simple or straightforward, not only because the evidence is spotty, but more fundamentally because the opposition did not at first speak the same constitutionalist language as the learned Patriots who so thoroughly dominated the public discussion of the city's future. In August 1786, shortly after the Draft Regulation was published, the *Nieuwe Nederlandsche Jaarboeken* published the following excerpt from a petition addressed to the Patriot Burgercommittee:

That the undersigned declare to the Representatives of the Burgerij of the City of Deventer that they have learned that there are certain Articles in the Draft Regulation which are contrary to our *Burgerlijke* Reformed Christian Religion and the Laws, Privileges and Liberties of the Guilds; besides certain Articles that are intemperate and in which self-interest is chiefly evident; that they [the undersigned] will not accept them, but consider them null and void.[35]

In this relatively crude and inarticulate declaration, with its pious defense of both "*Burgerlijke*" Calvinism and guild traditions, we see the first signs of public opposition to the Draft Regulation. The *Jaarboeken* report went on to suggest that the most controversial issue was Article XV – the one that granted *burgerrechten* to Catholics. But the specific grounds for opposition to this article were not immediately evident. The opposition movement only later clarified its demands and took on a specific political identity.

The Burgercommittee, unsympathetic to criticism, simply ignored this petition, which then was addressed directly to the Magistracy and the Sworn Council in almost the same form on September 22, 1786. Again the petition did not specify which articles were objectionable, and again the request was

!

fruitless. An anonymous Patriot pamphleteer who sought to refute the "*Den-kwys*" (way of thinking) of the petitioners, identified these two petitions with members of "the several Guilds of Deventer" who reportedly signed in large numbers. It seems to have been common knowledge in this small political community that the chief obstacle to acceptance of the new constitution was the question of political and civil rights for Catholics, for the pamphleteer focused on this issue. Although he praised the "Patriotic" sympathies of the guildsmen, he roundly condemned any suggestion that Catholics could be denied *burger-rechten* and guild membership in the name of "true religion" and ancient guild laws.[36]

At the beginning of November, the movement in opposition to the Draft Regulation took a new tack. Derk Nijland (a baker) and L. van Weteringen (a butcher), identifying themselves as the *generale ouderlieden* (elders) of the guilds, asked the Magistracy to approve new elections of "Representatives of the Burgerij." This request, too, was denied on the grounds that the existing Burgercommittee had been legally constituted in August 1785 and their commission never revoked. Undaunted, the opposition at the end of November requested that 26 "*wettige aangestelde*" (legally appointed) representatives of the guilds and Burgerij be recognized in the place of the existing Burgercommittee.[37] Again the Burgemeesters and Sworn Councilors denied their request.

At the end of 1786, then, on the eve of the Patriots' *coup d'état*, the points at issue remained obscure, at least to anyone who depended on the public press rather than the local rumor mill for information. The Municipal Commission, which had written the Draft Regulation, was charged with the task of examining the petition of this new "Burgercommittee," and in a special published report the Commission not only elaborated its reasons for refusing to recognize the new Committee, but also attacked what it saw as the petition's underlying assumptions. Once again, it was taken for granted that the real issue at stake was the question of *burgerrechten* for Catholics. But the Commission detected something else. Its report noted ominously that the "so-called Representatives of the Burgerij" included not only people whose capabilities were not sufficient to the task,

but also certain persons of whom it is known throughout the entire City that they adhere to the party of the Stadhouder; and far from wishing to see improvements in the political system by which the Stadhouder's influence might in some measure be weakened, [they] would employ all their means to stop the proposed improvements . . .[38]

Thus, to the Commissioners, opposition to their Draft Regulation was being contaminated by association with Orangism. And to be Orangist was, of course, to be the enemy of the people.

As the battle lines were being drawn, the new opposition movement was still known chiefly by its reputation. It had repeatedly invoked the rhetoric of piety and tradition, but it had not yet addressed the constitutional issues that the Patriots had mooted in their proposed constitution. Not until the stage was fully set for the Patriot Revolution did the "representatives of the guilds and the Burgerij" publicly elaborate their demands at length. On January 19, 1787, just six days before the Patriots' purge of the Zwolle Magistracy, the new Burger-committee finally addressed a lengthy petition to the Sworn Council of Deventer.[39] The 24-page document answered many obvious questions about the opposition movement and, in particular, confirmed the suspicion that opposition to the new constitution had been combined with support for the Stadhouder. But even more strikingly, the petition gave the opposition move-ment a new kind of voice. Straightforwardly pious defenses of "true religion" gave way to complex legal and historical arguments about sovereignty and corporative privilege. The reason for the change was quite simply that it was not this time the guild leaders, but ex-Burgemeester E. H. Putman, the first casualty of the Patriot movement in 1783, who wrote the petition.

Addressing the Sworn Council as the "immediate representatives" of the Burgerij, the petition was an attempt to clarify and defend "the most reasonable and legitimate" requests that had been repeatedly denied by the government. The petitioners were especially agitated by the recent report of the Municipal Commission which attacked the personal qualities of the petitioners and ascribed to them an 'improper factiousness and party spirit." The petitioners felt obliged, at the outset, to declare that they would spare no "legal and constitutional" means to maintain their "inalienable" rights and privileges. The petition itself would be proof of the purity of their opinions and the legitimacy of their demands.

Before specifying their demands, the petitioners, like the constitution-writers before them, "reminded" the Councilors of a number of fundamental prin-ciples. These principles echoed the introductory articles of the Draft Regu-lation on some points, but crucial differences identify for us the chief areas of disagreement between two opposing perceptions of the political future. Like the Patriots' draft constitution, the petition asserted that supreme authority in the sovereign city of Deventer rested in the Burgerij. In this document, however, the Burgerij was defined as the "Guilds and the enfranchised Burgers and Residents" – a peculiarly enigmatic definition whose repeated use by the petitioners indicates the special importance of guilds in the opposition's con-ception of politics. Citing no less an authority than Van der Capellen as support, the petitioners argued that the province's Governmental Regulation had been instituted in 1748 with the tacit approval of the Burgerij and must therefore be considered the fundamental constitution of government, unalterable except with the expressed consent of the majority of the Burgerij. All authority not delegated by mutual consent in the Governmental Regulation to the Stad-houder was vested in the Burgerij and was merely delegated to the Sworn

Council and Magistracy. To the petitioners, then, it seemed to follow that "the People" had always retained the right to elect both Burgemeesters and Sworn Councilors, even though in practice the elections had been entrusted to the Sworn Council! Amplifying these basic principles, the petition argued that historical precedents, and especially the extraordinary election of 1703 (see chapter 2), proved that guilds and enfranchised Burgers had previously exercized their sovereign authority with "felicitous results." The petitioners were further convinced that far from compromising the sovereignty of the people, the Governmental Regulation was necessary to protect the guilds and the Burgerij against possible domination by the Magistracy and the Sworn Council. Accordingly, they opposed the initiative in the provincial Estates to absolve the regents of their oath to the Regulation. To absolve the regents of their oath to the constitution, it seemed, would be to allow them to force through their Draft Regulation against the expressed wishes of the people.

The petition recounted the recent history of the city's constitution-making efforts with bitter sense of betrayal. Under the guise of correcting abuses in government, the Patriot Burgercommittee and the Municipal Commission had proposed to "overthrow the whole constitution of the province of Overijssel." This the Patriots had accomplished in "a more or less covert way" using "very intricate" petitions that the unsuspecting majority of the Burgerij had signed. Then, "instead of being summoned to judge the importance or interest of some grievances presented to the Burgercommittee by a very small number of Burgers, [the Guilds and the Burgerij] were presented with a conceited proposal for a completely new, exceedingly imperfect municipal Constitution."[40] As the petitioners saw it, the new constitution destroyed the Stadhouder's prerogatives, undermined the "most holy and inalienable privileges" of the guilds and the Burgerij, and was so complicated that "only the grossest of confusions, intrigues, and calamities perpetuated by clever persons" could be expected to result from it.

While they objected generally to the tone of the first 18 articles of the Draft Regulation, the petitioners focused on two articles in particular. Article VII, which posited the illegality of the Stadhouder's Governmental Regulation, was considered "contrary to the good intentions of the unprejudiced majority of the Guilds and the Burgerij." And Article XV, which opened *burgerrechten* to Catholics, represented "nothing less than a sidling blow intended at once to extinguish the privileges of the Guilds and Burgerij and to intrude into the electoral process . . . persons who were not enfranchised according to time-honored municipal traditions."[41] Obviously sensitive to the considerable criticism already directed at them, the petitioners cited the *Stadregt* (Charter) and numerous municipal resolutions to justify their opposition to Catholics. In an elaborate, legalistic defense, they argued that the guilds and Burgerij had possessed for more than a century and a half the right to exclude "Foreigners,

Roman Catholics, and Mennonites" in order to protect the interests of those who were the champions of the "true Reformed Christian Religion."

Thus, in the final analysis, the petitioners claimed the right to exclude not only Catholics, but also Mennonites and "Foreigners" of all kinds. It was apparent, moreover, that the interests being protected by exclusive membership in the guilds and the Burgerij were not only the purity and integrity of "true" religion but also the economic interests of the petitioners themselves.[42] The petition asserted that at the beginning of the century the guilds had bitterly opposed granting *burgerrechten* to Mennonites. Countering the then current argument that commercially ambitious Mennonites would enhance the general prosperity of the city, the guilds had insisted that Mennonites coming from outside the city would compete directly in established trades and commercial enterprises to the obvious disadvantage of the Reformed Burgerij. Still, by "connivance and usurpation," many Mennonites had achieved Burger status and joined guilds, with the expected damaging results. Now the same arguments were being advanced on behalf of Roman Catholics, and the petitioners wanted no part of it. What seemed especially insidious was the insistence of the Burgercommittee and Municipal Commission that Catholics and Mennonites take part in the deliberations over the Draft Regulation, thus granting these "outsiders" the right to vote for the dispensation of privileges that they did not legally possess.

In light of this extended, even impassioned, clarification, the petitioners' specific demands seem rather straightforward.[43] They asked: (1) that all deliberations leading to adoption of the Draft Regulation and abolition of the existing Governmental Regulation be halted immediately, with the proviso that the grievances of the Burgerij be considered in the proper manner at a later date; (2) that the Sworn Council pledge in writing to preserve and maintain the privilege of the Burgerij and guilds to exclude outsiders from access to *burgerrechten* and guild membership; (3) that "no Roman Catholics, Mennonites, Foreigners, or minors" be allowed to take part in deliberations over the rights and privileges of the guilds; and (4) that the old Burgercommittee be abolished and the "Representatives and Electors of the Guilds and the Burgerij" be recognized as the spokesmen of the people. Finally, the petition ended with a solemn and ominous declaration: if this request, too, were either rejected or ignored, the guilds and the Burgerij, "however reluctantly and regretfully, would have to resort to whatever ways and means there remained" to protect their "most beloved Rights and Privileges."

Obviously the movement in opposition to the Patriots' Draft Regulation had matured since its first impulsive denunciation of the document in August 1786. As the petition shows, Everhard Putman, a patrician lawyer himself, spoke the same constitutionalist language as the authors of the Draft Regulation. It was abundantly clear, however, that despite wide areas of agreement – with regard to the general principles of popular sovereignty and democratic representation, for example – a chasm of distrust and misunderstanding divided the political leaders of Deventer. The very same people whose harmony and "unanimous" political action had been seen as a national example were now a source of embarrassment and serious concern for the Patriot movement: two political factions, both claiming to represent the same Burgerij, opposed one another over issues that seemed to be irreconcilable.

To defend the privileges of the Stadhouder and the exclusiveness of the guilds simultaneously was to violate the most sacred tenets of the proposed constitution. Accordingly, on January 27, 1787, eight days after the "Orangist" petition had been published, the Municipal Commission issued a lengthy report that attacked, point by point, the opposition's arguments.[44] On January 30, the delegates from Deventer voted with the majority of the Estates to absolve themselves of their oath to the Governmental Regulation. And in the first days of February, the government proscribed the Orangist Burgercommittee and prohibited any further political activity by the guilds – the very same guilds that had been instrumental in organizing the Patriot movement. The revised draft of the Draft Regulation, which appeared on February 10, qualified the controversial Article XV by adding that Catholics would be given *burgerrechten* "without prejudice to guild privileges."[45] But that was too little, too late.

DIFFERENT PATHS TO THE REVOLUTION

Before we analyze more closely the social dimensions of the ideological divisions that emerged in revolutionary Deventer, we will do well once again to situate Deventer in a comparative context. In Kampen and Zwolle, too, the grievances of the Burgerij were translated into proposals for constitutional change. Indeed, the timetable for that process was almost identical: petitions for abolition of the Governmental Regulation were signed in August 1785; grievances were solicited and analyzed by January 1786; draft constitutions were published in the summer of 1786. Meanwhile, collective action gave way to quiet deliberation as the rank and file of the Patriot movement entrusted their leaders with the task of drafting the political agenda for the future. Having started from different points, however, Kampen and Zwolle experienced the constitution-writing process differently, and those differences serve to highlight for us essential characteristics of the conflict that was emerging in Deventer.

In Kampen, as was noted in chapter 4, the popular movement, lacking a natural organizational base in independent guilds, remained weak and sporadic.[46] We do not know how many persons signed the petition demanding constitutional reform and popular election of the Sworn Council in late August 1785, but the municipal government quickly acceded to the demand and created a special commission, comprised of four Magistrates and four Councilors, to undertake the task of designing a new Governmental Regulation. Only then did the Patriots in Kampen create a Burgercommittee, not to spearhead a new wave of popular agitation but for the limited purpose of receiving and reporting on the grievances of the citizenry.[47] Given this lethargic pace, it is not surprising that, by comparison with Deventer where the Burgercommittee was inundated with a wide range of popular grievances, the Burgercommittee in Kampen had a very easy task; it received just two sets of grievances: a series of 24 complaints from five Burgers and a series of nine points submitted by just one Burger. To these the Burgercommittee appended two sets of its own grievances regarding provincial and local government when it reported to the government's special commission on January 31, 1786.[48]

The Burgercommittee's report was quite short and clearly focused on its designated task – that is, simply to communicate the grievances of Kampen's Burgerij regarding provincial and local government. The Municipal Commission, in turn, quickly issued its report on provincial government in the spring of 1786[49] but did not issue its report on local government until November of 1786.[50] In its second report, the Municipal Commission concluded that the only real problem with the city's existing constitution was the matter of the Stadhouder's interference in municipal elections, and accordingly the Draft Regulation which it proposed focused especially on establishing a "free" electoral process in which all Burgers would indirectly elect new members of the Sworn Council and each year review their performance in office with an eye to removing those who were deemed unworthy by two-thirds of the electors. As the Commission saw it, the new constitution's primary objective was to prevent intrigues and cabals from perverting the electoral process.

In sharp contrast to Deventer, then, the constitution-writing process in Kampen did not produce a general declaration of the rights and obligations of the good citizen – a basic set of principles by which municipal government could be redefined and restructured. Likewise, there would be no Patriot *coup* in the beginning of 1787 by which Magistrates unwilling to accept the fundamental transformation of local power would be removed from office. At the insistence of the Sworn Council and under the tutelage of the ruling oligarchy, Kampen seemed to be headed toward a limited electoral reform along democratic lines that was designed to insulate the elite from outside interference without undermining their authority at home.

It would be mistaken, however, to infer from this that all was well with Kampen. One of the few grievances not strictly related to the local constitution of government complained, for example, that nothing was being done about increasing the city's population which, after two big floods and two "fatal years of death," was seen to be declining precipitously. But more dramatically, in the course of 1786, an anonymous pamphleteer expressed the accumulated frustrations of guild-based artisans and tradesmen who had not been able to develop an independent voice through popular mobilization:

There is no Guild in the City that does not have its grievances – in one, the same people are always chosen [as elders] and some Guild Brothers are always excluded; in another, the moneys that could be used for the benefit of the Needy and Unfortunate are wasted in expensive Banquets, – the Sworn Councilors are Commissioners, Procurators, and Guild Masters – the Magistrates pass Resolutions for the benefit of one Faction or another without recognizing the Council, the true Representatives of the People. – But if one or another part of a Guild addresses its complaints to the Magistracy and the Council, it finds its Antagonists in the Council's chambers, since in almost all the Guilds a Councilor serves as director, – if one expresses grievances concerning the Civic Guard, – the Councilors are Captains, Lieutenants, etc. – the Magistracy does not want to antagonize its friends in the Council, – the Requests are either ignored or, at best, after hearing oral testimony, they recommend that the matter be resolved internally.[51]

In this light, what is striking about Kampen is not absence of grievances and problems, but rather the apparent inability of ordinary people to articulate their frustrations, to defend their interests and to seek resolution of their problems through direct political action and/or participation in the constitution-making process.

In Zwolle, by contrast, the Patriots had mobilized a strong and independent popular movement around the bedrock support of the majority of the guilds and in opposition to a generally uncooperative Magistracy (see chapter 4). Unfortunately, we do not know much about the grievances that were submitted by the Burgerij in Zwolle following the creation of a special Municipal Commission to reform the Governmental Regulation. From the Commission's report on the grievances we know that they had received only five sets of complaints, which seems like a small number for such an active movement, but the Commission, defining its task narrowly, focused on only those grievances which related directly to the constitution of provincial and local government.[52] Thus, they did not even report on the content of two of the five lists, and they skipped over a number of specific points in a third. Like their counterparts in Deventer, then, the members of the Municipal Commission in Zwolle asserted the primacy of constitutional reform over the resolution of "lesser" grievances, regardless of their cogency or urgency. But while this critical decision served only to divide the Patriot movement in Deventer, the dynamics of the conflict were sufficiently different in Zwolle that the issues of constitutional reform actually did seem primary to the rank and file of the Patriot movement. At the same time, however, the Municipal Commission in Zwolle also specifically noted that, while it was not a strictly constitutional issue, they judged it to be entirely reasonable to protect local manufactures against foreign competition whenever possible – this in sharp contrast to the Deventer Commission's report which explicitly rejected the corporative legitimacy of the guildsmen who had articulated similar demands for economic protection.

For the moment, the most obvious difference between developments in Deventer and Zwolle in 1786 was the tenacious intransigence of the Zwolle

Magistracy. In conjunction with its report on the local grievances, the Municipal Commission produced a very brief and limited Draft Regulation for popular election of Sworn Councilors in May, 1786 – an even more modest document than was produced in Kampen – but it was accompanied by a frontal assault on the existing Regulation as an illegal imposition and bolstered by arguments asserting that all constitutions are subject to change, even if they have been legally adopted. Though much learned discussion ensued, the decisive reaction finally came in November in the form of an official resolution voted by a narrow majority of the Zwolle Magistracy which reaffirmed the legality of the old Regulation – a decision that threatened to stalemate both local and provincial reform.[53] At this point, direct popular action, largely absent in the previous year, again seemed necessary, and a gathering of more than 1,000 persons in the Grote Kerk produced a declaration that a scheduled election to fill a vacancy on the Sworn Council by the old method of co-optation would not be recognized as legitimate. When the government nevertheless proceeded with the election in mid-December, the chosen candidate was intimidated by Patriot crowds and forced to resign immediately.[54]

Thus, at the beginning of 1787, the battle lines in Zwolle were clearly drawn between a thoroughly divided oligarchy and a thoroughly politicized and readily mobilized populace. The immediate issue that divided them was clear and unambiguous: whether or not Sworn Councilors would be subject to popular election and recall. The local Burgercommittee, repeatedly organizing demonstrations of popular support, focused its efforts on the weak and ineffectual Sworn Council, and on January 17, just prior to the annual election of Burgemeesters, produced a series of 24 non-negotiable points that needed to be included in a new constitution, the emphasis being placed on the classic concerns of popular elections, secret ballots, balance of powers, and the prevention of cabal and intrigue.[55] Under heavy pressure and to great popular acclaim, then, the Council finally declared unilaterally the abolition of the old Governmental Regulation and on January 25 purged the Magistracy of nine Burgemeesters who refused to accept the Burgercommittee's 24 points as the basis for a new constitution.[56] Hardly a Declaration of Independence or a storming of the Bastille, these developments in Zwolle, nevertheless, comport well with our traditional expectations of what should have been the dynamics of "democratic" revolution.

Returning finally to Deventer, we are struck not by the existence of controversy and conflict, *per se*, but by the peculiar dynamics of the impending struggle. While in Zwolle the Magistrates finally decided to resist the Patriots' modest proposals for constitutional change, in Deventer the Magistrates were in the strange position of defending the Patriot Burgercommittee's push for constitutional change and the Municipal Commission's fundamental redefinition of urban politics against unwanted opposition from the Orangist Burgercommittee. And while in Kampen guildsmen were frustrated by existing conditions yet unable to influence the agenda for reform, in Deventer spokesmen for "the Guilds and the Burgerij" simply created a new Burgercommittee when the old one which they had helped to create and had previously supported so consistently no longer seemed to be representing their interests. To be sure, the peculiar issue that divided the people of Deventer – the question of whether or not Catholics should be granted access to *burgerrechten* and guild membership – jars our twentieth-century sensibilities. Lest we assume that bigotry was the exclusive trait of guildsmen in Deventer, however, we should note that in both Kampen and Zwolle, Catholics were already allowed to join guilds, which meant that political enfranchisement of Catholics was a much less frightening proposition. Still, guildsmen in both Kampen and Zwolle were agitating to deny *burgerrechten* and guild membership to Jews, though in neither case did this become a major issue.[57] In order to understand why the acceptance of Catholics should have been so divisive in Deventer, we need to look beyond the specific issues to the people for whom they held such significance.

NOTES

1 W. Suermond, *Leerrede gehouden op den Keurdag der Regeering van Deventer den 22 Febr. 1786* (Deventer, 1786), p. 40. The text from Ecclesiastes reads as follows (New International Version). "Woe to you, O land whose king is a child . . . Blessed are you, O land whose king is of noble birth."

2 This incident is reported briefly in the Book of Resolutions of the Magistracy for 14 Ferbruary 1788: GA Deventer, Republiek I, 4, vol. 45. Cf. "Deventer in de Patriottentijd III," *Salland*, 29: 30 (16 April 1935); the author of this article mistakenly reports that the event occurred in 1785.

3 *NNJ*, 1785, pp. 1483–4.

4 *NNJ*, 1786, pp. 71–91.

5 *Rapport over de Verbetering van de Provinciale Regeeringswyze . . .* (Deventer, 1786).

6 *Tweede Rapport . . . over der Verbetering van de Stedelyke Regeeringswyze uitgebragt in Augustus des jaars 1786* (Deventer, 1786).

7 *NNJ*, 1786, pp. 869–70.

8 See, for example, the *Derde Rapport van Gecommitteerden uit Raad en Gemeente rakende zekere Adressen door pretense Gecommitteerden uit de Burgerij aan Schepenen en Raad geadresseerd* (Deventer, 1786).

9 The "Act of Appointment" itself was not published, but the names of the new Committeemen were printed on several occasions; see, for example, *NNJ*, 1786, p. 71.

10 J. Lindeboom, "Het Deventer Professoraat van F. A. van der Marck," *VMORG*, 54 (1938), pp. 115–37.

11 See, for example, *Redenvoering van F. A. van der Marck, over de liefde tot het Vaderland . . .* (Deventer, 1783).

12 The report of the Burgercommittee was printed in its entirety in *NNJ*, 1786, pp. 71–91; this is the text that I have used. Cf. *Rapport van de Burger-Commissie der*

Stad Deventer. Betreffende de ingeleverde bezwaaren der burgery. Overgegeven aan de commissie uit Raad en Meente, den 6 Jan. 1786 (Deventer, 1786).

13 Cf. GA Deventer, Collectie Dumbar, 84: "Stukken over de toelating der Doopsgezinden in de Gilden te Deventer, 1700."

14 This was marked as letter B in the Committee's report. The original petition is not extant. Cf. *De Politieke Kruyer*, no. 307, pp. 713–16. If we assume that the 250 Catholics who signed this petition were adult males, as was characteristic of Patriot petitions, then they represented approximately 12 percent of the adult male population – certainly a political force to be reckoned with.

15 Letter D in the Committee's report. The bakers' guild also asked that the annual *"Vette-Beesten"* (fatted cattle) Market be revived. It had probably been cancelled in recent years because of a serious outbreak of cattle plague; cf. *NNJ*, 1775, pp. 1120–4, and 1785, pp. 1482–3.

16 Letter C in the Committee's report. This sounds like it could have been a grievance of members of the retail merchants' guild, although it was not identified as such.

17 Letter E in the Committee's report.

18 Letter M, the last, in the Committee's report.

19 Letter L in the Committee's report; no author is named.

20 GA Deventer, Republiek I, 4, 17 July 1781.

21 M. van der Heijden, *De Dageraad van de emcipatie der Katholieken in Nederland* (Nijmegen, 1947), p. 13. The influential Patriot journal, *De Politieke Kruyer*, no. 105, p. 1520, had also published a letter by "Ultrajectinus" (dated January 31, 1784) which criticized the corporative power of the guilds. Attempts to restore the power of the guilds, Ultrajectinus argued, had nothing to do with democracy because decisions within the guilds were commonly made by casting lots – that is, chance – and because guilds were exclusive, especially on the basis of religion.

22 *Tweede Rapport*, p. v. The report also invoked the example of the United States as a strong recommendation for the system of representative democracy.

23 Its great length notwithstanding, the Draft Regulation was not intended to be comprehensive. Where they were not superceded by the new constitution, the *Stadregt* and the city's ancient customs and traditions would still determine the conduct of public affairs.

24 I am grateful to Professor R. R. Palmer for pointing out this striking similarity.

25 *Tweede Rapport*, p. 1.

26 These constitutional principles are as radical and unequivocal as can be found anywhere in the eighteenth century. Certainly they belie R. R. Palmer's suggestion in *The Age of the Democratic Revolution*, vol. 1 (Princeton, NJ, 1959), pp. 365–6, that the Patriots did not proceed from the principle of the sovereignty of the people to the act reconstituting government by means of constitutional documents. The same goes for I. Leonard Leeb's general contention in *The Ideological Origins of the Batavian Revolution. History and Politics in the Dutch Republic, 1747–1800* (The Hague, 1973) that the Patriots did not become "truly" revolutionary until after the defeat of 1787.

27 Here, for the first time, the authors of the Draft Regulation invoked the city's ancient rights and privileges as preserved by the Union of Utrecht.

28 *Tweede Rapport*, p. vi.

29 Cf. Gordon Wood, *The Creation of the American Republic, 1776–1787* (Chapel Hill, NC, 1969).

30 The authors were especially careful to incorporate many of the traditional ceremonies (*plechtigheden*) into the new electoral process.

31 *De Politieke Kruyer*, no. 395, pp. 422–6.

32 Ibid., no. 405, pp. 585–92.

33 Ibid., no. 395, pp. 427–36.

34 *Advis van Otto Nicolaas Westenink, Lid der Gezworen Gemeente der Stad Deventer . . . ter Vergadering overgegeven den — October 1786* (Deventer, 1786).

35 *NNJ*, 1786, pp. 869–70. The petition was not printed in its entirety.

36 *Aanmerkingen over het adres en de Denkwys van veele Leden der respectieve Gilden in Deventer* (Deventer, 1787).

37 These petitions were not published; we only know of them from reports in the *Nieuwe Nederlandsche Jaarboeken* and in the *Derde Rapport* of the Municipal Commission.

38 *Derde Rapport*, p. 7.

39 *Addres aan de Gezworen Gemeente van Deventer op naam van Gildens en Stemgeregtigde Burgerij door 26 personen gepresenteerd den 19 Jan. 1787 met de Resolutie van Raad en Gemeente van den 20 ditto* (Deventer, 1787).

40 Ibid., p. 9.

41 Ibid., p. 11.

42 On the economic foundations of the Catholic question, see also *De Politieke Kruyer*, no. 307, pp. 713–16.

43 *Addres aan de Gezworen Gemeente*, pp. 22–3.

44 *Rapport van Heeren Gecommitteerden uit Raad en Gemeente der Stad Deventer, Rakende het Addres, den 19 Jan. 1787 aan Ed. Achtb. Gezw. Gemeente van Deventer gedaan door 26 Personen . . .* (Deventer, 1787).

45 See *Concept Reglement of de Regeering van de Stad Deventer* (Deventer, 1787); in this revised edition of the constitution, the controversial Article XV became Article XIV.

46 In addition to the works cited in chapter 4, see GA Kampen, Oud Archief, 299; "Bij de stadsregeering ingekomen stukken van patriottisch gezinden, betreffende stedelijke aangelegenheden. Met stukken betreffende de patriotten in het algemeen, 1784–1796."

47 W. A. Fasel, "De Democratisch-Patriottische woelingen te Kampen," *VMORG*, 74 (1959), p. 94.

48 *Bericht van de Burger Commissie der Stad Campen, Betreffende de Inleveringe van Bezwaren aan de Commissie uit Raad en Meente Gedaan den 31 January 1786* (Kampen, 1786).

49 *Rapport over de ingeleverde Provinciale bezwaren, uitgebragt door de Heeren tot onderzoek derzelver . . .* (Kampen, 1786).

50 *Rapport over de verbetering van de Regeeringsbestelling der Stad Campen, Door Heeren Gecommitteerden uit Raad en Gezwoorene Gemeente uitgebragt in November 1786* (Kampen, 1786).

51 *Brief van een Burger uit Campen, aan een Burger te Deventer* (Kampen, 1786), p. 10.

52 See "Brief van een Zwolsch Volks Vriend, over en ten geleide van het gewigtig Rapport, door eene Commissie uit Raad en Meente, over der Burger-Bezwaren, onlangs uitgebragt . . .," *De Politieke Kruyer*, no. 349–51, pp. 543–90.

53 *Resolutie van de Heeren van de Magistraat der Stad Zwolle . . . over Het Rapport door de Commissie uit Raad en Meente tot de bezwaren uitgebragt . . .* (Deventer, 1786). See also,

for the on-going discussion of the proposed constitutional changes, *Advis van de Heeren Burqemeesteren Theussink, van Sonsbeek, Gelderman, van der Wyck en van Marle. Over het Rapport van de Commissie uit Raad en Meente tot de burger bezwaren* (Kampen, 1786) and *Aanmerkingen op het Rapport van de Commissie uit Raad en Meente te Zwolle over de bezwaren, door een Zwolsch Burger* (Zwolle, 1786).

54 *NNJ*, 1786, pp. 1643–7.
55 *De Burger-gecommitteerden der stad Zwolle aan hunne Committenten* (Zwolle, 1787).
56 *NNJ*, 1787, pp. 168–75, 355–62.
57 M. van Dam, "Kampen," in *Herstel, Hervorming of Behoud? Tien Overijsselse steden in de Patriottentijd, 1780–1787*, ed. M. A. M. Franken and R. M. Kemperink (Zwolle, 1985), pp. 85–6, and P. J. Lettinga, "Zwolle," in ibid., p. 56.

6

A City Divided

For all practical purposes, the Orangist petition of January 1787 ended the debate over Deventer's new constitution and initiated the battle for control of the city. Cut off almost as soon as it began, the constitutional discussion was on the whole as one-sided as it was short-lived. Indeed, matters that we today commonly consider crucial to the institution of representative democracy were hardly discussed at all. Thus, for example, the complex sections of the Draft Regulation which attempted to separate legislative, judicial, and executive authority in the municipal administration seem not to have been particularly controversial as such. The Orangist petitions simply branded the bulk of the new constitution too "intricate and complicated." On the contrary, the major sticking points appeared to be matters of transparent self-interest and traditional prejudice rather than philosophical disagreement. Defending the "rights" of the Stadhouder and the guilds, the Orangist petition attacked especially the seventh and fifteenth articles of the draft constitution which posited the illegality of the old "aristocratic" Governmental Regulation and gave *burgerrechten* to Roman Catholics, respectively. Thus, the Patriots could easily and self-righteously dismiss the opposition to the new constitution as a particularly insidious combination of Orangist cabal, aristocratic selfishness, and religious bigotry.

During the next eight months, the Patriot and Orangist leaders of Deventer traded invectives rather than ideas. Each side held to apparently fixed political demands, and all attempts at reconciliation seemed to be doomed to failure. In May, for example, there was an attempt to unite the city behind a series of 13 general constitutional principles, but even these relatively conciliatory articles proved to be divisive.[1] It was not immediately clear, however, whether the rhetoric of the leadership corresponded to political and social realities in Deventer. After all, both sides claimed to represent the interests and to enjoy the support of the established Burgerij. Only in the course of the struggle, as it became increasingly difficult to remain neutral or indifferent, would the outline of the revolutionary fracture in Deventer society become clear, but even then contemporary observers had difficulty describing the opposing forces in other than traditional "party" terms.[2]

Our purpose here is to go beyond the traditional labels and to situate the rhetoric of the opposing leaders within the social reality of both the immediate revolutionary situation and the long-term structural changes we discerned in chapter 1. We will examine, first of all, the nature of the revolutionary coalition that took control of Deventer in 1787. The Patriots had sustained some casualties in the battle that erupted over the Draft Constitution, but they appeared to be winning the war nevertheless. On the other side, the Orangists proved to be remarkably determined to press the fight despite the odds against them, and we will try to uncover the social and political foundations of this new counter-revolutionary coalition. Having thus described the internal divisions as they emerged in 1787, we will turn finally to the question of what was peculiar or exceptional about the dynamics of municipal revolution in Deventer.

MEASURING THE REVOLUTIONARY COALITION

The social profile of the Patriot movement is relatively easy to discern because the Patriots seized the political initiative early in 1787 with a major petition drive. Following several months of increasing tension and on the eve of the annual *Petrikeur*, the Patriots circulated a petition demanding that the Sworn Council engineer a decisive break with the past: they sought to abolish the old Governmental Regulation, to require that all Burgemeesters pledge their support for efforts to devise a new constitution providing for popular election of the Sworn Council, and to swear in the new Magistracy without the Stadhouder's approval.[3] Surely, to sign this petition was, in the charged atmosphere of 1787, an important political act. Large numbers of people, who for the past 18 months had been largely spectators as various leaders claimed to represent their best interests, now were forced to decide for or against the Patriot Revolution as it had come to be defined in liberal constitutional terms. Because of the seriousness of the situation, the Patriots made every effort to maximize the number of signatures, and on the eve of the annual election, they presented to the Sworn Council a petition with 740 signatures – a modest increase of 26 signatures over the petition of February 1783; again, the signatories represented more than one-third of the city's adult male population. The Sworn Council was obviously receptive, and in the *Petrikeur* two days later, five Orangist Burgemeesters were replaced by five well-known Patriots, all of them officers in the Vrijcorps.[4]

Of the 740 Patriot signatories, I have been able to identify the occupations of 378 or slightly more than half, and as table 6.1 indicates, some major shifts took

Table 6.1 Occupational profile of Patriot signatories, February 1787

Occupation	Census 1795 (%)	Petition Feb.1787 (%)	Index census= 100	Change since 1783
Manufacturing	38.6	39.9	103	−23%
Trade and transportation	16.9	24.9	147	−13%
Social services	5.3	11.9	225	+129%
Agriculture and fishing	6.4	5.0	78	+56%
Unskilled labor	8.4	6.9	82	+306%
Miscellaneous	6.7	5.3	79	+43%
Inactive	17.6	6.1	35	+7%
Total	100.0 (n=1,929)	100.0 (n=378)		

place within the Patriot coalition even though the total number of signatories remained essentially constant. In the first place, the two largest occupational groups, which were consistently over-represented in the earlier petitions, both recorded declines in their share of the total since the petition of February 1783. Although those working in trade and transportation were still decisively over-represented (index of 147), manufacturing dropped to an index of just 103. Conversely, the smaller occupational groups all recorded significant increases in their share of the total, with those in social services becoming by far the most over-represented group (index of 225). Still, the most dramatic change since the petition of 1783 was evident in the category of unskilled laborers, whose share of the total more than tripled. The smaller occupational categories, with the exception of social services, remained relatively under-represented, but for the first time they constituted more than one-third of the total signatories.

It is immediately obvious from the petition of February 1787, then, that the Patriot movement had undergone a major transformation since it first demanded fundamental reform of the constitution of government in August of 1785. The precise nature of that transformation becomes readily apparent if we compare the petitions of 1783 and 1787 more closely. Breaking down the largest categories of manufacturing and trade and transportation, we find that only one occupational group retained an essentially constant share of the total number of signatories: those in commerce increased their share 3 percent. For the rest, the shifts were more dramatic – between 30 and 300 percent. Borrowing the vocabulary of a daily stock market report we can identify the prominent gainers and losers. As table 6.2 indicates, almost all of the decline was registered in five categories of manufacturing, supplemented by a large decline in transportation. The losses were more than offset by dramatic gains in the social service and unskilled labor categories plus more modest gains in three types of manufacturing and agriculture and fishing. As a result of these shifts,

Table 6.2　Changing participation by occupation, 1783–7

	Losers Signatories				Gainers Signatories		
Occupation	1783	1787	Change	Occupation	1783	1787	Change
Metalworking	15	9	−6	Construction	19	26	+7
Woodworking	22	10	−12	Textiles	6	14	+8
Leatherworking	36	20	−16	Misc. Trades	18	26	+8
Garments	30	24	−6	Social Services	18	45	+27
Food							
processing	35	22	−13	Agriculture and fishing	11	19	+8
Transportation	28	14	−14	Unskilled labor	6	26	+20
Total	166	99	−67	Total		78	156	+78

nearly two-fifths of the signatories were signing a Patriot petition for the first time. On the other side of the coin, the most serious consequence for the Patriot movement was that 92 of the 152 people we identified as the core of the Patriot movement in 1782 and 1783 – its most faithful petition-signers – failed to support the Patriots' *coup d'état* in 1787.

This last point is dramatically underscored if we examine more closely those occupational groups whose support declined. Among artisans and tradesmen, precisely those occupational groups which were clearly over-represented in the core of the Patriot movement in 1783 (for comparison, see table 4.4; index of more than 200) now appear in the "loser" column of table 6.2. In metalworking, for example, seven members of the blacksmiths' guild, all of them faithful members of the Patriot core in 1783, were conspicuously absent from the Patriot petition in 1787. Likewise, seven coopers, 19 shoemakers, 20 tailors, 13 bakers and five boatmen, all of them guildsmen and many of them part of the movement's faithful core, disappeared from the ranks of the Patriot movement. In some cases, the effects of these defections were mitigated by new recruits in the same or similar occupations. In the garment trades, for example, journeyman tailors and hat and wig makers, many of them new recruits, replaced members of the tailors' guild who defected. But in the woodworking trades, chairmakers and cabinetmakers who had no guild disappeared along with the members of the coopers' guild. In all, 80 percent of those who defected from the Patriot core were artisans, and these were overwhelmingly identified as members of guilds. Fully half were tailors, shoemakers, bakers, and blacksmiths – that is, involved in the traditional service trades oriented to the local market.

What was left of the core of Patriot support after these important defections represents an interesting distortion of the original profile of the Patriot coalition (table 6.3). Nearly half of the remaining Patriot faithful were guild members, but now the emphasis was on commerce rather than manufacturing. There were a few members of the artisanal guilds who continued to support the Patriot

Table 6.3   The core of Patriot support, 1787

Occupation	Census 1795 (%)	Patriot core (%)	Index census= 100	Change since 1783
Manufacturing				
Construction	5.8	5.0	86	-15%
Metalworking	2.2	1.7	77	-76%
Woodworking	3.2	3.3	103	-50%
Leatherworking	5.4	3.3	61	-72%
Textiles	6.1	0.0	0	0
Garments	6.0	8.3	138	-42%
Food	5.7	15.0	263	+27%
Miscellaneous	4.5	3.3	73	0
Subtotal	38.6	40.0	103	-35%
Trade and transportation				
Commerce	12.1	41.6	344	+86%
Transportation	4.8	3.3	69	-44%
Subtotal	16.9	45.0	266	+59%
Other	44.5	15.0	34	+42%
Total	100.0 (n=1,929)	100.0 (n=60)		

cause: among others, two coopers, four tailors and two bakers remained part of the core, which helps to account for the fact that their occupational groups were still relatively over-represented among the most faithful petition-signers. Still, in all, guild solidarity was the rule in the artisanal guilds, and as a result of their large-scale defection, the category of manufacturing as a whole declined 35 percent in its share of the Patriot core. Likewise, transportation followed the same downward course with the defection of formerly faithful boatmen and innkeepers. The alimentary trades were a striking anomaly in that their share of the smaller total actually increased, but now bread bakers, whose market was local, were overshadowed by specialty *koek* bakers, brewers and distillers – all of whom were oriented to markets beyond the local community.

By contrast with manufacturing and transportation, commerce dramatically increased its share of the total. Indeed, the majority of the guild members who remained part of the Patriot core were merchants – members especially of the silk merchants' and the retail merchants' guilds. The silk merchants, who remained solidly Patriot, were now the largest block of guild members in the Patriot core while the members of the larger retail merchants' guild appear to have been thoroughly divided. Though proportionally not many of them were originally part of the Patriot core, just over half of the retail merchants who had signed all three petitions in 1782 and 1783 remained true to the Patriots' cause. More broadly, nearly two-fifths of all the people who can be identified with this guild signed again in 1787. In the end, then, merchants accounted for 42 percent of the remaining Patriot faithful, a share nearly three and a half times larger than their proportion of the working population.

Around this remnant of the original core of the movement, the Patriots were forced to build a very different, much broader coalition. Indeed, only 16 percent of the signatories in 1787 had signed all the previous petitions, and among those whose participation increased – the gainers – social diversity is an immediately striking characteristic. At one end of the spectrum, unskilled laborers, not previously part of the core of Patriot support, suddenly became a significant element in the coalition. More than two-thirds of these wage workers and day laborers were signing a Patriot petition for the first time. At the other end of the spectrum, among the educated religious and liberal professions, there was an exceptionally high degree of continuity – three-quarters of those signing in 1783, signed again in 1787 – but these were supplemented by an increased number of people in minor municipal offices, many of whom were new or less consistent signers. In agriculture and fishing, there was relatively little continuity and a high number (nearly three-fifths) of people signing for the first time. The overall proportions of peasants, market gardeners, and fishermen, however, remained essentially constant.

There were, by contrast, major qualitative shifts among the three artisanal groups whose participation increased. In textiles, the weaver and spinner who signed in 1783 and identified themselves as "master" (*baas*) failed to sign in 1787 and were replaced by larger numbers of unorganized spinners, weavers and rope-makers, most of whom had never signed before. Similarly, in the category of miscellaneous trades, five of the seven members of the glassmakers' guild who signed in 1783 failed to sign in 1787; they were replaced by five basket-makers and four wagon-makers who signed for the first time and were outside the guild-regulated sectors of the economy. Indeed, basket-making was probably the largest of the protoindustrial *fabrieken*. In the construction trades, there were very few who signed for the first time, but six of the seven members of the construction guild (*Vier Gekroonde Gilde*) failed to sign in 1787. They were replaced by increased numbers of carpenters, masons and hodcarriers, most of whom had signed at least one of the earlier petitions but none of whom had apparently been admitted to the exclusive membership of the guild.

In all, despite their economic and social diversity, what those occupational groups which increased their participation in the Patriot movement had in common was their lack of guild organization. They were overwhelmingly what the earlier petitions had termed "*particulieren*" – individuals and private persons. Even in the miscellaneous and construction trades, where there was considerable guild participation evident in 1783, there was a decisive shift toward *particulieren* and toward new recruits in 1787. The result was that among the gainers only a very small fraction (2 percent) were guild members. This pattern also holds more generally for the Patriot coalition as a whole in 1787. Guild participation, as high as 64 percent in December 1782 and 46 percent in February 1783, dropped to just 11 percent in 1787.

This image of the Patriot coalition – of a movement largely deprived of its original base in the artisanal guilds and now overwhelmingly a movement of *particulieren* – is reflected as well in the membership of the Patriots' Vrijcorps. Along with the Burgercommittee, this free militia had been designed deliberately to bring *"het Volk"* into the political process. During much of its existence, its function seemed largely symbolic – that is, to demonstrate the Patriots' new-found muscle when the Burgercommittee presented its petitions to the municipal government, and while the annual municipal elections were being held. Since, from the very beginning, the Vrijcorps had close connections with the Sworn Council through its officer corps, it seemed unlikely that it would ever be inclined or forced to take the Stadhuis by storm.

Once the Patriots actually came to power in 1787, however, the needs of the Patriot movement were transformed. The Burgercommittee, divided and battered by the challenge of the new Orangist opposition, all but dropped from sight, and the Vrijcorps became the essential prop of the revolutionary regime.[5] That role as the strong arm of the revolutionary movement culminated in a direct challenge to the Orangists at the end of June. Patriot militiamen, having provoked a confrontation outside the Orangist Burger Society, opened fire on the opposition crowd. Five unarmed Orangists were killed, and in the following days, the Burger Society was banned and all those who refused to pledge their allegiance to the Patriots' regime were disarmed by the loyal members of the Vrijcorps.[6] In short, however symbolic its original intent, the Vrijcorps was called on for serious business once push came to shove.

Of the 349 members of the Vrijcorps, whose membership list was drawn up in late 1786, I have been able to identify just 153 or 44 percent in the census of 1795.[7] On the whole, the members of the Vrijcorps whom I could identify were not the same people who faithfully signed Patriot petitions. Twenty-three percent signed none of the Patriots' petitions, and another 21 percent signed in 1787 for the first time. Just 8 percent of the members of the Vrijcorps signed all of the petitions. For this there are two obvious reasons. On the one hand, many of the militiamen, especially the drummers and pipers but also some of the musketeers, were very young and thus not likely to be solicited as petition-signers. On the other hand, more than half of the officer corps were members of the municipal government and thus on the receiving end, not the signing end, of the petitions. Despite differences in personnel, however, the profile of the members of the Vrijcorps (table 6.4) is generally similar to that of the Patriot signatories in 1787.

Among the Vrijcorps members who were heads of households in 1795, artisans once again predominated, but it was qualitatively a different group than

Table 6.4   Occupational profile of the Patriot Vrijcorps, 1786

Occupation	Census 1795 (%)	Vrijcorps 1786 (%)	Index census= 100
Manufacturing	38.6	51.6	134
Trade and transportation	16.9	17.0	101
Social services	5.3	9.2	174
Agriculture and fishing	6.4	2.6	41
Unskilled labor	8.4	7.8	93
Miscellaneous	6.7	3.3	49
Inactive	17.6	8.5	48
Total	100.0 (n=1,929)	100.0 (n=153)	

had previously set the tone for the Patriot movement. Blacksmiths were outnumbered by coppersmiths, tailors by hat- and wig-makers, and bakers by basket- and brush-makers – all of which indicates a clear shift from the guild-based artisanal groups to the newer entrepreneurial manufactures. The result was that, of the 79 craftsmen I could identify, only three appear to have been members of the artisanal guilds. Overall, just 6 percent of the members of the Vrijcorps can be identified as guildsmen, and they were mostly in commercial occupations. Though trade and transportation dropped below its usual share, merchants as well as educated professionals were especially prominent in the officer corps of the militia. As was the case with the Patriot signatories in 1787, the smaller occupational groups claimed a larger share of the total (nearly one-third) than they had in the petitions of 1782 and 1783. Those in social services were once again the most over-represented group, but most remarkably, perhaps, there were nearly as many unskilled workers and day laborers (12) in the ranks of the Vrijcorps as there were merchants and shopkeepers (13). In short, the Patriots had recruited more broadly than either the rhetoric of the pamphleteers or the traditional wisdom of the historians would suggest.[8]

   Indeed, the breadth of the coalition that supported the revolutionary regime in Deventer is both striking and surprising. Having lost the allegiance of many of their most reliable and easily mobilized supporters in the artisanal guilds, the Patriots were forced to look more broadly for support among the *particulieren* who stood outside the organizational network of the guilds. The result was that the smaller occupational groups increased their share of the total of both Patriot signatories and militiamen. In fact, that segment of the working population which is usually assumed to have remained outside the political movements of the eighteenth century – unskilled wage workers and day laborers – recorded the largest increases and now became a prominent element in the rank and file of the Patriot movement. Likewise, journeymen and unorganized tradesmen joined the movement in unprecedented numbers. Though the Patriots still claimed to represent the interests of the established Burgerij, it is clear that they depended on the support of large numbers of more marginal residents, many of whom might not have been enfranchised to vote for members of the Sworn Council or eligible to serve in political office.[9]

Deprived of its original backbone, this motley coalition of *particulieren* was most certainly more difficult to mobilize for the sort of massive petition drives that marked the Patriots' rise to prominence and power. But by 1787, the situation called for new kinds of allegiance and a new repertoire of collective action. Once the Patriots actually controlled the municipal administration, the protection offered by the Vrijcorps was far more important than the popular pressure that the Burgercommittee could offer by means of petition drives. What is more, the Vrijcorps more than made up for lost organizational resources of the guilds; while guilds, whose primary purpose was economic regulation, had proved to be useful for political purposes, the Vrijcorps had explicitly political intentions from the beginning. The rank and file of the Vrijcorps could, moreover, be expected to respect and follow the orders of the officers they elected. The result of this shift in both the repertoire of action and the movement's internal organization was a leaner but undoubtedly more disciplined and reliable base of popular support.

At the same time, there can be little doubt that officers of the Vrijcorps rather than the members of the Burgercommittee set the tone and the political agenda for the Patriot movement as it came to power. The members of the Burgercommittee were, by definition, outside the municipal administration, and the committee chosen in 1785 proved to be representative enough of the Patriots' original coalition that four of its members failed to sign the Patriot petition in 1787; and the only member from one of the major artisanal guilds (Jan Vunderink of the bakers' guild), actually became a member of the Orangist Burgercommittee at the end of 1786. Thus divided˙and compromised, the Burgercommittee was eclipsed by the leaders of the Vrijcorps who were closely connected with the Patriot regime. Of the 32 officers of the Vrijcorps, no less than 18 were regents – in 1787, 13 were members of the Sworn Council, but five were elevated to Burgemeester when the Orangist minority in the Magistracy was removed from office. As was typically the case in the regent elite, 15 of them held university degrees in law, though only one appears to have been practicing law. Of the 17 officers who can be identified as heads of households in 1795, then, one was an attorney, three held high political office, five were merchants, and one a teacher, while just two were artisans – a tailor and a *koek* baker. The remaining five either listed no occupation or called themselves *rentiers*. Thus, the Patriot leadership in 1787 can hardly be said to represent the social diversity of the Patriot movement, but it does clearly reflect the importance of the merchants and educated professionals who were so prominent among the most consistent supporters of the movement. Indeed, their political connections were so good that four officers of the Vrijcorps sat on the nine-man Municipal Commission that wrote the new constitution.

Losing the allegiance of 60 percent of its most faithful supporters on the eve of the *coup d'état* was obviously a serious blow for the Patriots. But the movement did more than just survive. On the one hand, the Patriots proved that they could still enlist the support of a large segment of the local populace, picking up new support for its most radical petition from precisely those more marginal groups who were under-represented on the earlier petitions. On the other hand, the Patriots moved into the brave new world of democratic representation in some ways more unified and better organized than ever before. As the activist leadership of the Burgercommittee, a hodgepodge of often competing interests, gave way to the protection of the Vrijcorps, with its intimate connections to the now-dominant Patriot faction of the regent oligarchy, the Patriots were no longer plagued by internal tensions and thus better equipped to meet the new challenge of maintaining their position of strength.

This, then, is the coalition of forces that demanded immediate suspension of the old constitution of government, removed from office those Burgemeesters who would not support the project of constitutional reform, and laid the foundations for the institution of democratic representation in municipal government. At the top were merchants, *rentiers* and especially lawyers; in the middle a variety of craftsmen, shopkeepers, farmers, and minor municipal officials; and at the bottom a surprisingly large number of wage workers and day laborers. Since each was in his own way an outsider in the corporative world of the old regime, they were especially well suited to unite behind an individualist conception of the democratic future of the city. The significance of this peculiar coalition is revealed, however, as much by the nature of its opposition as by its own stated intentions.

THE SOCIAL FOUNDATIONS OF COUNTER-REVOLUTION

The social profile of the counter-revolutionary Orangist movement is rather more difficult to discern. Documents like large petitions or organizational membership lists that might reveal the extent and nature of Orangist support are simply not available. We must rely, therefore, on fragmentary evidence to sketch a partial image of the Orangist coalition. The pattern of Orangist allegiance and mobilization that emerges from the available sources is nevertheless sufficiently clear to compensate for the lack of symmetry in the analysis of the opposing forces.

The sheer weight of numbers in support of the early Patriot petitions demonstrates that there could have been no substantial Orangist support – thus no Orangist movement – during the early stages of the Patriot Crisis. Still there were some individuals who could be identified as advocates of the Stadhouder's influence in municipal and provincial politics. The outspoken Orangism of Burgemeester E. H. Putman, for example, was all the more remarkable because of his isolation in a sea of Patriot protest. Putman was certainly not the only Magistrate whose politics reflected his dependence on the patronage of the Stadhouder, but he was singled out by the Patriots as a test of the Prince's strength and resolve. In the election of 1783, Putman was demoted, in defiance of the Stadhouder's recommendations, from Burgemeester to Sworn Councilor, in which position he remained until he was again elevated to the position of Burgemeester under the Orangist restoration (see chapter 3).

To the Patriots, who were characteristically inclined to accept conspiracy theories, E. H. Putman seemed to symbolize the Orangist cabal at work in Deventer; he was the very incarnation of the "*verdervende hand*" (corrupting hand) that they saw sowing the seeds of dissension among good Patriots. According to Professor Ruckersfelder, for instance, he was responsible for encouraging the tailors, shoemakers, and boatmen to demand popular election of the Sworn Council in 1784 when that idea was still novel and divisive.[10] But despite Putman's best efforts to divide and conquer the Patriot movement, there is no evidence of a popular Orangist movement in Deventer until after the opposition Burgercommittee was created in 1786 to resist the implementation of the Patriot's Draft Constitution. Although the committeemen claimed to have been elected by a large number of citizens, we have no specific evidence of the extent or nature of their support. But the men whose names appeared on petitions signed by the opposition Burgercommittee in late 1786 and early 1787 provide our first glimpse of the nascent counter-revolutionary movement.[11]

Of the 27 men who signed the Orangist petitions, I could identify 20 (74 percent) as heads of households in the occupational census of 1795. Except for one *rentier*, the Orangist committeemen were all active in commerce (six) and manufacturing (13). While there was a wide variety of artisanal occupations represented, none of the smaller occupational groups – social services, agriculture and fishing, or unskilled labor – was represented. Most importantly, however, 85 percent of the Orangist committeemen had signed Patriot petitions in 1782 and 1783, eight of them having signed all three petitions. Not surprisingly, the Patriot petitions also reveal that at least 14 of the 27 were members of guilds. To judge by the composition of the opposition Burgercommittee, then, the core of the Orangist movement consisted of people who formerly were the core of the Patriot coalition. The remarkable case of Jan Vunderink illustrates this important fact: a baker and a member of the bakers' guild, Vunderink had served on the Patriot Burgercommittee at the beginning of 1786 but had joined the Orangist Committee by the end of the year.

Whether the break-up of the Patriot coalition was due to the machinations of E. H. Putman is a moot point, but the split in the Patriot movement clearly worked to the advantage of Orangists like Putman. The *Nieuwe Nederlandsche Jaarboeken* reported, for example, that during the month of January 1787, 16 members of the new Burgercommittee had "undertaken negotiations" with the Count of Heiden Hompesch, the Stadhouder's most visible ally in the provincial nobility.[12] Not surprisingly, the guildsmen who, as we have seen, had only recently defected from the Patriot coalition were assumed to be the backbone of the Orangist movement. Derk Nijland and Lodewyk van Weteringen, *generale ouderlieden* (elders) of the guilds, were the committee's public spokesmen, and the committee apparently held its meetings at the Gildehuis.[13] Accordingly, when the revolutionary government acted to repress the Orangist movement in February 1787, it not only prohibited any further petitioning by the Orangist Burgercommittee, but forbade all political discussions in the meetings of the guilds.

Deprived of its organizational base in the Burgercommittee and the guilds, the Orangist movement in Deventer turned to a private Burger Society to coordinate its activities.[14] The leaders of the Burger Society, like the leaders of the Burgercommittee, had been active in the Patriot movement in 1782 and 1783: Adriaan van Dalen, a baker and guild member, was Director and Simon van Brackel, a sugar refiner, was Secretary. Following the tragic confrontation between Patriot militiamen and Orangists outside the Burger Society in June 1787, the Society was abolished and its records confiscated by the municipal government. Unfortunately the membership list of the Society, which was reported to have had between 400 and 500 members, has not survived, but at the same time the Patriot government reportedly disarmed 400 men who would not pledge to resist the tyranny of the Prince of Orange.[15] If these reports are not hopelessly exaggerated, they suggest that the Orangist movement had attracted considerable support, although the Orangists do not appear to have organized their armed supporters in an independent militia comparable to the Vrijcorps.[16]

Our broadest measure of the Orangist coalition is the counter-revolutionary government elected by "Representatives of the Guilds and the Burgerij" on September 20, 1787, the day Prussian troops occupied the city. The new government consisted of 16 Burgemeesters and 48 Sworn Councilors, most of whom were new faces in municipal government.[17] The corps of Burgemeesters included, naturally, the five Burgemeesters who had been removed from office for their Orangist sympathies earlier in the year. Six others had previously been Sworn Councilors – a small Orangist minority in the Patriot-dominated Council. Only five of the Orangist Burgemeesters had held no political office previously, but four of these newcomers had signed Patriot petitions in 1782 and 1783. Occupationally, the Burgemeesters were typical of the old-regime oligarchy: 11 were listed as *rentiers* in the occupational census and 12 had university degrees in law, while only two pursued active occupations. Both of them were merchants and one was a member of the retail merchants' guild.

By comparison, all except one of the Orangist Sworn Councilors were new office holders. Of course not all members of the Orangist Burgercommittee

Plate 1 Map of Deventer by J. Blaeu from *Toneel der steden van de Vereenighde Nederlanden*, 1649. Following the liberation of Deventer in 1591, the city's medieval wall was replaced by the most modern fortifications, in the style known as the *trace italienne*, which made a frontal assault nearly impossible. Within the outline of the old city, two large, public spaces are clearly visible: the Brink (see plate 2) toward the upper right and the Grote Kerkhof (see plate 4) in the center, near the IJssel River (Courtesy of the Gemeente Archief Deventer)

Plate 2 "De Waag en Hoofdwagt te Deventer," engraving by Jan de Beijer in *Hedendaagsche Historie of Tegenwoordige Staat ... van Overijssel*, volume 3, Amsterdam, 1781. The Brink, the largest market area within Deventer, was bounded on one side by the city's magnificent Weighing House; just behind it (not visible here) was the Gildehuis, the locus of much political activity in the 1780s. To the right in this scene is the Hoofdwagt, the headquarters of the largely ceremonial Civic Guard (Courtesy of Museum de Waag, Deventer)

Plate 3 '''t Plunderen te Deventer,'' engraving by R. Vinkeles and C. Bogerts, ca. 1793. Following the invasion of Prussian troops in September 1787, the houses of several leading Patriots were attacked by Orangist crowds in Deventer. In this scene the house of F. A. van der Marck, head of the Patriot Burgercommittee, is being ''plundered,'' its windows were broken and the contents of the house were destroyed (not stolen) and scattered in the street (Courtesy of Atlas van Stolk, Rotterdam)

Plate 4 "Het Grote Kerkhof met de Duimpoort," drawing in pen and pencil by Jan de Beijer, 1746. The Grote Kerkhof was the scene of many Patriot demonstrations in the 1780s, especially when petitions were presented to the city's regents or on the occasion of the annual *Petrikeur*. The building on the extreme left of this drawing is the Landshuis which housed the office of the Clerk of the provincial Estates and served as a meeting place for the Estates' committees. The building next to it with the small portico was the Stadhuis (City Hall), whose facade had been reconstructed in 1690. Further down the row was the Latin School and, at the end, the Duimpoort, which led to the IJssel River. The enormous St Lebuinus Church or Grote Kerk is just out of view on the right of this scene (Courtesy of Museum de Waag, Deventer)

were rewarded with seats on the new Sworn Council; in fact, just 12 members of the Committee were elected to the Sworn Council. But like the members of the Burgercommittee, the Councilors were overwhelmingly refugees from the Patriot movement; no less than 43 of the new Councilors (90 percent) had signed Patriot petitions in 1782 and 1783, and of these, 18 had signed all of the first three petitions. Thus here, too, we see the origins of the Orangist movement in the disintegration of the Patriot coalition. Most of the Orangist Councilors (70 percent) can be identified as heads of households in the census of 1795, but a special list of the new Council members which reported the occupation of each one indicates more clearly than the census data what distinguished the rank and file of the Orangist movement from their former allies in the Patriot movement.[18]

Occupationally, the Orangist Council was a radical departure from the old-regime elite (table 6.5). Except for two *rentiers* and one member of an old patrician family who listed no occupation, all of the new Councilors were active in commerce and manufacturing. As was the case with the Orangist Burgercommittee, the smaller, more marginal occupational groups were not represented at all, and there appear to have been, *mirabile dictu*, no lawyers among the 48 members of the new Council.[19] Among the artisans, the shoemakers, tailors, bakers, and blacksmiths, who collectively accounted for more than half of the desertions from the Patriot coalition, were all represented by at least one member of the Council, as were glassmakers, carpenters, and masons. In trade and transportation, there were both boatmen and innkeepers alongside a variety of merchants. Though the small numbers involved tend to exaggerate the indices, there emerges a pattern of over- and under-representation in the Orangist Council that is remarkably similar in crucial respects to the remnant of Patriot faithful in 1787 (see table 6.3).

Several artisanal groups – construction, woodworking, textiles and garments – were equally or even less well represented in the Orangist Council than they were in the Patriot core. This is especially striking in the woodworking trades where a large-scale defection of coopers and chair-makers from the Patriot movement did not translate into representation on the Council: while only three of the ten known members of the coopers' guild still supported the Patriots in 1787, none of their number appeared either in the new Burgercommittee or in the Orangist Sworn Council. The only woodworker on the Council was P. Zichler, a cabinetmaker, who was actually a member of the construction guild. Several other groups, including metalworking, leatherworking, miscellaneous trades, and transportation, were clearly better represented among the Orangists than the Patriots. Metalworking was especially boosted by two members of the small silversmiths' guild, the miscellaneous trades by three glassmakers, and transportation by three innkeepers. Still, the most striking indices are those of the alimentary trades and commerce, for both are dramatically over-represented at the core of both political coalitions.

Table 6.5   Occupational profile of the Orangist Sworn Council, 1787

Occupation	Census 1795 (%)	No.	Orangist Council (%)	Index census= 100
Manufacturing				
Construction	5.8	2	4.2	72
Metalworking	2.2	4	8.3	377
Woodworking	3.2	1	2.1	66
Leatherworking	5.4	3	6.3	117
Textiles	6.1	0	0.0	0
Garments	6.0	3	6.3	105
Food	5.7	9	18.8	330
Miscellaneous	4.5	4	8.3	184
Subtotal	38.6	26	54.2	140
Trade and transportation				
Commerce ·	12.1	15	31.3	259
Transportation	4.8	4	8.3	172
Subtotal	16.9	19	39.6	234
Other	44.5	3	6.3	14
Total	100.0 (n=1,929)	48	100.1	

Those who worked in the food preparation trades were arguably the most politicized and divided group in the working population of Deventer; indeed, they were represented by an equal number of men (nine) in both the Patriot core and the Orangist Council. Though it is not immediately clear why we find two corn chandlers on each side, there is an obvious qualitative difference between the brewers, distillers and specialty *koek* bakers who were among the most faithful Patriots and the bread bakers and butchers who appeared in the Orangist Council. The former represented the entrepreneurial *fabrieken* which stood outside traditional guild regulation; the latter were among the oldest guild-regulated trades oriented especially to the local market.

The same sort of distinction emerges in the commercial occupations represented on the Orangist Council. Unlike the census, which used the very ambiguous term "*koopman*" for all manner of commercial occupations, the list of the Orangist Sworn Council distinguished between various kinds of merchants. Thus we learn that most of the Orangist merchants were small shopkeepers, especially grocers (seven), who can be identified from Patriot petitions as members of the retail merchants' guild. By contrast, no less than eight of the Patriot merchants were members of the wholesale silk merchants' guild. In addition, the ranks of the Patriot faithful included three book publishers/

salesmen, the men who enabled the Patriots' domination of the public press, as well as two wine merchants and several undifferentiated merchants who cannot be identified on the Patriot petitions as guild members. In any event, the distinction between the wholesale merchants and *particulieren* who character-ized the Patriot movement, and the guild-based small shopkeepers and artisans who dominated the Orangist Council, clarifies the conflict that tore at the social fabric of Deventer in 1787.

To judge by the counter-revolutionary government, then, the Orangist coalition was made up of two distinct groups. Like the Patriots, the Orangists drew a significant number of their leaders from the thoroughly divided patrician oligarchy, but in contrast to the Patriots' relatively young leadership drawn especially from the dissident faction of the Sworn Council, the Orangists were led by some of the oldest and most established members of the Magistracy.[20] Coupled with this Orangist minority of the political elite of Deventer, we find the ranks of the Orangist movement filled with artisans and shopkeepers, many of whom can be identified as guild members and most of whom were erstwhile Patriots. These were in many cases the seasoned veterans of four years of popular political action, the very people who had been instrumental in the rapid mobilization of popular opposition to the Prince of Orange and his noble allies in 1782 and 1783. But when they perceived their interests to be compromised by the Draft Regulation, they just as quickly rejected the Patriots' constitutional vision of the future and made peace with the Stadhouder.

Though the available evidence is limited, it is nevertheless clear enough that the Orangist vision of the future had precious little to do with the Prince of Orange; rather, its cutting edge was the established artisans' and shopkeepers' defense of economic interests defined in old-regime corporative terms. As we have already seen, the tailors', shoemakers', and boatmen's guilds had muddied the political waters as early as 1784 by demanding corporative influence in the election of Sworn Councilors. In 1785, when they had the opportunity to express their specific grievances, the bakers' guild made an urgent plea for relief from the competitive disadvantages of the city's high excises on flour; shopkeepers pleaded that wholesale fairs be abolished and that wholesalers be required to sell their products through established retailers; and butchers, bakers and innkeepers demanded that their counterparts in the countryside be taxed at the same rate as they were (see chapter 5). To be sure, these demands were coupled with continued support for the project of political reform. But the economic situation appears to have been very difficult for these established tradesman, and many of them tied both their economic and their political future to a strengthening of their corps. That included the right to exclude outsiders from their guilds.

To the artisans and shopkeepers who joined the Orangist movement, the Patriots' Draft Regulation naturally seemed a rejection of their economic interests and their political aspirations. Indeed, the lawyers who made the constitution insisted that economic matters, no matter how urgent, were secondary to the central task of redefining the polity in terms of free and equal individuals. In fact, the second article of the Constitution explicitly denied a political role to exclusive corps like guilds. Fearing the worst – that is, convinced that granting *burgerrechten* to Catholics would only increase competition in an already difficult local marketplace – these erstwhile Patriots sought refuge in the only haven available to them, in alliance with the Orangist faction of the oligarchy. But these established craftsmen and tradesmen, who considered themselves the backbone of their community, demanded and apparently got a high price for their support of the Stadhouder whom they had only recently rejected.

An unpublished manuscript by Everhard Putman indicates the political bargain that was struck within the Orangist coalition.[21] As a member of the Sworn Council, ex-Burgemeester Putman wrote an extended critique of the Draft Regulation for consideration by his colleagues on the Council. Putman mainly registered the same objections to the new constitution that appeared in the Orangist petition of January 1787 – in some instances, he even used the same words and phrases. But in addition, Putman put forward an alternative vision of the future of Deventer, a vision suffused with the aspirations of the tradesmen with whom he was allied.

To begin, Putman pleaded for prompt action to save the city's economy. In sharp contrast with both the Patriot Burgercommittee and the Municipal Commission, Putman argued that Deventer's economic health would have to be restored *before* its people could truly enjoy political liberty. He recommended several proposals for tax reform and improvement of water transport facilities, but he urged as well that a panel of experts, including both merchants and manufacturers, be assembled to investigate ways to revive existing economic enterprises to create new forms of employment for the poor. And finally, as an essential part of his economic package, Putman urged that the privileges of guilds be reaffirmed and that all guild charters be printed and circulated at public expense.

Although Putman expressed a profound suspicion of all attempts to alter the Governmental Regulation, he did reluctantly admit, undoubtedly in deference to his coalition partners, that adjustments in the election of the Sworn Council and the Magistracy were warranted in order to prevent "family government." In place of the "intricate" electoral system proposed in the Draft Regulation, Putman suggested electoral procedures that combined individual and corporative influence in the nomination of candidates to fill vacancies. For each vacancy in the Sworn Council and Magistracy, the guilds would nominate two and the rest of the Burgerij would nominate one candidate. From this list of candidates the Sworn Council would make its selection, subject to the approval of the Prince of Orange. Putman also outlined a complex procedure by which the guilds and the Burgerij could recall Burgemeesters and Councilors. Finally, Putman added a corporative twist to the notion of representation.

Whereas our sovereign, free Rijkstad (whose exalted government wields legal jurisdiction without appeal . . . in both criminal and civil cases) exercizes such considerable influence in the provincial constitution, and at the same time, must provide for its welfare principally from commerce, therefore the Magistracy should be so arranged that it include at all times six practicing lawyers, six so-called *Costumieren* [experts in ancient customs and usages] who understand the interests, the origins and the complexities of the nation and the city, and four able merchants . . .[22]

Thus conceived, representation would insure that demonstrated expertise was brought to bear on the diverse functions and responsibilities of municipal government.

E. H. Putman's critique of the Draft Constitution was in many ways idiosyncratic – a personal testimony of his political vision. Yet it is evidence of his considerable political savvy that Putman absorbed so thoroughly the corporative aspirations of his coalition partners into his political program. Under a thin veneer of concern for the Prince's prerogatives, this vision of the future was rooted in a conception of the golden past when guilds and Burgerij had exercized "sovereign authority" with "felicitous results." Legalistic rhetoric based on alleged historical precedents should not, however, disguise the fact that these nominally conservative opponents of the new constitution were making radical claims for power they had never exercized in the history of the Republic. Historically, the corporative "privileges" of the Sworn Council and the Magistracy were more firmly established, but exceptional circumstances demanded and selective historical memory allowed these privileges to be compromised by the "will of the people."

For the Orangists in Deventer, then, it would seem that the future held a larger, rather than a smaller role, for their corps. Indeed, the Orangist agenda for reform would have enormously strengthened the guilds' corporative position in the political and economic life of Deventer. Old-regime corporatism was, of course, based on the concept of privilege, and an essential aspect of corporative privilege was the right to exclude. At all levels, corporations – guilds, the Town Council, even the city itself – restricted their membership to preserve their identity and to protect their interests. Beginning in 1785, however, the Patriots, including many guildsmen, had attacked the privileges of the oligarchy, while they staunchly defended the privileges of the sovereign city in opposition to the Stadhouder. But when they perceived their collective economic interests to be at stake, many guildsmen were willing to sacrifice the corporative autonomy of the city and make peace with the Stadhouder. Obviously theirs was not so much a principled defense of corporatism *per se*, as it was a defense of political and economic self-interest conceived in familiar corporatist terms.

Thus, to the extent that the Orangist movement offered an alternative agenda for political reform, it reflected more clearly the economic interests and political aspirations of guild-based artisans and shopkeepers than it did the political program of the Stadhouder and his patrician allies. It should be noted, of course, that however tenaciously these "Orangist" guildsmen defended their right to be exclusive in their corps, their political demands were not entirely exclusive of others. There was always some room for the rest of the Burgerij – for those *particulieren* who were not organized in guilds. But Putman's formula of two nominations for the guilds as opposed to one for the rest of the Burgerij probably reflects the guildsmen's sense of their importance in the larger community. In the final analysis, then, this was hardly a definition of the political community that could have broad popular appeal, especially in a social and economic world that was increasingly characterized by *particulieren*. Indeed, to judge by the signatories on the Patriot petition of January 1787, it did not even appeal to all guild members, especially those, like the silk merchants, connected with wholesale commerce.

In the end, the Orangist movement seems to have attracted primarily those independent artisans and shopkeepers whose importance in the community had been undermined by the economic and social evolution of Deventer in the recent past, who felt most threatened by the prospect of increased competition from Catholics in the local marketplace, *and* who had the option of defending their interests by means of established guilds. They had both something to lose and a ready means of collective self-defense. More broadly, the available evidence suggests that the Orangist movement had only limited appeal to the city's working population. In 1786, one Catherina Smit was prosecuted for inciting a crowd to harass the local Vrijcorps, but this appears to have been an isolated incident. Outside the few lawyer/politicians in the oligarchy who remained true to their patron, the Prince of Orange, there was no natural Orangist constituency in Deventer. Though there were some *particulieren* in the Orangist Burgercommittee and Sworn Council, one looks in vain for any evidence of Orangist support among agricultural or unskilled workers, the most marginal elements of the urban population who are often said in Holland, at least, to have been sentimentally attached to the House of Orange.[23] Even in the highly charged and partisan atmosphere of 1787, "*het grauw*" – that is, the mob or the rabble, what C. H. E. de Wit loosely calls the "*proletariaat*" – is conspicuously absent from the Orangist coalition. To the extent these people were involved at all, they appear to have been mobilized by the Patriot movement.

AN EXPLOSIVE MIXTURE

To summarize, then, the fracture lines that ran through Deventer society in 1787 divided people from one another in a complex though not unpredictable pattern. At the top, among the patrician elite, there was a solid faction of Patriots, rooted in the Sworn Council and extending after the *coup* into the Magistracy, and a smaller faction of Orangists, originally in the Magistracy but limited to the Council by the Patriots' *coup*. But surprisingly enough, when Deventer's august regents were no longer afforded the luxury of hedging their bets, the majority of those already in power were willing to favor the Patriots' drive to transform the political structure. Also, among the relatively small group of educated professionals who stood outside the ruling oligarchy of office-holders, there is evidence of significant support for Patriot movement, not only in the faculties of the Atheneum and the Latin School, but also among the Reformed clergy who defy their traditional image as defenders of the status quo. At the other extreme, the numerous unskilled workers and day laborers, those in whom historians traditionally expect to find a sentimental attachment to the Prince of Orange, undoubtedly felt much less pressure to choose sides and become involved. Still, among these least advantaged members of the working population, there was a surprising level of involvement in the Patriots' Vrijcorps while there was little evidence of support for the Prince.

Between these extremes, the divisions were a good deal more complex, but not surprising. Given that one of the most prominent issues dividing Patriots from Orangists was the right of guilds to exclude outsiders and especially Catholics, the prominence of guild members among the Orangists who defended those rights is certainly predictable, as is the preponderance of *particulieren* – individuals who stood outside the corporative structure – on the Patriot side. But the Patriot Revolution in Deventer did not simply or neatly divide guildsmen and *particulieren* along institutional lines, for there were guildsmen and *particulieren* on both sides. Beyond the rhetoric of corporatism versus individualism stood the economic reality of decidedly different orientations in the marketplace. The guildsmen who abandoned the Patriot movement and joined the Orangists were typically from the older service crafts and trades – shoemakers, tailors, grocers, blacksmiths – which were oriented to the local market and who therefore sought protection from outside competition. By contrast, the proprietors of the protoindustrial *fabrieken*, which were oriented to markets outside the city – basket-making, brewing and distilling, and leather tanning – were recruited to the Patriot cause whether or not they were members of guilds. Thus it was that in 1787 many shopkeepers were opposed to wholesale merchants, bread bakers were divided from specialty *koek* bakers. Though there is some indirect evidence of division between masters and journeymen in the construction and garment trades, on the whole the pattern was one of solidarity within occupational groups.

Beyond this pattern of division and conflict lay the sharp competition for leadership of the movement between two key groups of actors, both of which enjoyed special corporative privileges under the old regime: artisans, who were organized in guilds, and lawyers, who sat for life in the Sworn Council. Clearly these artisans and lawyers had cooperated in the birthing of the Patriot movement in Deventer, but during the constitution-writing process, the lawyers seized the initiative and openly attacked the corporative interests of the guilds. At the same time, guild leaders became defensive about their corps. When defense of the corporative privilege of the guilds was finally tied to defense of the Stadhouder's political prerogatives, the enmity between these groups was sealed, and their political differences were no longer negotiable. Undoubtedly the history of this competition hinged to some extent on the strong personalities involved: E. H. Putman, the Orangist ex-Burgemeester who continued to agitate behind the scenes; F. A. van der Marck, the law professor who headed the Patriot Burgercommittee after 1785; and Jan Vunderink, the baker who served on both the Patriot and Orangist Burgercommittees in the same year. Still, another brief comparison with Kampen and Zwolle will suggest the special conditions that made the mixture of artisans and lawyers so explosive in Deventer.

In Zwolle, as we have seen, the conflict between a very strong and determined popular movement and an equally uncompromising Orangist Magistracy came to a head in the Patriots' *coup* in January 1787. Of the 16-man Burgemeester corps, nine were newly appointed, having first been forced to accept the Patriot Burgercommittee's controversial 24 points as the basis for the city's constitutional future. Yet contrary to popular expectations, a new day of democratic political harmony had not yet dawned in Zwolle. Amid ongoing discussions of such matters as secret ballots, division of legislative, executive, and judicial powers, and the extent of the franchise, the Municipal Commission finally produced a Draft Regulation in the summer of 1787 – a proposal which once again set up an opposition between the Burgercommittee and the local government.[24] According to the Burgercommittee, the Municipal Commission, contrary to its pledge in January, had produced a Draft Regulation which ignored several of the Committee's critical demands. As a result, the Committee attacked the "aristocratic tendencies" in the revolutionary regime it had installed a few months earlier, and in August the Committee published its own Draft Regulation, even establishing its own procedures and timetable for revision and adoption of the new constitution.[25] But time had run out for the Patriots, and Prussian soldiers occupied Zwolle on the very day established by the Burgercommittee as the deadline for general comment and criticism of its proposed constitution.

Ironically, the two draft constitutions – that of the Municipal Commission and that of the Burgercommittee – differed very little with regard to their electoral provisions. Both eliminated property qualifications for the franchise, and both provided for complex indirect elections and secret ballots. The most striking difference was in the preliminary articles. The Municipal Commission began with three articles which briefly asserted the constitutional independence of the city, popular sovereignty with regard to the Regulation, and popular election of the Council, but in a fourth article it put severe restrictions on the role of the Burgercommittee. The Burgercommittee, by contrast, drafted some 17 preliminary articles which dramatically expanded the meaning of popular sovereignty and specified new mechanisms for popular influence on local government, even providing for popular referenda on controversial legislation. Arising out of the specific needs of the situation, these articles may not pass muster as an enduring expression of universal democratic principles, but they are an unequivocal symbol of the most independent, aggressive, and united popular movement in Overijssel. At the same time, the very need to draft its own constitution betrays the weakness of the Burgercommittee's ties to the political elite in Zwolle and its inability, as a result, to effect change through more or less legal or official channels.

In Kampen, the strongest and most consistent voice for constitutional change came from the Sworn Council, and in the absence of either independent guilds or a strong Burgercommittee, popular action remained weak and sporadic. Since the thrust of the proposed constitutional change was simply to remove the last vestiges of the Stadhouder's influence and the Magistracy was willing to go along with this limited revolution, there was no occasion for a political purge such as occurred in both Deventer and Zwolle at the beginning of 1787. Still, the Council continued to press its limited vision of reform, and in a very learned and reasoned report published in March 1787, the Council pushed especially for secret balloting in order to reduce the possibility of intrigue or cabal in the election of Councilors.[26] It is certainly a credit to the Council's influence that a revised Regulation, published in July and submitted for the approval of the Burgerij, included secret balloting in the new electoral process.[27]

Still, as we have seen, there was popular discontent, especially among traditional artisans, that was not being addressed by the official constitution-writing process. In March, 1787, in the context of increasing tension nation-wide, this popular frustration may have given rise to two independent petitions, signed by more than 450 burgers, which pressured the Magistracy to provide for better defense of the city and for the general armament of all able-bodied citizens between 16 and 60 years of age.[28] Apparently fearful of the political effects of this kind of general mobilization, the government dragged its feet until May when a delegation of burgers refused to leave the Stadhuis until the Magistracy and the Council had acted on its demands. Though they called the emergency meeting that was demanded, the Burgemeesters subsequently took precautions, including proclaiming the threat of using the Civic Guard, to insure that "unqualified" persons never presented demands like that again. With that, independent action by the citizenry again disappeared. But when the Draft Constitution was submitted for popular approval, the good Burgers of Kampen apparently boycotted the referendum, and the new constitution was approved by just 23 persons![29] Once again a troubled silence characterized the situation in Kampen.

In broad structural terms, the different dynamics of the municipal revolutions

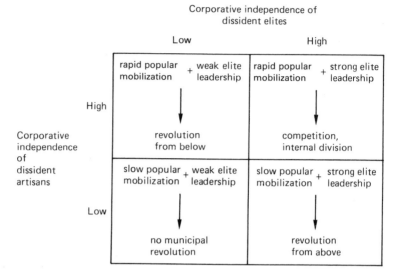

Figure 6.1   Internal dynamics of municipal revolutions.

in the three *hoofdsteden* can be summarized by the interaction of the two variables presented in figure 6.1. In the broadly similar social and political environments of these provincial capitals, the specific institutional legacy of the old regime could be decisive in determining the dynamics of the revolutionary process. In Kampen, there was a strong and independent Sworn Council which pushed for limited reform while the Burgerij, in the absence of independent guilds, was generally unable to undertake sustained political action of its own. The result can be seen as a pattern of "revolution from above" (lower right quadrant in figure 6.1). In Zwolle, independent guilds were able to mobilize a very strong and persistent popular movement, but the relatively weak Sworn Council there was unable to promote the interests of the popular movement effectively through "legal" or official channels. There the result can be described as a pattern of "revolution from below" (upper left quadrant). In Deventer, there was a strong and independent popular mobilization rooted in politicized guilds alongside a Sworn Council which was willing and able to enter into a mutually beneficial alliance with the popular movement. The result was a growing competition for leadership between artisans and lawyers that was mirrored in a more fundamental division in the revolutionary coalition in 1787 (upper right quadrant). By extension, this analysis suggests, where neither lawyers nor artisans enjoyed a reasonable degree of corporative independence under the old regime, the likelihood of an independent municipal revolution would be small (lower left quadrant).

In any case, from a comparative perspective, it is the rough parity between two very different, but equally important components of the original Patriot coalition that distinguishes Deventer from its sister cities and seems to have set the stage for a particularly tense revolutionary struggle. To be sure, the intensity of the competition between corporatist artisans and constitutionalist lawyers was not inevitable, since in the face of a common and determined enemy, these sorts of differences were easily blurred within the Patriot coalition in Zwolle. But under the conditions that obtained in Deventer it was possible both for constitutionalist lawyers to push for an especially radical redefinition of the urban polity in individualist terms, and for guild-based artisans to project an equally radical vision of the political future in which their corporative influence would be significantly extended. In the final analysis, then, the very strength of the original Patriot coalition in Deventer turned out to be its fatal weakness.

NOTES

1 *Artikelen opgedragen ter beoordeling aan de Burgers en Ingezetenen van Deventer* (Deventer, 1787).
2 This was especially evident in the *Nieuwe Nederlandsche Jaarboeken* in 1787; in their reports on Deventer they talked about *Oude Staatsgezinden* and *Nieuwe Staatsgezinden* – old and new partisans of the Estates, the traditional name for opponents of the Prince being *staatsgezind* – even though it was clear that the Estates or the Prince had little to do with the developing conflict in Deventer. Modern historians have occasionally shared the confusion.
3 GA Deventer, Republiek II, 140: "Adressen van burgers en ingezetenen aan het Gezworen Gemeente, houdende verzoek voor de aanstande keur het oude Regeeringsreglement af te schaffen en de alsdan gekozenen ook zonder approbatie des Stadhouders te beëdigen." The archive inventory mistakenly dates this petition from 1786.
4 *NNJ*, 1787, pp. 582–5.
5 See, for example, *NNJ*, 1787, pp. 146–52.
6 GA Deventer, Rechterlijk Archief, 76: "Stukken overgelegd door twee advocaten-fiscaal a. h. tot staving van hunnen eisch tegen L. Bannier c. s. wegens geweldpleging tegen eenige leden der Oranje-societeit te Deventer op 29 Juni 1787." Cf. *NNJ*, 1787, pp. 2166–71.
7 GA Deventer, Republiek I, 84: "Rangeerlijsten van de vier compagnien infantrie en het detachment artillerie der 'Vrije burgermilitie te Deventer.'" The archive inventory mistakenly dates these lists from 1783. By checking the ages reported for members of the Vrijcorps against the local birth registers, I have estimated that the lists were made up in the fall of 1786.
8 The notion that the militias were thoroughly middle-class seems to derive from the experience of the larger cities of Holland, but it seems only to be based on impressionistic sources. One ought not to take too seriously the Patriots' claim that they represented the wisest, best, and wealthiest people in Dutch society. On the

extent of popular support for the Patriot cause in Amsterdam, based on research using judicial sources, see I. van Manen and K. Vermeulen, "Het lagere volk van Amsterdam in de strijd tussen Patriotten en Oranjegezinden, 1780–1800," *Tijdschrift voor sociale geschiedenis*, 6 (1980), pp. 331–54, and 7 (1981), pp. 3–42.

9 The proposed constitution did not include property qualifications for either the franchise or for office-holding; it did, however, restrict the franchise to those who held the status of Burger – something the working poor would have had very little incentive to purchase – and excluded those who received poor relief. Office-holding was further restricted to those who professed the Reformed Calvinist faith.

10 W. H. de Beaufort (ed.), *Brieven van en aan Joan Derck van der Capellen van de Poll* (Utrecht, 1879), p. 836.

11 *Adres aan de Gezworen Gemeente van Deventer op naam van Gildens en Stemgerechtigde Burgerij door 26 personen gepresenteerd den 19 Jan. 1787* (Deventer, 1787). The names of the 26 signatories appeared on page 24. Cf. *Derde Rapport van Gecommitteerden uit Raad en Gemeente rakende zekere Adressen door pretense Gecommitteerden uit de Burgerij aan Schepenen en Raad geaddresseerd* (Deventer, 1787); in this report, one additional name is associated with the earlier petitions.

12 *NNJ*, 1787, p. 579.

13 Ibid., pp. 148–61, 579–82.

14 Information on the Orangist Burger Society is scanty; some data can be culled from the trial records in GA Deventer, Rechterlijk Archief, 76.

15 *NNJ*, 1787, p. 2171

16 It is possible that many Orangists were members of the largely ceremonial Civic Guard; this would help to explain why so many had weapons. Cf. J. Zandstra, "Deventer," in *Herstel, Hervorming of Behoud? Tien Overijsselse steden in de Patriottentijd, 1780–1787*, ed. M. A. M. Franken and R. M. Kemperink (Zwolle, 1985) p. 41.

17 See H. Kronenberg, "Schepenen, Raden en Gezworen Gemeente te Deventer van 1787–1795," *VMORG*, 38 (1921), pp. 79–87.

18 GA Deventer (uninventoried): "Boekje, houdende naamlijsten van burgemeesteren, schepenen en raden, gezworen gemeente, gecommitteerden en keurnoten, enz." I am grateful to H. J. Nalis of the Deventer Archive who brought this little booklet to my attention. It lists the occupations of all but one of the Sworn Councilors. I have also discovered that no less than 12 of the 48 Sworn Councilors were born outside the city; cf. GA Deventer, Republiek I, 95, which lists the names and places of birth of new burgers. It is possible, I suppose, that the Prince's patronage network depended on the appointment of "outsiders" in order to insure loyalty to him rather than to the city in which they served.

19 The preponderance of lawyers in the municipal administration of Deventer is striking; based on the *Naam-Register van alle Heeren Leden der Regeering in de Provincie Overijssel* (Zwolle, 1787), the comparative figures for the three cities are as follows (lawyers as a percentage of all members):

	Magistracy %	Sworn Council %
Deventer	100	52
Zwolle	50	46
Kampen	42	3

20 The average age of 17 regents associated with the Vrijcorps was 39 years of age, while the average for the restoration Magistracy was 50 years of age.

21 GA Hasselt, Oud Archief, 189: "Stukken betreffende de patriottische woelingen, 1784–88." How Putman's statement on the Draft Regulation ended up in the archives of the town of Hasselt I do not know. It is possible that Putman sent it to his Orangist allies there.

22 Ibid. (unpaginated). To call Deventer a *Rijkstad* – a free Imperial city – seems like a deliberate attempt to play on the traditional chauvinism that was rooted in its origins under the German Empire before the time of the Hapsburgs and the Republic.

23 Though this is almost a cliché in Dutch historiography, C. H. E. de Wit gives it a special polemical significance in *De Nederlandse Revolutie van de Achttiende eeuw, 1780–1787* (Oirsbeek, 1974); his subtitle *"Oligarchie en proletariaat"* tells it all.

24 *Rapport van de Commissie uit Raad en Gemeente tot de Burger Bezwaren en Concept Reglement van Regeering voor de Stad Zwol* (Zwolle, 1787).

25 *Concept-reglement van Regeering voor de Stad Zwolle. Uitgebragt door de Burger-Gecommitteerden, En aan derzelver gezamentlyke Committenten ter beoordeelinge aangeboden* (Zwolle, 1787).

26 *Advis en Consideratien van de Gezworene Gemeente der Stad Campen. Over het Rapport ter verbetering van de Regeerings bestelling deezer Stad . . .* (Kampen, 1787).

27 *Concept-reglement op de Regeerings-bestelling der stad Campen* (Kampen, 1787).

28 M. van Dam, "Kampen," in *Herstel, Hervorming of Behoud?*, pp. 87–91.

29 W. A. Fasel, "De Democratisch-Patriottische woelingen te Kampen," *VMORG*, 74 (1959), p. 99.

—

PART III

The Limits of Municipal Revolution

7
Friends and Enemies of Deventer's Revolution

As they entered the critical constitution-writing phase of their drive for control of Deventer, the Patriots acted on an extraordinary faith rooted in their city's long history and articulated in the third article of their draft constitution: "The *Burgerij* of this City has the right to govern itself and to regulate its internal affairs without the assistance or approval of anyone outside it."[1] The virtual sovereignty of their city, as they envisioned it, provided them at once with an enormous challenge and a great opportunity. The challenge – that of rethinking and rewriting the essential contract between government and the governed – linked them with the aspirations of democratic revolutionaries everywhere in the north Atlantic world. And the opportunity – to seize control of their political future so directly within their community without immediate reference to outsiders – they shared especially with the burghers or citizens of other virtually independent cities in northwestern Europe – not only in the Dutch Republic, but in western Germany and the Austrian Netherlands as well.

Constitutionally, then, the Patriots believed and acted as if they existed in a vacuum, but politically they knew better and planned accordingly. From the very beginning of the Patriot Crisis, the Patriots of Deventer consciously sought to work with friends elsewhere, not only in the other cities of Overijssel, but more broadly in the Republic and even beyond. By 1787, when developments within Deventer had put the Patriots on the defensive, they depended on a vast network of contacts, friends and allies who supported their revolution in a variety of ways. But they also accumulated a long list of enemies who were threatened by the Patriots' success and were allied in various ways with the Orangists in Deventer. The importance of these political alliances was abundantly evident in the late summer of 1787, by which time Deventer had become an armed camp.

In the last days of August, representatives of the "armed Militias, Vrijcorps, and Associations" in Overijssel held an urgent meeting in Zwolle to discuss plans for defense of the province.[2] Though there had long been concern for possible violent repression of the Patriot Revolution, an unexpected incident in late June had added a new dimension to the Patriots' problems. In her audacious attempt to return from virtual political exile in Gelderland, Princess Wilhelmina had been detained on her way to The Hague by a Patriot militia patrol at Goejanverwellesluis (near the city of Woerden in Holland) and, after a humiliating night in Patriot hands, was sent back to Gelderland.[3] Wilhelmina's brother, King Frederick William of Prussia, was demanding "satisfaction" from the Patriots in Holland, and Prussian troops were being moved ominously to the area around Lingen on the eastern border of Overijssel.[4] In this crisis atmosphere, on August 31, the association of Vrijcorps finally approved plans for a volunteer provincial army, modeled on a larger Patriot army being assembled in Holland. The association then adjourned until September 12, when the Vrijcorps leaders would bring back lists of volunteers from their local units.

When the militia leaders reconvened, however, their plans for a provincial army were upstaged by even more immediate concerns. On September 11, the provincial Estates, meeting in Kampen, had received a letter from the King of Prussia.[5] The letter created an uproar in Patriot circles. Because of the "intolerable insult" to his sister, he formally requested permission for his troops to march through Overijssel en route to the province of Holland to demand "an appropriate satisfaction" from the Estates of Holland. The Patriot journals fumed about this "vengeful" demand and compared the Prussian King unfavorably to even Philip II of Spain and the Duke of Alva. The Estates of Overijssel, dominated by the Patriots, gave an equivocal reply; they did not dare to reject the King's request outright. They spoke instead of the need to consult the Estates General and pledged that all efforts would be made meanwhile to convince the Estates of Holland to satisfy the King.

To the more militant representatives of the Vrijcorps, the situation called for more decisive and resolute action.[6] On September 13, they delivered a sharply worded declaration to the provincial Estates which demanded that they do everything possible to resist the attack on Holland by the opponents of "the People's Liberty and the supporters of the HEREDITARY TYRANT" who sought to spread riot and discord within Overijssel. Claiming to represent "a considerable number of Citizens and Residents" of Overijssel, they pushed their proposal for a citizens' army and asked that the special Defense Commission of the Estates be authorized to do whatever the situation demanded. Some members of the Estates were apparently offended by both the tone and substance of the document, and the editors of the *Nieuwe Nederlandsche Jaarboeken* declared that such an "ill-considered" declaration amply demonstrated the danger of entrusting public affairs to those who lacked the necessary knowledge, insight, and experience. But after a delegation from the associated

Vrijcorps hurried to Kampen to explain their intent to the official Defense Commission, the Estates quickly moved to implement the documents' suggestions.

As it happened, however, there was little anyone could do to save the Patriot Revolution. On the same day when the Vrijcorps were demanding action, nearly 900 Prussian hussars entered the city of Ootmarsum in northeastern Overijssel.[7] As we have already seen, the Prussians moved quickly across the province from east to west, disarming Patriot militias and re-establishing Orangist control within the province. Despite their bravado, the Patriots militias were not strong enough locally to offer open resistance, but in some places, like Zwolle, a generally uncooperative populace did manage to make life miserable for the Prussian occupation forces in the following weeks and months.[8] On the other side of the coin, several writers had predicted a general wave of counter-revolutionary terror, but only in Deventer did the arrival of Prussian troops unleash a significant burst of violence and even there relatively few houses were plundered.[9] Nevertheless, the Patriot writers turned out to be painfully right in their assessment of the political situation: that the King of Prussia's quarrel with the Estates of Holland was a threat to Patriots everywhere; that the King, along with the "enemies of Liberty," was using the incident at Goejanverwellesluis as a pretext to restore the political fortunes of the House of Orange; and that the Patriots everywhere would stand or fall together.

And fall they certainly did. In retrospect, however, we must resist the temptation to overemphasize the Patriots' failure to prevent or resist Prussian intervention. Their military failure was, to be sure, absolute, but their political weakness was only relative. For us, the Patriots' frantic, if futile, attempts to shore up the province's defenses in the last days of the revolution highlight both the strengths and weaknesses of the complex coalition that united the revolutionaries in Deventer with "Patriots" elsewhere, even beyond the Republic's frontiers. At the same time, the Prussian invasion and its aftermath underscores the essential characteristics of the Orangists' counter-revolutionary coalition and its connections with the world outside. My goal here is to sketch the changing patterns of alliance among the friends and enemies of Deventer's revolution in order to understand more fully the political processes at work in the Patriot Revolution.

DISSIDENTS, OUTSIDERS, AND *"VADERLANDSCHE REGENTEN"*

From the very beginning of the processes of politicization and mobilization in 1782, the Patriots of Deventer sought consciously and publicly to work with political allies elsewhere. The petition on behalf of John Adams, for example, recited a litany of economic troubles caused by the disastrous war with England

– from the paper-making industry across the IJssel River in the Veluwe (Gelderland) to the linen industry of Twente and Westphalia – all of which brought the chair-makers, hat-makers, woolspinners and boatmen of Deventer together with entrepreneurs and wage workers elsewhere in a common political cause.[10] In October 1782, the massive petition addressed to the Magistrates of Deventer took up the issue of the *drostendiensten*, the irksome labor services required of peasants by the powerful *drosten*, and for the first time artisans, wage workers, and peasants closed ranks against a common political enemy (see chapter 4). At the same time, in the copy of their petition sent to the Sworn Council, the Patriots referred to recent land invasions in the nearby village of Bathmen which were a protest against the enclosure of common land by Burgemeester E. H. Putman, the most outspoken Orangist in Deventer.[11] By the time they wrote their petition of February 1783, Deventer's Patriots were also championing the rights of the so-called *kliene steden* against the intrusion of the Stadhouder and the *drosten*.[12]

All of these are tokens of largely informal and ad hoc alliances based, apparently, on the oldest of political principles: the enemy of my enemy is my friend. The common enemy here was clearly the Stadhouder, William V, and his political allies within the province. Yet even these informal associations were not automatic; they required information, communication, and perhaps some persuasion to make the connection between otherwise disparate issues and interests. The linchpin in the informal network that bound the diverse Patriot coalition in Deventer with equally diverse groups elsewhere was J. D. van der Capellen who was in continuous conflict with the Prince and the *drosten*.[13] This "Burgerbaron", a classic political broker, was able to bring disparate parties together through his voluminous correspondence and tireless effort, this in spite of obviously failing health. At its peak, Van der Capellen's network of personal contacts extended from the peasants of Twente to leaders of the American Revolution like Livingston, Adams, Washington, and Franklin. Though Van der Capellen had occasionally difficult and competitive relationships with other leaders, such as the "matadors" (his name for the leading regents of Holland) and the Deventer Burgercommittee, he nevertheless remained until his death in June 1784 the movement's one universally recognized leader and thus an important friend of the Deventer Patriots.

After Van der Capellen's death, other prominent people in Overijssel were able to pick up some of the many threads of this larger coalition. For example, A. W. Van Pallandt tot Zuidheim in the Ridderschap, G. W. Van Marle in Zwolle, and Gerhard Dumbar, Jr in Deventer emerged as important leaders, not only in Overijssel but nationally. And in the person of Carel de Vos van Steenwijk, the younger brother of two Patriot supporters in the Ridderschap, the Patriots of Overijssel even enjoyed direct contact with the "Patriots" of North America; in 1783, this young nobleman accompanied the first Ambassador to the United States and, as he traveled the length and breadth of that new republic, he met many of the leaders of the American Revolution.[14] Still, no one in Overijssel could come close to matching Van der Capellen's reputation or to recreating Van der Capellen's extended network of friends. But that was not necessary, for the Patriots had self-consciously moved to formalize and solidify their contacts and alliances even before Van der Capellen's death in 1784.

The Burgercommittees were the first such attempt (see chapter 3). Like the American committees of correspondence, they were intended to communicate among Patriots in different communities, and they served that purpose well in Deventer and Zwolle for a time. There were also Burgercommittees in several of the smaller cities of the province, but they were never universal enough to meet the organizational needs of a broad provincial, much less a national, movement. For that, the Patriots came to depend on two complementary and sometimes competing networks involving dissident regents and militia officers. The first of these more formal networks began with a festive celebration of the Patriots' first victories in the spring of 1783 and blossomed into a formal association of *"Vaderlandsche Regenten"* (Patriotic Regents) which held at least six national meetings to discuss common problems and to coordinate strategies. The second began with an informal meeting called by the Patriot Vrijcorps of Utrecht in 1784 and expanded by 1787 into a network of provincial and national militia associations committed to defending Patriot victories against the threat of violent counter-revolution. Together, these networks allow us to see the broadest outlines of the revolutionary coalition – those people with whom the Patriots of Deventer were allied – and to discern important changes within the movement in the course of the 1780s.

According to H. T. Colenbrander, the idea of holding regular meetings among opposition regents was launched in April of 1783 at a well-publicized "patriotic" dinner at Amsterdam celebrating, among other things, Van der Capellen's reinstatement to the Ridderschap of Overijssel, and the first in a series of more formal meetings was held in August of 1783.[15] The association was open only to current office-holders in any of the seven United Provinces, and in all we know the names of 156 persons who attended between 1783 and 1786. Initially these *Vaderlandsche Regenten* seem to have been drawn together only by their opposition to the Prince of Orange, but as the crisis developed, the association increasingly concerned itself with the general reform of aristocratic government and eventually spoke out in favor of democratic representation of *"het Volk."*[16] In the absence of centralized political institutions, this voluntary association of opposition regents was instrumental in bringing the disparate elements of the Patriot coalition together on a national scale, and its changing composition mirrors larger shifts in the nature of opposition politics.

The first meeting in April 1783 comprised just 25 people who clearly reflected the traditional base of regent opposition to the Prince of Orange in the urban and commercial west: two-thirds of them were from the province of Holland and more than a quarter (seven) from Amsterdam alone. Overijssel was represented by the formidable but solitary figure of Van der Capellen while Gelderland was represented by three members of the Ridderschap of Nijmegen and Friesland by four officers of the rural *grietenijen*. In short, the cities of Holland were allied with essentially rural sources of early regent opposition to the Prince in the outer provinces. The second meeting in October of 1783 had an attendance of 32 and included 17 new faces, but they were essentially more of the same kinds of people: five more noblemen from Overijssel, Gelderland, and Utrecht; three new *grietenij* officials from Friesland; and nine more urban regents from Holland. All in all, those who attended the first two meetings constituted a fairly distinguished group – no less than 14 noblemen and 20 lawyers among 42 members – but with the notable exceptions of Burgemeester Hendrik Hooft of Amsterdam and Pensionary Cornelis de Gijzelaar from Dordrecht, this was not a particularly well-connected or powerful group. Among the urban regents of Holland, for instance, the members of the broad but not particularly powerful municipal councils (*vroedschappen*) outnumbered ruling magistrates (the Burgemeesters) 18 to three. Likewise the rural noblemen and *grietenij* officials from the outer provinces represented minority factions outside the circles of the Stadhouder's patronage network.

The *Vaderlandsche Regenten* apparently held no regular meetings in the course of 1784, but at the next full meeting, attended by 62 regents in August 1785, the political characteristics of the group changed in significant ways. For the first time, perhaps as a reflection of the way popular mobilization emboldened the Prince's opponents in the east, the cities of the outer provinces were represented, though there were still new recruits from the Ridderschap of Gelderland as well. Deventer was represented by Burgemeester A. J. Weerts and Secretary Gerhard Dumbar, and there were 12 other representatives from Zwolle, Kampen, and the cities of neighboring Gelderland. There were also new officers present from five cities in Holland which had not previously been represented. The result was that the association had gained a broader geographical base even though there were still no representatives from either Zeeland or Groningen. At the same time, it is striking that the new recruits included as many Burgemeesters as town councilors; these were, however, mainly from the outer provinces and the smaller towns of Holland – only one (Burgemeester O. Gevaerts from Dordrecht) came from a major city in Holland.

During the following year, so critical for the development of the conflict in Deventer as in the whole Republic, the *Vaderlandsche Regenten* held urgent meetings in August and October (with attendance of 74 and 89, respectively), the latter symbolically held at Utrecht where a new Patriot administration had been installed during the summer. At these meetings, they continued to attract new ruling magistrates from the outer provinces – there were five new faces from Deventer alone in the course of 1786 – and the smaller towns of Holland, but now the number of new town councilors, from both Holland and the outer provinces, grew at an even faster rate. Not surprisingly, the embattled cities of Gelderland continued to send large delegations while the revolutionary cities of Utrecht and Wijk-bij-Duurstede sent the association its first popularly elected regents. The result of all these changes was evident in the meeting of October 1786: there were as many new recruits as there were experienced members; town councilors outnumbered magistrates more than three to one; the small town of Elburg, which would soon bear the brunt of William V's counter-offensive, was as well represented as the city of Amsterdam; and nearly 40 percent of those present had gained political office since the beginning of the Fourth English War. Still, they remained a distinguished and well-educated group; as in the first meeting, 14 bore noble titles and at least half were lawyers.

All in all, then, the association of *Vaderlandsche Regenten* shows how the Patriot movement recruited significant and ever-greater support among the thoroughly divided regent oligarchy. Its members came together voluntarily as individuals, not as formal representatives of their corps or their cities, but beyond their undoubtedly diverse motives for opposing the political status quo in their cities and provinces, they shared a common position at the margins of republican politics. Not unlike the old-regime officials who supported the French Revolution,[17] these opposition regents – outsiders – of the old regime aspired to be the political brokers – insiders – of the new regime. And as the Patriots came to power in Overijssel, for example, we can see their political importance for the movement as a whole. Burgemeesters D. J. van Doorninck (Deventer) and G. W. van Marle (Zwolle) became provincial delegates to the Estates General in 1787; Burgemeesters A. J. Weerts (Deventer) and J. D. van der Wijk (Zwolle) were appointed members of the provincial executive com-mittee; and Burgemeester Weerts (Deventer) along with A. W. van Pallandt tot Zuidheim (Ridderschap) and Burgemeester D. Thomassen à Theussink (Zwolle) became members of the Defense Commission created by the provin-cial Estates.[18] These *Vaderlandsche Regenten* were, thus, among the principal leaders of revolutionary Overijssel – the kind of men the officers of the Patriot militias consulted with in their frantic attempt to shore up the province's defenses in September of 1787.

POPULAR LEADERSHIP FOR A NEW ERA

The second national network established by the Patriots – the union of revolutionary militias – projects a decidedly different image of the revolutionary movement and its development in the 1780s. Beginning in December 1784, the leaders of the various *schutterijen*, *exercitie genootschappen*, and *vrijcorpsen* held a series of national meetings to discuss common political concerns and to prepare for the defense of the Fatherland against its internal and external enemies. Though their most obvious concerns were military, "it was," as Simon Schama has suggested, "in the deliberations of these assemblies that the practical politics of the Patriots was shaped."[19] Thus, at the association's third meeting in June 1785, the militias adopted an *Acta van Verbintenis* by which they pledged to defend a "true Republican constitution" and committed themselves to the promotion of the "*volksregeering bij representatie*." In doing so, they clearly committed themselves to the fight against both the tyranny of the Stadhouder and the selfishness and corruption of the "Aristocracy."

Though the national association of Patriot militias has not been studied as systematically as the association of *Vaderlandsche Regenten*, several distinguishing characteristics of this broad network are nevertheless immediately clear.[20] In the first place, the militiamen who came together in this association did so, not simply as individuals, but as representatives of larger local and provincial organizations. Perhaps the most striking feature of the association of Vrijcorps is that in 1783 the geographical distribution of its delegates – reflecting more broadly the strength of the Patriots' early popular mobilization – is almost a mirror image of the distribution of *Vaderlandsche Regenten*. At the first meeting, called by the association "Pro Patria et Libertatia" in Utrecht, for example, the delegates from Holland – none was from Amsterdam – were outnumbered nearly two-to-one by those from Utrecht and Overijssel; Gelderland, which generally sent the second largest delegation to the *Vaderlandsche Regenten*, was not represented at all. Holland was outnumbered three-to-one in the numbers of militiamen these delegates represented; Overijssel alone reported some 2,000 men under arms (53 percent of the total).

As the national association of militias grew and matured, eventually including representatives from all seven provinces, it is also striking that it gradually took on the confederal structure of the polity in which it operated. At the national meeting of February 1785, Friesland was reported to have formed a provincial association of some 22 local militia units which sought collectively to join the national coalition, and in the summer of 1785, a meeting of 53 delegates from local militias within Holland adopted its own political declaration, the so-called "*Leidse Ontwerp*," which stands as perhaps the most famous democratic manifesto of the whole period.[21] In February 1785, the militias of Overijssel, too, created their own provincial association although they did not begin to hold frequent meetings until the spring of 1786. These provincial organizations undoubtedly included representatives from numerous small militia units which would not otherwise have been represented in the national association, but the end result of the growth of the provincial organizations was that large national conventions of delegates from local organizations – such as the one which adopted the Acta van Verbintenis in 1785 – gave way to much smaller meetings of delegates from the provincial associations. The latter were probably more efficient for the planning of the defense strategies when civil war seemed imminent but were not as directly or as clearly reflective of the diversity of the Patriot coalition.

For our purposes, the association of "armed Civic Guards, Vrijcorps, and Associations" in Overijssel is of special interest because it allows us to see more clearly the characteristics of the Patriots' network – the friends of Deventer's revolution – at the provincial and local level. After its initial meeting in February of 1785, the provincial association did not hold another formal meeting until May of 1786. By that time, however, the perceived need for armed defense of the Patriot cause was enough to bring them together more frequently: there were three more meetings in the summer and fall of 1786 and at least six meetings in 1787 before the Prussian invasion on September 13. In July of 1786, the representatives of some 19 local organizations reported nearly 3,000 men under arms in the province, and the notes of the many meetings in 1787 mention at least 30 different local units (see map 3). Many of these militia units may have been merged or associated with one another at various times, so that an accurate count is not possible, but however small or shadowy they may have been, it is undoubtedly true that each, like the Vrijcorps of Deventer, had its own history and distinctive character.

The province's largest militias were, of course, in the voting cities. Deventer's unit seemed quite stable with a membership in the range of 300 to 350, while the number of militiamen in both Kampen and Zwolle continued to grow. Zwolle reported a membership of 425 in December 1784 and 530 in the summer of 1786; on the eve of the Prussian invasion in 1787, the Zwolle Vrijcorps reported no less than 600 volunteers for the proposed provincial army. Kampen reported nearly 400 men under arms in 1785 and 500 in 1786, but these were divided between the traditional "Burger-regiment" – numbering nearly 300 men in 1785 and firmly under the control of the municipal administration – and a smaller independent *genootschap*. Even if the reported growth were primarily in the size of the Vrijcorps, it would still have been outnumbered in 1786 by the more conservative Civic Guard; in 1787, then, Kampen reported only 130 volunteers for the provincial army.[22]

Though the three *hoofdsteden* consistently accounted for a major share of the Patriots' armed strength in Overijssel, they were by no means alone in their defense of the Republic and their promotion of political reform. Most of the smaller chartered towns (11 of 14), ranging in size from 600 to 2,500 population, had voluntary militias which participated in the provincial association; in 1786, they accounted for two-fifths of the province's reported militia strength. Hardenberg and Ommen reported the smallest numbers – 64 and 65, respectively, in 1786 – while Oldenzaal, Ootmarsum, Enschede, Almelo, Steenwijk, and Vollenhove all had units with more than 100 members; the largest was in Almelo with 186 members in 1786 and 80 volunteers in 1787. This pattern of small-town mobilization comports well with the pattern of official involvement in the league of small cities which lobbied for more political independence *vis-à-vis* the *drosten* and the provincial Estates throughout the 1780s.[23] The absence of Hasselt in both the militia network and the league of small cities is

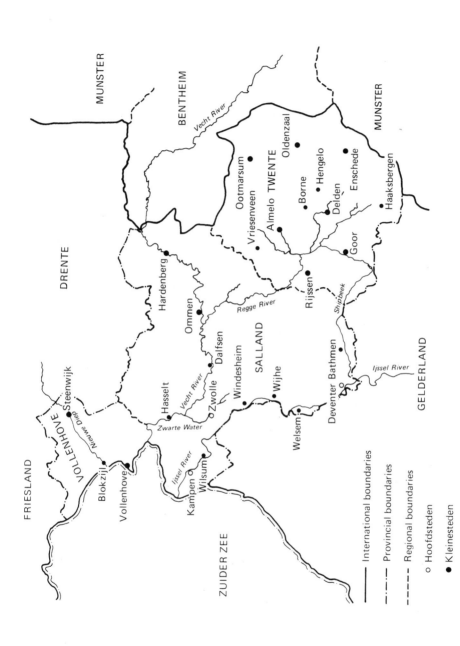

Map 3 Location of Patriot militias in Overijssel.

especially conspicuous, for in 1787 its municipal administration attempted to betray the province by bringing a garrison of Orangist troops into the city. By the same token, the presence of the Steenwijk, Ommen and Almelo militias, which had been formed against the expressed wishes of their local governments, reminds us that the small-city militias did not always enjoy official approval.[24]

The militia units established outside the walls of the three voting cities and outside the jurisdictions of the smaller towns are more difficult to enumerate and evaluate. At least nine rural Vrijcorps sent representatives to the provincial association in the course of 1787, but there are indications in the records of the association that there were as many as ten more units in the countryside. Most of these rural militias did not report their size to the provincial association, but if those which did are representative of the rest, there may have been more than 1,000 rustics under arms, which would represent approximately 30 percent of the total strength of the Patriot militias in 1787. In any case, in the preliminary figures of September 1787, 16 percent of the volunteers for the provincial army came from the rural militias. Though the rural militias were established in all parts of the province, the heaviest concentrations were in the areas of extensive protoindustrialization in Twente and along the IJssel and Vecht rivers, which were the main commercial waterways in the province.

We have very little comprehensive information about the social composition of the membership of the Patriot militias. Still, the available information suggests that through the militias the Patriots drew together a broad and extremely diverse coalition (see table 7.1).[25] In Deventer, as we have seen, the Vrijcorps comprised members of all sectors of the working population, but included surprising numbers of unskilled workers who served alongside educated professionals and disaffected members of the regent elite. In the absence of militia lists for Kampen and Zwolle, we might assume that the membership of these large urban militias was broadly representative of their working populations as well. But in light of the fact that the resentment to the established regime was especially strong among the guilds in Kampen, and that in Zwolle the original alliance between guildsmen and *particulieren* remained strong till the end, we might expect that in these cities established artisans and tradesmen would be better represented in the Patriot militias than they were in Deventer.

The militia units of the smaller cities naturally reflected the local and regional diversity of the province. In Steenwijk, a city of nearly 1,800 people in the northwest corner of Overijssel, the core (52 percent) of the Patriot militia consisted of a variety of skilled artisans – bakers, shoemakers, tailors, and carpenters were all well represented – who were supplemented by roughly equal numbers of merchants (nine), on the one hand, and unskilled workers (ten), on the other.[26] The importance of the commercial exploitation of nearby marshlands is reflected, in particular, by a sizeable contingent of broom-

Table 7.1   Membership of select Patriot militias in Overijssel

Occupation	Deventer (%)	Steenwijk (%)	Ommen (%)	Vriesenveen (%)	Windesheim/ Wijhe (%)	Bathmen (%)	Total (%)
Manufacturing	58	53	46	27	25	30	46
Commerce	18	17	18	16	9	5	16
Agriculture	3	1	6	33	44	40	15
Social services	11	16	8	6	16	5	11
Unskilled labor	10	13	22	8	5	20	13
Total	100	100	100	100	99	100	101
	n=137[a]	n=76	n=50	n=51	n=55	n=20	n=389

[a]Total does not include "Inactive;" cf. table 6.4.

makers, many of whom lived outside the city in Zuidveen. Agriculture was, by contrast, poorly represented – there was just one market gardener among the members I could identify – although some of the unskilled laborers may have found seasonal work in agriculture. In Ommen, one of the smallest towns, with a population of just 700, in the central district of Salland, the Patriot militia also found the core of its membership (45 percent) among skilled artisans – tailors were the most numerous – again supported by a number of unskilled laborers (22 percent).[27] Here, however, the special importance of commercial traffic along the Vecht River is reflected in the solid block of barge captains (*schippers*) who alone constituted 12 percent of the militia membership; also, a small group of button-makers appears to have joined along with a specialized button merchant/entrepreneur.

Further east, in the cities of Twente, we encounter variations on similar themes. In Almelo, for example, R. M. Kemperink suggests that the Patriot militia drew especially on the skilled workers of the large textile manufacturing industry, which employed 50 percent of the working population.[28] He also notes a special Patriot constituency among the small, but influential Mennonite religious minority, many of whom were the principle textile entrepreneurs.[29] Farther east, in Ootmarsum, a smaller town less dependent on the textile industry, it seems clear that the Patriots drew heavily on the large Catholic community (roughly two-thirds of the population); indeed, when the Patriots elected representatives to monitor the troubled finances of the city, they were careful to elect equal numbers of Calvinists and Catholics.[30] And in 1787, when they tried to increase the membership of the militia to 300, the Patriots of Ootmarsum began deliberately to recruit among the peasantry in the surrounding countryside for whom the city served as an important market center.

In the countryside, the Patriots' militias naturally drew more heavily on the province's agricultural population, but by no means exclusively. For example, in Bathmen, a small village to the east of Deventer, opposition to enclosure of common land by outside investors led to an exceptionally high level of Patriot mobilization: if a report of a 150-man militia in 1787 is correct, then the Patriots had recruited more than half the adult males in this predominantly agricultural district.[31] Still, among the volunteers for the Patriots' provincial army, we can identify as many non-agricultural residents from the village – several craftsmen, an innkeeper, and the assistant *schout* – as farmers (*boeren*) and cotters from the surrounding district. In addition, there were a number of unskilled laborers, most likely employed for the most part in agriculture. In Vriezenveen, a village in Twente with special and long-standing trade relations with Russia, skilled artisans (weavers were the most numerous), merchants, and barge captains outnumbered peasant farmers, who nevertheless made up one-third of the militia's membership.[32]

The villages of Windesheim and Wijhe, along the IJssel River between Deventer and Zwolle, illustrate another possible constellation of forces in the countryside: in their combined Vrijcorps, the small settlement at Windesheim contributed primarily yeoman farmers (*boeren*) while a majority of the members from the larger village of Wijhe were skilled artisans, merchants, and educated professionals; altogether, then, *boeren*, cotters, and unskilled workers made up just half of this fairly substantial militia unit.[33] The proportion of those involved primarily in agricultural work may have been similar in the village of Haaksbergen in southern Twente. The Patriot militia there, in response to the call for volunteers for the provincial army, reported that membership in its 70-man militia dropped to just 34 in the summer when large numbers of local craftsmen migrated to Amsterdam for seasonal work in the construction trades.

All in all, the image that emerges of the membership of the Patriot militias in Overijssel is one of amazing social diversity. Around a solid, though locally variable core of skilled artisans, the Patriots built a diverse coalition that extended from one end of the province to the other and included cotters and day laborers as well as innkeepers, merchants, and low-level government officials.[34] What these friends of Deventer's revolution had most clearly in common was their formal exclusion from the inner circles of aristocratic politics under the old regime. Having been politicized during the Fourth English War, this broad array of political outsiders managed not only to break the Orangist regime's monopoly of coercive force but to make politics the routine and on-going concern of large numbers of ordinary people.

The Patriots of Deventer did not, for the most part, enjoy individual or direct contact with their broadly diverse allies elsewhere in the province. Rather, their collective needs and aspirations were represented within the broader coalition by a more select group of leaders. J. D. van der Capellen may not, in fact, have been wide of the mark when he portrayed the militias as a microcosm of the ideal democratic society: free and equal individuals joined together, drew up a mutually acceptable compact to govern their affairs, elected their leadership, but in the end were expected to be orderly, disciplined, and obedient to the decisions of their officers.[35] The popular movement's fundamental commitment to this kind of *volksregeering bij representatie* was most clearly expressed in the nearly universal institution of popular election of militia officers. By extension, then, the election of officers and delegates to the provincial militia association gives us an indication of whom the rank and file in this broad popular movement might have wished to project into the leadership of the Patriots' new democratic regime.

Again our evidence is fragmentary, but the leadership of the militias was naturally as variable as the militias themselves. In Deventer, as we have already seen, the officer corps of the Vrijcorps reflected the strength of the local alliance of the popular movement – five merchants, two artisans, and a school teacher were among the elected officers – with the dissident faction of the Sworn Council – more than half the officers were lawyer/politicians. In the village of Vriezenveen, by contrast, we can identify two *boeren*, a merchant and a baker among the officers. Similarly, in the village of Bathmen a cotter served alongside a carpenter and the assistant *schout* in the officer corps, while in Wijhe/Windesheim the leadership included a *boer* and a cooper as well as two Protestant pastors and two distinct-level government officials. Among the militia officers in the small cities, we can identify two barge captains, a merchant, a surgeon, and a watch-maker in Ommen and two merchants, a medical doctor, and a carpenter in Steenwijk. Thus, it was not uncommon for simple rustics – cotters and *boeren* – as well as skilled craftsmen to appear at important provincial meetings to debate the political future of the Republic.

The bulk of the leadership of the militia association was, nevertheless, a more select group, far removed from the world of manual labor. Among the most distinguished delegates to the important association meetings in the spring and summer of 1787 were a number of Burgemeesters from the voting cities – A. G. Besier and G. J. Jacobsen from Deventer, D. J. van der Wijk from Zwolle and H. J. Corff from Kampen – three members of the Ridderschap – J. A. de Vos van Steenwijk tot Nyerwal and R. W. Sloet tot Merksvelt from the city of Vollenhove and J. E. Mulert tot de Leemkuile from the village of Dalfsen – and a former member of the Council of Justice for the Netherlands Indies, J. van der Wyk from the village of Hengelo. These men represented the popular movement's ability to project itself into the inner sanctums of aristocratic politics even before the institutions of government had been formally opened to popular influence. But as important as these men were as symbols of the Patriot movement's success in 1787, they were not necessarily the voices that prevailed in the association's deliberations.

The effective leadership of the Overijssel militia association appears to have come from men who stood somewhere between the rustics and the regent elite.[36] This was especially evident at the critical meeting on September 12, 1787, when the association adopted its less-than-delicate declaration admonishing the Estates to stand firm against the King of Prussia.[37] Presiding at the meeting was G. J. Pijman, a former army officer who was Commandant of the Zwolle Vrijcorps, and the official Secretary was Solomon van Deventer, an attorney, a regent and, like Pijman, a delegate from the Vrijcorps at Zwolle where the meeting was held. Those who bore primary responsibility for the militia's request to the Estates, however, all came from outside the *hoofdsteden*: Jan Bannier from Wijhe and William de Lille from Vollenhove drafted the document and A. Vosding van Bevervoorde from Ootmarsum and J. E. Mulert tot de Leemkuile from Dalfsen suggested important changes. Later, when members of the Estates reacted negatively to the tone and content of the document, De Lille, Vosding van Bevervoorde, and H. J. Colmschate from Almelo were dispatched to Kampen to resolve the difficulties with the provincial Defense Commission. All five would be prosecuted for their "insulting and seditious" behavior under the Orangist restoration.[38]

What these men represented was a new kind of political leadership that emerged within the militia network. To be sure, their personal political fortunes varied considerably. De Lille (former Secretary of Steenwijk) and Vosding van Bevervoorde (Burgemeester of Ootmarsum) were typical of a larger group of politically ambitious professionals from the small cities – secretaries and magistrates for the most part, lawyers all – who were pressing demands that the small cities gain more political autonomy and be admitted, alongside the *hoofdsteden*, to the provincial Estates.[39] Bannier and Van Mulert, by contrast, exemplified political careers rooted in the countryside. Jan Bannier – the son of J. J. Bannier, a Patriot Sworn Councilor in Deventer who was elevated to Burgemeester in the *coup* of 1787 – was Schout of Heino and Assistant Schout of Wijhe and thus an appointee of the provincial Estates.[40] Van Mulert was an anti-Orange member of the Ridderschap. Though they were not yet voicing specific demands for direct political representation of the countryside, it is clear that these men, like the magistrates and secretaries of the small cities, aspired to political roles under a new Patriot regime. Well educated and well connected, the new leaders emerging within the Vrijcorps Association would represent the interests of the small towns and the countryside in the larger political world once dominated by the interests of the voting cities.

ORGANIZING THE COUNTER-REVOLUTION

Together the Patriots' two formal networks – the *Vaderlandsche Regenten* and the united Vrijcorps – describe a potent, if changing, coalition of which Deventer was an integral part. At one end, the many militias – not only in Overijssel, but in all seven provinces – provided the strength of numbers, of thousands of men under arms. At the other end, dissident oligarchs provided the political experience, expertise, and contacts that helped the Patriots to establish important political connections at home and abroad. But the strengths and weaknesses of this particular constellation of forces are revealed as much by its opposition as they are by its own internal self-definition. In order to assess Deventer's particular position within this larger revolutionary world, then, we must trace the outlines of the Orangist coalition as well.

The political coalition that opposed the Patriot movement in the 1780s was, of course, rooted in the first instance in the structure of power of the old regime.[41] The Prince of Orange, as Stadhouder, did not exercise direct legislative, administrative or judicial authority within the seven sovereign provinces, but rather influenced governmental policy – especially foreign policy – through an elaborate patronage network. By controlling access to local political office and preferment to positions of regional and national power and authority, William V had become the most powerful of the Dutch Stadhouders, and indeed his political opponents, like. J. D. van der Capellen, were wont to portray his influence as tyrannical or even absolute. As the political crisis escalated, however, the indirect influence of the patron proved to be extremely vulnerable. Increasingly William was forced to depend on his other principal source of power and prestige within the Republic – his position as commander-in-chief of the Dutch army and navy. But here, too, he proved to be vulnerable as provinces, controlled by Patriot regents, put severe limits on the disposition of troops specifically in their pay or removed the Prince from the office of Captain-General altogether. Though many army officers had greater loyalties to the Prince than to the provinces which employed them, the critical fact was that even his military might was, in the long run, dependent on his ability to influence political decisions at the provincial and local level.[42]

Thus, the patronage network that the Stadhouders had cultivated and developed following the Orangist restoration of 1747 remained the bed-rock foundation on which a counter-revolutionary Orangist coalition was built in the 1780s. The character and effectiveness of this network varied considerably from province to province, reflecting institutional differences and variations in the Stadhouder's specific prerogatives, but in all cases, it involved local contact persons – often called "lieutenants" or "premiers" – who served as the principal political brokers within the important centers of republican power.[43] Within Overijssel in particular, the Prince's most important correspondents or lieutenants were Louis Rouse, Burgemeester of Zwolle since 1753, and the Count of Heiden Hompesch, member of the Ridderschap since 1755.[44] With these men the Stadhouder carried on extensive correspondence regarding local and regional politics, and on them he depended for advice and information. A man like Heiden Hompesch, who was a political power in his own right, even dared on occasion to reprimand the Prince.[45]

As the Patriot crisis developed, the fragility of the Prince's influence over the political elite in Overijssel was evident in the steady erosion of his prerogatives in the province. To be sure, Burgemeester Rouse was able to delay the progress of several Patriot reforms in Zwolle, and to the end a majority of the Ridderschap remained loyal to the Prince.[46] But the independence and built-up resentment of many urban regents combined with the pressure of the Patriots' popular mobilization was, in the end, too strong to prevent the desertion of a significant number of Magistrates and Sworn Councilors in all of the cities, both large and small. Thus, the Patriots managed to eliminate the Stadhouder's "recommendations" for municipal elections in all three voting cities by 1784, to abolish the Governmental Regulation, and with it the Prince's appointment of the highest provincial officials, in March of 1787, and finally to remove William as Captain-General of the province's troops in June of 1787 (see chapter 3).

In other provinces, the erosion of the Stadhouder/patron's support within the oligarchy may not have been as extensive as in Overijssel[47] or it may have been reversed significantly when the Patriot movement began to attack the aristocracy as well as the Stadhouder,[48] but in many cases, the oligarchs who remained loyal to the Prince, like those in Deventer, were forced to seek popular support through new kinds of political alliance. These alliances are more difficult to describe than the Patriots' because they were largely local, personal, and informal, but the broadest outlines of what can be called an Orangist counter-revolutionary coalition are still visible. Indeed, it is possible to discern a gradual transformation of Orangist politics in the course of the 1780s as well.

In the important crises of 1672 and 1747, Orangist forces had, of course, built on massive waves of popular protest, especially in Holland, Zeeland, and Friesland, to restore and enhance the Stadhouder's position in provincial and national politics.[49] But in the 1780s, for the first time, the main thrust of popular mobilization on a national scale clearly worked to the Prince's disadvantage. To be sure, there were demonstrations of popular support for the Prince, and the specter of a general uprising of "*het grauw*" (the mob or rabble) looms large at times in the Patriot literature. In the famous Orangist demonstrations in Rotterdam in 1784, at least, the infamous Kaat Mossel, who was charged with inciting and leading protests against local Patriots, appears actually to have received both encouragement and practical support from the Prince's court in The Hague,[50] but when apparently spontaneous peasant resistance to a Patriot-sponsored *levée-en-mass* invoked the name of the Prince in 1785, William was forced to repudiate his supporters publicly.[51] As it turned out, however, crowd actions in support of the Prince, like those in the cities of Holland, were sporadic and largely ineffective as a reaction to the Patriots' early success. The relatively undisciplined and ephemeral old-regime crowds turned out to be no match for the Patriots' new voluntary militias.[52]

Having been out-hustled and out-organized by the Patriots in their traditional bases of popular support, the supporters of the Prince eventually turned to a counter-mobilization in kind, depending on new voluntary associations not unlike the Patriots'.[53] On the one hand, they tried to develop a network of support outside the urban elites by encouraging and sponsoring the creation of

"*Oprechte Vaderlandsche Sociëteiten.*" These were deliberately tied to a central or mother organization in The Hague and promised to improve communications among otherwise atomized pockets of Orangist support. But as it happened, these societies enjoyed only limited success in just a few cities and in any case lacked the resources of numbers and arms that their opponents possessed. Not surprisingly, then, we can see some Orangists also turning to the creation of militias to counter the Patriots on their own terms. Lacking anything like national or even provincial networks, however, these appear to have remained locally specific reactions to Patriot challenges and success.[54]

All of these elements of popular mobilization on behalf of the Prince can be seen in Overijssel in particular. In the rural district of Den Ham, for example, there was significant peasant resistance to the Patriots' attempt to register all able-bodied men for universal military service in 1785,[55] and in Deventer, Catherina Smit was prosecuted in 1786 for inciting and leading a crowd that attacked the Patriot militia.[56] These crowd actions remained isolated incidents, however, amid a larger wave of more organized Patriot mobilization. In Deventer, as we have seen, there was also an Orangist *Burgersociëteit* which, after an Orangist Burgercommittee had been abolished and the guilds had been forbidden to meet for political discussions, served as the focus of local dissent against the revolutionary Patriot regime in the summer of 1787 (see chapter 6). It is doubtful that there were other such groups in Overijssel, and it is unclear whether this society was connected with the *Oprechte Vaderlandsche Sociëteiten* in Holland. It was, in any case, abolished after the fatal clash between its members and a unit of the Patriot militia.

In several small cities – Steenwijk, Ommen, and Almelo – the mobilization of Patriot militias was met with the counter-mobilization of Orangist militias.[57] In each case, the Orangist militia was created reactively with some form of official support – that is in alliance with an important faction within the local elite – after local Patriots had appealed successfully to the provincial government for the right to form their militias. In Steenwijk, where the local administration even paid for the Orangist militia's weapons, a strikingly large proportion of the Orangist militiamen, at least by comparison with the Patriot militiamen we saw earlier, were unskilled laborers and agricultural workers – the Patriots charged that many were dependent on municipal charity. In Ommen, half of the members of the Orangist militia were artisans and shopkeepers, but they may have recruited as well in the surrounding countryside, especially from Den Ham where there had been demonstrations on behalf of the Prince. In Almelo, the bulk of the Orangist militia may very well have been tenants of the Vrouw van Almelo – the locally powerful seigneurial lord – who was locked in a protracted struggle with the Patriots for control of the city's administration. Though sporadic violence punctuated the relations between these opposing militias, the Patriots were eventually able, in each case, to use the provincial government to disband the Orangist militias – that is, like the Patriots of

Deventer, they were able to deny their enemies the resources and opportunities they claimed for themselves.

How the workers, artisans, and peasants of Steenwijk, Ommen, and Almelo were brought together with the artisans and shopkeepers of Deventer in a larger Orangist coalition opposed to the Patriots' regime is not altogether clear. In Deventer, at least, the guildsmen's alliance with ex-Burgemeester Putman connected them ultimately with the Count of Heiden Hompesch and the Prince. The same pattern of alliance through the old-boy networks of the patronage system are most likely to have obtained in the cases of Steenwijk, Ommen, and Almelo as well. In any case, there is no evidence that these essentially isolated pockets of popular Orangist mobilization were connected by independent networks through Burgercommittees, militia officers or even informal direct contacts. Still, to judge by the Orangists of Deventer, at least, the popular elements of the Orangist alliance could demand and get significant political concessions from their coalition partners within the political elite, concessions especially concerning real and urgently felt problems at home. While these local issues may have had little to do with the politics of the Stadhouder, as such, what most obviously drew these artisans, peasants and day laborers together and made them in a profound sense "Orangists" was the common perception that a Patriot victory over the Stadhouder/Prince would be detrimental to their interests.

The relatively weak Orangist coalition in Overijssel cannot be said to be typical of the other provinces, but in fact, the Orangists were unsuccessful, except in the provinces of Zeeland and Gelderland, in pulling together broad coalitions that were capable of rivaling the new voluntary associations on which the Patriots had capitalized in their rise to power. Instead, the ultimate victory of the Orangists in the fall of 1787 was especially attributable to a third network that extended well beyond local and provincial politics, a network comprised, in Alfred Cobban's phrase, of "ambassadors and secret agents." In this largely secretive and conspiratorial realm of international diplomacy and intrigue, the main character was James Harris, England's envoy to the Dutch Republic from December 1784 on.[58]

One of the immediate consequences of England's declaration of war on the Dutch Republic in 1780 was to undo an enduring diplomatic legacy of Louis XIV's Dutch wars, that is, the generally warm relations – some called it a natural alliance – between England and the Dutch Republic despite the Dutch policy of strict neutrality in European affairs. With the departure of Joseph Yorke, the Dutch were finally open, from a diplomatic point of view, to French "influence." Though there was much traditional Calvinist resentment of Catholic France, French mediation of a potentially explosive dispute with Austrian Emperor Joseph II helped finally to clear the way for a formal defensive alliance, signed on November 10, 1785, between the Kingdom of France and the United Provinces. The event was celebrated as a major victory by the Patriots who had steadily whittled away the Prince's influence at The Hague. The despondent Prince of Orange, who had already left the seat of government for the more secure surroundings of Gelderland, even talked of abdicating.

In the midst of the Austrian dispute and the discussions of the Franco-Dutch alliance, William Pitt's government sent James Harris to The Hague to revive the so-called "English Party." With English influence at a low ebb, Harris had a hard time of it at first, but demonstrating enormous patience and cunning, he slowly developed a network of official Dutch friends and allies who were committed to the revival of both the English connection and the Stadhouder's fortunes even though they seemed to be losing out to the Patriots at every turn. At the same time, under strict orders to avoid war at all cost, Harris sought to enlist Prussian support for the effort to restore the Prince, but Prussian help was not forthcoming as long as Frederick the Great favored good relations with France and urged the Stadhouder to make a compromise with the Patriots. Even with the accession of Frederick William II, brother of Princes Wilhelmina, in 1786, Anglo-Prussian cooperation remained only a remote possibility. Consequently, Harris devoted himself especially to the promotion of an indigenous counter-revolutionary movement and to what he called "a plan of vigorous and systematic action."

Convinced that French agents were spending huge sums of money in support of the Patriots, Harris pleaded with the British government for equally large sums of secret service funds to support the Orangist cause. In one instance, he reported to the British foreign secretary that he needed £2,000 to £2,500 "to bring to reason three or four refractory pensionaries of the more insignificant towns" of Zeeland.[59] In another he asked for and got £2,500 "to feed the arrière-ban of our new party;" this was not, he explained, "to purchase friends of the *first class*, but to gain over inferior dispensers, *Dutch borough-mongers* and those who have influence in the streets and highways."[60] But undoubtedly the most important expenditure was a £70,000 "loan" to the Estates of Gelderland approved in May of 1787. This money was urgently needed to pay regular troops stationed in Gelderland which the Estates of Holland had ordered to withdraw; in addition, the money was to be used for the purpose of "seducing" regular officers, who were part of the Patriots' cordon around Holland, into defecting to the Prince.[61] Indeed, with this enormous infusion of cash, Harris's "English Party" was able to buy valuable time, to prevent the deterioration of their military situation, until the Prussians joined the fight.

No one could have planned or predicted the events that finally led to Prussian intervention in September of 1787, but the diligence and effectiveness with which Harris set about building international and domestic support for the Prince of Orange stands in sharp contrast to his French antagonists. Though French agents continued to promise military support to the Patriots and there were numerous rumours of lavish French expenditures, some of them specifically to support Patriot militias in Overijssel, there was no French "plan of vigorous and systematic measures" to counteract Harris's agitation. An alleged plan to assemble up to 12,000 French troops at Givet for eventual use in defense of the Patriots' regime turned out to be a bluff, and in the end, the French government was neither willing nor able to risk another war on behalf of democratic revolution.

Once the force of international arms had arbitrated the military stand-off between Patriot militias and Orangist troops, the way was again cleared for old-regime crowds to serve as an effective weapon of counter-revolution. And in some places, the Patriots paid dearly for their earlier suppression of Orangist dissent. In Deventer, as we have seen, the houses of several leading Patriots were plundered, but in Gelderland and Zeeland where the Orangists were strongest the sparks of crowd violence were the most spectacular.[62] In the small city of Zierikzee alone (Zierikzee was distinguished among the cities of Zeeland as having had both a large Patriot militia and a number of Patriot regents who were involved in the association of *Vaderlandsche Regenten*), more than 100 houses were plundered in the course of 1787 and 1788.[63] Though Orangist regents could generally turn this old-style crowd action to their long-run political advantage, they were often powerless to control the situation in the short run – either to mobilize crowds where they might have seemed useful or to demobilize them when they were no longer deemed necessary or desirable.[64] As it turned out, then, the Orangist restoration came finally to rest, in part at least, on a recreation of the same uneasy coalition between an elite tied through patronage to the Stadhouder and a variety of old-regime protesters. This was the coalition that had prevailed in 1672 and 1747, but had nearly been driven from the field by the Patriots in 1787.

THE FUTURE IN THE BALANCE

Drawing up a summary balance of the friends and enemies of Deventer's revolution is no easy task, for the conflict remained fluid and unpredictable until the end. In the course of 1787, the chances of a military confrontation between the two coalitions were undoubtedly growing, or at least everyone seemed to be expecting civil war, but it was by no means certain what form this war might take. The eventual outcome of a military confrontation clearly depended on the arena in which it took place. At the local level, especially within the political space afforded by chartered municipalities, the Patriots' militias were almost invariably dominant, suppressing, as they did in Deventer and more generally in Overijssel, old-regime crowds and rival militias alike. Even the mighty Burgemeesters of Amsterdam could not, in the end, withstand the pressure of an armed and organized popular movement.[65] In Holland more generally, the Patriots' inter-urban networks and solidarity also proved to be of critical importance in the rapid succession of urban revolutions that brought this most important of provinces into the revolutionary fold in the summer of 1787.[66] Dutch republican politics cannot, however, be seen as a simple aggregation of municipalities in which revolutionaries could easily triumph by breaking the regime's monopoly of coercive force by means of independent militias.

On a broader scale, the diverse structures of the various provincial Estates, the formal sovereigns in the Dutch confederation, offered the Patriots remarkably variable chances for political and military success.[67] Where independent cities were politically dominant, as in Holland and Overijssel, the simple aggregation of urban revolutions did gave the Patriots their best chance for control of provincial budgets and, by extension, provincial troops. In Gelderland, by contrast, where the allies of the Prince were relatively invulnerable to popular pressure, the Orangists were able to use provincial troops to repress Patriot mobilization at the local level.[68] In Utrecht and Friesland, where internal divisions produced stalemates that resulted in the creation of rival versions of the provincial Estates, both of which laid claim to provincial sovereignty, it was clear that the final outcome of the conflict would depend on the relative strength of national and international coalitions.

On the national scale, the friends of Deventer's revolution did not, on the face of it, serve it well. As the conflict escalated in 1787, the leaders of the national militia association concentrated their military preparations on the formation of a cordon, combining regular troops and militia volunteers under the command of the Rhinegrave van Salm, around the province of Holland. Though the cordon was eventually expanded to include the city of Utrecht, it left the outer provinces to fend for themselves. Even requests for supplies were regularly denied by the national leadership.[69] Still, the outlook for the Patriots was not bad in the long run. Deprived of the fiscal support of Holland, Overijssel, and Groningen, and subject to firm challenges in Utrecht and Friesland, William's grip on the military situation was gradually slipping. Since money to pay troops would eventually run out, time seemed to be on the Patriots' side.[70] And since the Patriots were firmly in control of Overijssel, the Patriot revolution in Deventer was, for the moment at least, secure.

If only the Prussians had not invaded . . . R. R. Palmer notes ruefully in *The Age of the Democratic Revolution* that the Dutch Patriots, like their counterparts in Geneva and the Austrian Netherlands, had the misfortune of living in a small polity which made them easy prey to outside intervention.[71] By extension, the revolutionaries in Deventer had the multiple misfortune of living in a small provincial capital in one of the Republic's smallest provinces. On the face of it, all their attempts to reshape their political world would seem to have been undone by the Prussian invasion against which they had no reasonable defense. It remains to be seen, however, what actually were the long-term consequences of their revolutionary conflict.

NOTES

1 *Tweede Rapport . . . over de Vebetering van de Stedelijke Regeeringswyze vitgebragt in Augustus des jaars 1786* (Deventer, 1786), p. 1.
2 GA Zwolle, Oud Archief, A-75; *NNJ*, 1787, pp. 5051–4.
3 This incident is famous – one that all Dutch school children seem to remember. For the latest, hour-by-hour retelling, see W. A. Knoops and F. Ch. Meijer, *Goejanverwellesluis, De aanhouding van de princes van Oranje op 28 juni 1787 door het vrijkorps van Gouda* (Amsterdam, 1987).
4 Alfred Cobban, *Ambassadors and Secret Agents. The Diplomacy of the First Earl of Malmesbury at The Hague* (London, 1954).
5 *NNJ*, 1787, pp. 5036–43.
6 Ibid., pp. 5043–51; RAO, Staten Archief, 4819–20: "Stukken van het voor het drostengericht van Salland gevoerde process tussen dr. W. Klopman als fiscaal van de Provincie – en – J. E. Mulert tot Leemcuile wegens crimen lesae majestatis, 1788–1793."
7 *NNJ*, 1787, pp. 5056–7.
8 P. J. Lettinga, "Zwolle," in *Herstel, Hervorming of Behoud? Tien Overijsselse steden in de Patriottentijd, 1780–1787*, ed. M. A. M. Franken and R. M. Kemperink (Zwolle, 1985), pp. 63–6.
9 *NNJ*, 1787, pp. 5036–8; J. I. van Doorninck, "De omwenteling van 1787 te Deventer," *Kleine Bijdragen tot de Geschiedenis van Overijssel*, 11 (n.d.).
10 *Egte stukken betreffende het voorgevallene te Deventer* (Deventer, 1783), pp. 1–6.
11 Cf. Wayne te Brake, "Revolution and the rural community in the Eastern Netherlands," in *Class Conflict and Collective Action*, ed. Louise A. and Charles Tilly (Beverly Hills, Ca/London, 1981), pp. 53–71.
12 *Egte stukken*, pp. 35–40.
13 For a broader assessment of Van der Capellen's importance for the Patriot Revolution in Overijssel, see W. P. te Brake, "Van der Capellen en de Patriottisch Revolutie in Overijssel," in *De wekker van de Nederlandse natie*, ed. E. A. van Dijk et al. (Zwolle, 1984).
14 A. N. de Vos van Steenwijk, "Een Drents patriot," *Nieuwe drentse volksalmanak*, 29 (1975), pp. 25–44. The journal that young Carel de Vos kept on this trip to the new world has been preserved in the family's private archive; I am presently engaged in preparing a translation and edition of the work.
15 H. T. Colenbrander, "Aantekeningen betreffende de Vergadering van Vaderlandsche Regenten te Amsterdam, 1783–1787," *Bijdragen en Mededelingen van het Historisch Genootschap*, 20 (1899), pp. 77–192. The following analysis is based on the valuable biographical information about the members of the Association embedded in the notes of this article; in just a few instances, I have supplemented or corrected Colenbrander with information from my own research.
16 This interpretation of *Vaderlandsche Regenten* the differs substantially from C. H. E. de Wit, *De Nederlandse Revolutie van de Achttiende Eeuw* (Oirsbeek, 1784). De Wit seems to deny the possibility of a revolutionary regent; he applies quite different ideological labels to officials than he does to their allies.
17 On the importance of "outsiders" in the French Revolution, see Lynn Hunt, *Politics, Culture, and Class in the French Revolution* (Berkeley, Ca, 1985).

18 *Naam-Register van alle Heeren Leden der Regeering in de Provincie Overijssel*... (Zwolle, 1787).

19 Simon Schama, *Patriots and Liberators. Revolution in the Netherlands, 1780–1813* (New York, 1977), p. 94.

20 The following analysis of the Patriot militias is based, unless otherwise noted, on the very diverse documents collected in GA Zwolle, Oud Archief, A –73–75.

21 *NNJ*, 1785, pp. 1427–34.

22 In this light, the absence of active government-controlled Civic Guards is a testimony to the independence of the popular movements in Deventer and Zwolle. But by comparison with the large number of volunteers in 1787 from Zwolle, Deventer's relatively small number of 150 volunteers for the provincial army may reflect the internal crisis of the Patriot movement in Deventer.

23 M. de Jong, Hzn, *Joan Derk van der Capellen, Staatkundig levensbeeld uit de wordings tijd van de moderne democratie* (Groningen/Den Haag, 1921); many of the records of the association of small towns can be found in GA Ommen, 144: "Stukken betr. de vergadering van de committeerden der kleine steden van Overijssel, gehouden teneinde middelen te beramen om van Ridderschap en Steden de uitoefening hunner oude rechten an privilegiën te herkrijgen, 1785–1787." Cf. A. A. W. van Wulfften Palthe, "Onderhandelingen omtrent het regeeringsreglement van Overijssel in 1786," *VMORG*, 18 (1891), pp. 57–68.

24 RAO, Staten Archief, 4818; GA Steenwijk, 212–14.

25 The methods used to identify Patriot and Orangist militiamen in the smaller towns and the countryside were the same as those used for Deventer; see appendix II.

26 For the difficult history of the Patriot militia in Steenwijk, see GA Steenwijk, 212–14, and W. Logtmeijer, "Steenwijk," in *Herstel, Hervorming of Behoud*, pp. 182–96.

27 RAO, Staten Archief, 4818, parts 2 and 3: "Stukken betreffende het onderzoek door dr. Fabius, fiscaal van Salland, naar de werking der exercitie-genootschappen en de Orangistische beweging te Ommen, 1785–1787;" cf. G. Steen and W. Veldsink, *Geschiedenis van Ommen* (Ommen, 1948), pp. 36–7.

28 R. M. Kemperink, "Almelo," in *Herstel, Hervorming of Behoud?*, pp. 113–30.

29 On the problem of Mennonites, who were traditionally non-violent, joining the Patriot militia, see W. H. Kuiper, "De Almelose doopsgezinden en het beginsel der weerloosheid in de patriottentijd," *VMORG*, 88 (1973), pp. 60–6.

30 P. H. L. Spee, "Ootmarsum," in *Herstel, Hervorming of Behoud?*, pp. 131–52; GA Ootmarsum, 81; Oudhiedkamer Twente, SOm, A32–38. See also, C. J. Snuif, "Het gewapend Burger-Vrijcorps van Ootmarsum," *VMORG*, 45 (1928), pp. 260–1.

31 Te Brake, "Revolution and the Rural Community."

32 GA Zwolle, Oud Archief, A–75.

33 GA Zwolle, Oud Archief, A–74; see also *Crimineel Proces, tegen W. L. van Warmelo, Predikant te Wijhe in Overijssel*... (Amsterdam, 1792).

34 For a comparative perspective on this provincial coalition, see W. Ph. te Brake, "*Burgers* and *boeren* in the Dutch patriot revolution," in *1787: De Nederlandse revolutie?*, ed. Th. S. M. van der Zee et al. (Amsterdam, 1988), pp. 84–99.

35 *Post van den Neder-Rhyn*, no. 221, pp. 591ff.

36 On the problem of leadership and friction within the Patriot coalition in Overijssel more generally, see Te Brake, "*Burgers* and *boeren*," pp. 90–2.

37 This account is culled from RAO, Staten Achief, 4819–20.

38 See, for example, GA Ootmarsum, 61, regarding the trial of Voslding van Bever-voorde.

39 See the rich portrait of Jacob van Riemsdijk, Secretary of Hardenberg, in H. G. Hoffman, "Hardenberg," in *Herstel, Hervorming of Behoud?*, pp. 160–2.

40 A number of *schouten* appear to have been related to prominent families in the *hoofdsteden*; see, for example, the official *Naam-Register* for 1787.

41 This is the leitmotif of C. H. E. de Wit's analysis of the counter-revolutionary coalition in *De Nederlandse Revolutie*.

42 This is confirmed by the eventual strategy of James Harris, the English envoy in the Republic, to raise large sums of money to pay troops loyal to the Prince; see Cobban, *Ambassadors*, and the discussion of Harris below.

43 Cf. De Wit, *De Nederlandse Revolutie*, chapter 1.

44 Heiden Hompesch was for years Drost of Twente, but in 1786 he became Drost of Salland, in which capacity he served as presiding officer of the provincial Estates.

45 Cf. De Jong, *Capellen*.

46 The specific breakdown of the vote within the Ridderschap regarding the decision to abolish the provincial Governmental Regulation in 1787, for example, was eight votes in favor and 25 opposed (*NNJ*, 1787, pp. 577–8). This kind of division within the Ridderschap deserves a fuller analysis in relation to noble wealth and princely patronage than would be warranted in a book on municipal revolution; such a study might finally break down the enduring image of an essentially monolithic Ridders-chap in the eastern provinces.

47 This may have been the case in Zeeland; cf. Cobban, *Ambassadors*.

48 This was most notably the case in Friesland; cf. W. W. van der Meulen, *Coert Lambertus van Beijma. Een bijdrage tot de kennis van Frieslands geschiedenis tijdens den Patriottentijd* (Leeuwarden, 1894). Despite the prominent example of Burgemeester Rendorp in Amsterdam, this was probably not the norm in Holland.

49 See D. J. Roorda, *Partij en Factie. De oproeren van 1672 in de steden van Holland en Zeeland, een krachtmeting tussen partijen en facties* (Groningen, 1978), P. Geyl, *Revolu-tiedagen te Amsterdam* ('s-Gravenahge, 1936), and J. A. F. de Jongste, *Onrust aan het Spaarne. Haarlem in de jaren 1747–1751* (Amsterdam, 1984).

50 On this very colorful figure, see G. van Rijn, "Kaat Mossel," *Rotterdams Jaarboekje*, 1890, pp. 159–231. On the role of women more generally in the Dutch Revolutions, see Wayne Ph. te Brake, Rudolf M. Dekker, and Lotte C. van de Pol, "Women and political culture in the Dutch Revolutions, 1780–1800," in *Women and Politics in the Age of Democratic Revolution*, ed. Darlene Levy and Harriet Applewhite Ann Arbor, MI, 1989.

51 *NNJ*, 1985, pp. 93–7.

52 I have developed this argument more fully in an unpublished paper, "Rhetoric and reality in the Patriot Revolution," presented at the University of Amsterdam and the Erasmus University Rotterdam, May/June 1985.

53 See H. T. Colenbrander, *De Patriottentijd*, vol. 3 ('s-Gravenhage, 1899), pp. 192–204, and R. A. M. de Bogt, "De Oranjesocieteit in Gouda" (unpublished scriptie, University of Leiden, 1985). I am very grateful to Mr De Bogt and to Dr Jan de Jongste for allowing me access to this unpublished research.

54 Cf. De Wit, *De Nederlandse Revolutie*.

55 RAO, Staten Archief, 4818, part 1.

56 GA Deventer, Rechterlijk Archief, 60, vol. 1, pp. 657–9.

57 See the sources for these communities cited above.

58 Colenbrander, *Patriottentijd*, Cobban, *Ambassadors*, and De Wit, *De Nederlandse Revolutie*, all tell different variations on this story. Colenbrander's extensive use of foreign sources, especially diplomatic correspondence, led him to portray both sides in the struggle between Patriots and Orangists as the tools or "puppets" of foreign agents. Cobban, of course, focuses on Harris's role in the building of the Orangist coalition, but he demonstrates a healthy respect for the integrity of the Patriots, suggesting that theirs "may even be accounted the first revolution on the pure democratic model. It exhibited for the first time the strength of a revolutionary democracy possessed of organization, leadership and an ideology" (p. 212). De Wit, in seeking to combat Colenbrander and what he calls the tradition of Orangist historiography, is at pains to find the indigenous roots of counter-revolution as well, but his exaggerated notion of the oligarchy's control of what he calls the "*proletariaat*" undermines the endeavor.

59 Cobban, *Ambassadors*, p. 111.

60 Ibid., p. 112.

61 Ibid., pp. 128–38.

62 De Wit, *De Nederlandse Revolutie*, pp. 95–239.

63 P. T. van Rooden, "De plunderingen op Schouwen en te Zierikzee, 1786–1788," *Archief van het Koninklijk Zeeuwsch Genootschap der Wetenschappen*, 1983, pp. 173–99.

64 This was, for example, clearly the case of Gouda; see De Bogt, "Oranjesocieteit in Gouda."

65 P. Geyl, *Geschiedenis der Nederlandse stam* (Amsterdam/Antwerpen, 1962), pp. 1306–52.

66 These were precipitated by the so-called *vliegende legertje*, a small militia detachment from Delft; this process deserves far closer scrutiny than it has received.

67 See W. Ph. te Brake, "Provincial histories and national revolution: The Dutch Republic in the 1780s" (paper presented to the Symposium "Decline, Enlightenment, and Revolution: The Dutch Republic in the Eighteenth Century," Washington, DC, March 1987) which presents a comparison of Holland, Friesland, and Overijssel.

68 H. A. Westrate, *Gelderland in de Patriottentijd* (Arnhem, 1903), and A. H. Wertheim-Gijse Weenink, *Democratische bewegingen in Gelderland, 1672–1795* (Amsterdam, 1973).

69 In exasperation, the Overijssel Defense Commission finally ordered Patriot volunteers to seize the important supply depot at Ommerschans; for the complaints of the Patriots in Friesland, see Van der Meulen, *Van Beijma*.

70 This was one of James Harris's greatest fears in the summer of 1787; even after the "Gelderland subsidy" had been approved, he was worried that the Orangist forces might not hold out through the winter. Thus, he was concerned that the Prussians act as quickly as possible. See Cobban, *Ambassadors*.

71 R. R. Palmer, *The Age of the Democratic Revolution*, vol. 1 (Princeton, NJ, 1959), p. 369.

8

Revolutionary and Counter-revolutionary Change

After years of increasingly bitter controversy and conflict, the immediate outcome of the Dutch Patriot Revolution was, quite simply, Orangist counter-revolution. What this meant, in the broadest and most obvious sense, was the restoration of Prince William V of Orange as Stadhouder of all seven provinces and as undisputed Captain-General and Admiral-General of the Union. This restoration was essentially what the conservative powers who intervened wished to achieve in the fall of 1787.[1] But the ambassadors and secret agents who could (and did) claim the victory as their own were not the only actors involved, nor was theirs the only political agenda on the table in the years to come. Indeed, to equate counter-revolution simply with restoration is to miss the long-range significance of the Patriot Revolution for Dutch politics and society. In communities like Deventer, at the base of Dutch republican politics, the essential processes of politicization and mobilization which the Patriot Revolution had set in motion could not so easily be undone, and while the Patriots had been denied the immediate realization of their hopes, the Orangist counter-revolution nevertheless confirmed the destruction of some essential elements of the old regime.

The most fundamental of these changes is suggested by a pamphlet published by Everhard Herman Putman a few months after his return to power as a ruling Magistrate of Deventer. Entitled *Voorlopig Berigt* (Provisional Report), this curious piece of political discourse was a rudimentary defense of Putman's politics against what he called "the prejudices which from time to time have been incited against him in the most excessive, bitter and vile manner by both secret and public Enemies and by biased Libelists . . ."[2] On the face of it, Putman's pamphlet does give eloquent testimony to the Orangist restoration, for the underlying purpose of this "Report" was to promote Putman for appointment to the "Generality Commission" or some other "Honorary or Profitable" position. This obvious self-promotion he accomplished by using "authentic documents" to demonstrate that the Putman family had for generations been faithful supporters of the House of Orange. Clearly the Prince of Orange, as patron-in-chief, was once again in control of political preferment in the Republic, and especially under the restored Governmental Regulation in Overijssel, William V held the key to Putman's political future.

Deventer's politics, however, had not simply returned to the patterns of old. In the first place, it is striking that Putman's self-promotion was a deliberate attempt to influence and use public opinion. Whereas before the Patriot Revolution one might have sought to advance through the Prince's patronage system by appealing to the Stadhouder's local "lieutenants,"[3] Putman was bypassing the likes of Burgemeester Louis Rouse of Zwolle and the Count of Heiden Hompesch, Drost of Salland, and allying himself instead with the "enlightened part of the People" (*verligte deel des Volks*) which, he said, knew how to distinguish truth from falsehood.[4] Thus, Putman's "authentic documents" include attestations to the purity of his politics made by the Orangist Burgercommittee of Deventer and leaders of the notoriously Orangist Kattenburg district of Amsterdam.[5] But even more pointedly, Putman ascribes his own political "restoration," not to William V, but to "the free and unbridled unanimous voice of the People expressed by the enfranchised and legally summoned Burgerij and Guildsmen" of his own city in the course of the "blessed revolution" of September 1787.[6] In this local account of the counter-revolution, then, the leader of the Orangist coalition in Deventer limits the Prince's political role to the simple approbation of an essentially popular election.

The "People" of Deventer had entered politics to stay. Not simply the rhetorical invention of self-serving Patriot pamphleteers or constitution-writers, "*het Volk*" had in the course of the 1780s become an armed and organized reality which proved to be easily capable, when united, of breaking into the urban political space. As unity gave way to division and conflict at all levels of society, however, the force and significance of the new popular politics was by no means extinguished. Thus, as we have seen, the counter-revolution in Deventer represented the victory of one segment of a newly politicized and activated "People" over another – not simply a restoration of aristocratic politics as usual. Indeed, the Orangist counter-revolution in Deventer unwittingly consolidated two momentous changes in the politics of this provincial city, the combination of which suggests that the character of urban politics was forever transformed: the private, aristocratic politics of the past had been shattered and the foundation had been laid for the public, participatory politics of the future.

THE CHANGING FACE OF MUNICIPAL POLITICS

The first of these changes – the destruction of aristocratic politics – was most clearly visible in the fragmentation of the urban oligarchy which was its foundation. To be sure, urban politics had always been plagued by factionalism among the office-holding elite, and in the second half of the eighteenth century the Prince's patronage had more clearly aggravated than cured the problem. During the early stages of the Patriot crisis, the oligarchy divided along more or less predictable lines: a majority of the Sworn Council, which sought to recover electoral and legislative authority eroded by the Prince's patronage system, kept pressure on a reluctant Magistracy, which was clearly dependent on the Prince's favor (see chapter 4). But as the conflict developed, this early factionalism gave way to more profound disagreements about the future of urban politics. The self-styled Patriots began to emphasize the power of constitutional reform as a means not simply to rid the city of the Prince's patronage – which they had broken in any case – but as a means of reforming society, of restoring the health of Deventer's economy and redressing its social ills. Establishing municipal government on the firm footing of popular sovereignty – that is, making local officials dependent on the will of *"het Volk"* rather than the Prince – promised to usher in a new era of republican peace and prosperity (see chapter 5).

Under pressure from a broadly based popular movement, the project of constitutional reform gained adherents not only within the Sworn Council, but within the Magistracy as well. Thus, when the Patriots finally seized power in 1787 only five "Orangists" had to be removed from the Magistracy for their implacable opposition to the new constitution for Deventer's government – a constitution written, after all, by the oligarchy's own commission. Arguing against the Patriots' constitution, Everhard Putman insisted on the urgent priority of economic reform and suggested that political reform, clearly of secondary importance, recognize the legitimacy of special interests and insure that special expertise of a variety of sorts be applied to the community's political and economic problems. In opposing the particular democratic reforms of the Patriots, Putman was not only giving new expression to the pious hopes and fears of his popular supporters, but also describing a new ideological cleavage within the office-holding elite between fundamentally different conceptions of the political future (see chapter 6). It was this ideological cleavage, clearly a by-product of the developing conflict and having remarkably little to do with the Prince of Orange, which made a simple return to the oligarchical factionalism of the past unlikely if not impossible.

The Orangist counter-revolution confirmed and consolidated the deep divisions within the oligarchy when it executed a wholesale change in the personnel of municipal government. Everyone who had cooperated with or supported the Patriots' regime was removed from office – not just Burgemeesters and Councilors but also Protestant pastors and a wide range of political appointees, the clients of the Patriot regime.[7] The result of this house-cleaning was the creation of a new regime which of necessity included new people even in the highest offices of the city (see chapter 6). To be sure, the core of the new Magistracy consisted of the dyed-in-the-wool Orangist regents who had stead-fastly refused to accept the Patriots' reforms, but even so five Burgemeesters under the Orangist regime had never held political office previously. The Orangist Sworn Council, in turn, consisted almost entirely of new men who represented a radical departure from the social profile of the traditional elite: none of the 48 members was a lawyer and only a few were *rentiers*, while the vast majority pursued active occupations in locally oriented commerce and manu-facturing. In short, the counter-revolutionary Council represents the kind of wholesale transfer of power to people – to political outsiders – that we usually expect of revolutionary regimes.

It is also clear that time could not quickly heal the wounds of the patrician elite. The political rehabilitation of even moderate or reluctant Patriots seems to have been out of the question in the short time that the Orangist restoration endured. On the contrary, despite the declaration of a general amnesty, former Councilor Lambert Bannier was even prosecuted *in absentia* for his role in the deaths of five Orangists in 1787. It is not surprising, then, that leading regents excluded from power in 1787 should appear among the leaders of the Batavian Revolution. In January 1795, under the pressure of French invasion from the south, the tables were once again turned in Deventer, and the Orangists were driven from the political stage.[8] In the city's first democratic election for municipal officers on March 31, 1795, no less than seven of the ten top vote-getters had been Burgemeesters in the Patriot regime of 1787, and among the next five, three had been Sworn Councilors in 1787.[9] To judge by these results, at least, the divisions within the patrician elite that had emerged only gradually in the 1780s became the immediate point of departure for the renewal of conflict and revolution in 1795.

While the formal constitutional destruction of aristocratic government in Deventer was not accomplished until the Batavian Revolution of 1795, this was clearly part of a larger process that was initiated by the Patriot Revolution of January 1787 and confirmed, ironically, by the Orangist counter-revolution of September 1787. Undoubtedly this was not the kind of outcome that the conservative powers of Europe intended when they intervened in Dutch politics on behalf of the Prince of Orange, but given the nature of the divisions invoked by the Patriot Revolution in Deventer, the Orangists had little choice but to make a fundamental break with the past. This break was, in the first instance, not a matter of institutional or constitutional change, for the Orangists quickly revived the Governmental Regulation of 1747 and thereby preserved the structures of old. But an essential precondition for the working of that system – the existence of an oligarchy which, however factional it might be, accepted the rules of aristocratic government – no longer existed. Division and conflict had, for the first time in Dutch republican history, led a major portion of the patrician elite to reject the fundamental principles of aristocratic government – especially its corporative exclusivity and secrecy – and to stake their political fortunes on the contrary principles of popular sovereignty and public scrutiny. Thus did the endemic factionalism of the old-regime elite give way to the ideological cleavages of the new.

A second change that was initiated by the Patriot Revolution and confirmed by the Orangist counter-revolution was no less important for the destruction of old-regime municipal politics. This entailed the fundamental realignment of popular politics within Deventer. Initially, the guildsmen of Deventer, fortified by their corporative organizations and practiced in the traditional forms of popular collective action, constituted the core of the popular Patriot movement, which seemed at the time to be the very model of successful mobilization (see chapter 4). Gradually, however, the leaders of the guilds were eclipsed by the university-educated lawyers and professors who dominated in the constitution-making process, and when the guild leaders perceived their interests to be threatened by the Patriots' Draft Constitution, these skilled craftsmen and shopkeepers turned against their erstwhile friends and became the core of a new counter-revolutionary Orangist movement (see chapter 6). At first this fateful decision subjected the Orangist guildsmen to systematic repression by the revolutionary regime, but with the Prussian invasion of September 1787, their fortunes and hopes were revived.

The members of the Orangist Burgercommittee – for the most part guild-based artisans and shopkeepers – working in concert with ex-Burgemeester Everhard Putman, were the principal architects of the counter-revolutionary regime in Deventer, the winners of the complex struggles that had divided the citizens of Deventer so deeply.[10] It was they, not the Prussian soldiers or the Prince's lieutenants, who so thoroughly cleaned house in the local administration and elected many of their number to membership in the Sworn Council, where lawyers and other educated professionals had for so long dominated. But their victory was short-lived, more apparent than real, given the larger structures of power which limited municipal autonomy and, by extension, their control of municipal politics as members of the Sworn Council. Following the special election of September 1787, which William V had little choice but to endorse, the Stadhouder was once again endowed, as patron-in-chief, with control over the annual election of the local Magistracy and the larger dimensions of political preferment in the Republic. As it happened, then, the long-term consequences of their becoming "Orangist" were soon apparent to the guildsmen of Deventer.

Following the Orangist restoration, the artisans and shopkeepers of Deventer who credited themselves with having defeated the Patriot movement were not prepared to retreat to their traditional obscurity in politics, but they repeatedly found themselves in conflict with a counter-revolutionary Magistracy that was unresponsive to their political demands. The guilds demanded, for example, that all politicians who had cooperated with the revolutionary regime be forever banned from office. Instead, a general amnesty was declared.[11] The guilds also claimed the right to discipline or expel members who had "made themselves unworthy" during the Revolution, but internal disciplinary action taken by some of the guilds was suspended by the Magistrates. In an effort to limit the political irritation, the counter-revolutionary Magistrates forbade meetings of the guilds for anything but the discussion of internal guild affairs, just as the revolutionary regime had done earlier in 1787.[12] When the guilds appealed directly to the Stadhouder for support, William V was as fearful of popular influence after 1787 as his father had been after 1747. Consequently, his appointed representatives, having investigated the situation in Deventer, sternly warned the guildsmen to stop meddling in affairs that were not their own and to obey "their lawful sovereigns."[13]

In the end, then, the militant guildsmen of Deventer were left without friends altogether. Their corporative political activism – their passionate defense of economic and political interests – proved to be as unacceptable to the Orangist regents they installed under the counter-revolution as it was to their former allies in the Patriot movement. In this sense, too, the counter-revolution unwittingly completed an important political process that had begun under the revolutionary regime, for the political isolation of Deventer's militant guildsmen cleared the way for an alternative configuration of popular politics rooted in the new voluntary associations that the Patriots had developed in the 1780s. During the Batavian Revolution of 1795, these voluntary associations – committees, clubs, and militias – quickly reappeared and easily filled the urban political space from which the guilds disappeared as a viable political force. This is not to say that artisans and shopkeepers retreated from political action altogether; rather, they were forced to compete in the new world of individualist popular politics on less advantageous terms. And just as they had feared in 1786, their privileged corporations, the last buttress of their formerly dominant position within the old-regime community, were abolished altogether before the century was out.[14]

In sum, the irony of the outcome of Deventer's municipal revolution is that the counter-revolution consolidated fundamental political changes within Deventer that might by some definitions be considered "revolutionary." Together, the fragmentation of the oligarchical elite and the realignment of popular politics spelled the end of old-regime corporatism. Under the pressure of a revolutionary movement increasingly identified with the political interests of *particulieren* and defined in essentially liberal and individualist terms, a coalition of militant guildsmen allied with a minority of the old-regime elite had defended critical elements of the old regime in essentially monopolistic and corporatist terms. Once this cleavage had emerged, it proved to be impossible simply to restore the old regime. In the short run, large numbers of new men entered the ranks of the municipal administration, but like the revolutionary coalition before it, the counter-revolutionary coalition discovered its internal differences once the common enemy had been defeated. Faced with a choice between the political activism of the popular movement, which had penetrated the formerly exclusive ranks of the Sworn Council, and the extreme insularity of the Magistracy as the last bastion of the old elite, the Prince of Orange chose the latter. In so choosing, William V, the last of the Dutch Stadhouders, unwittingly endorsed a new political reality: supported by just a small remnant of newly dependent aristocratic clients and isolated from the popular support he had gained during the darkest days of the Patriot Revolution, his "restoration" regime in Deventer fell as ignominiously in 1795 as his enemies' had in 1787.

THE VIEW FROM DEVENTER

In order to understand the significance of this outcome of the revolutionary process in Deventer, it is once again useful to place Deventer's experience in the larger comparative context of developments elsewhere. As we have seen throughout, the intensity of Deventer's conflict sets it apart from its sister cities, Kampen and Zwolle, but the political processes at work in Deventer were not different in kind. Rather, the exceptional qualities of the conflict in Deventer allow us to see with unusual clarity the essential qualities of eighteenth-century municipal revolutions. In the final analysis, the immediate outcome of Deventer's revolution was more precocious than it was aberrant.

In Zwolle, the victory of the Orangist coalition did not produce as extensive a counter-revolution as in Deventer. As we have seen earlier, the revolutionary coalition in Zwolle, constituting a thorough blend of guildsmen and *particulieren*, remained intact right up to the time of the Prussian invasion. Faced with continuing resistance from the regent elite, even after the *coup* of January 1787, the popular movement led by a unified Burgercommittee pressed for constitutional changes that would give it significant and on-going control over the administration of public affairs (see chapter 6). Given the breadth and unity of the revolutionary coalition in Zwolle, then, there was little opportunity for the kind of counter-revolutionary house-cleaning that occurred in Deventer. To be sure, under the protection of Prussian troops, a new Orangist administration was installed, but without popular support this regime had to steer an extremely cautious course through the troubled waters of municipal politics.[15] Still, it is not possible to speak of a simple restoration in Zwolle, for however cautious the revolutionary regime had been *vis-à-vis* the popular movement, it was held responsible for its support of the Patriot cause: just one man in the corps of 16 Burgemeesters remained in office. Here, too, the unity of the regent elite had been broken, though curiously some prominent Patriot leaders, like Solomon van Deventer, were allowed to retain their positions on the Sworn Council.[16]

In 1795, the Batavian Revolution seems to have resumed the revolutionary process in Zwolle precisely where it left off in 1787.[17] The provisional government installed in January 1795 included many regents who had been removed from office for their Patriot sympathies in 1787, and it was faced with strong popular challenges to its cautious politics until a more radical regime was finally installed in May. Once in power, however, the revolutionary coalition began to encounter the same kinds of problems on a national scale as had plagued the Patriots earlier within Deventer. Sensing the obvious significance for their own interests of the thrust toward individualist conceptions of democratic politics, the many strong and independent guilds of Zwolle appealed directly to the National Assembly for the preservation of their corporative privileges, but theirs turned out to be a defensive action that could hardly stem the tide toward liberalization of the economy as well as politics.[18] Thus, the guildsmen of Zwolle suffered the same fate as their counterparts in Deventer when first their demands were ignored by revolutionary leaders they had helped to install and finally their exclusive privileges were abolished by national legislation in 1798. This is not to say that guilds immediately disappeared in Zwolle (or, for that matter, Deventer); indeed, they proved to be remarkably resilient, reappearing for the next two decades in new guises after each attempt to abolish them.[19] But for those who continued to identify their long-term interests with the preservation of their exclusive corporations, the democratic revolution obviously became more of a menace than the blessing it may at first have seemed.

In Kampen, by contrast, the victory of the Orangist counter-revolution in 1787 produced virtually no changes in local politics. In the absence of a strong and independent popular movement to apply pressure on local regents, the Patriot Revolution had amounted to little more than a modest revolution from above. Though it was eventually rejected by popular referendum, the new system for popular election of Sworn Councilors proposed by the administration's constitutional commission would have done little to restructure local politics, at least not in the short run, while it would have released the local elite from the outside pressures of the Prince's patronage system (see chapter 6). Not surprisingly, then, Prussian intervention brought only a nominal Orangist restoration to Kampen in September of 1787. Since the local Magistracy voluntarily disarmed the local Patriot militia, the city was spared Prussian occupation, and since the city fathers voted immediately for the restoration of the Governmental Regulation in the Estates of Overijssel, there was apparently no need for the Prince to replace or restore anyone in the local administration to accomplish his immediate goals. Thus, Kampen retained its image of tranquillity, even becoming a refuge for Patriots fleeing their homes elsewhere in the Republic.[20]

In Kampen, too, the Batavian Revolution started out in 1795 essentially where the Patriot Revolution had left off in 1787. The remarkably resilient ruling oligarchy of Kampen tried once again to adapt itself to changing times by cooperating with a citizens' committee in the creation of a provisional revolutionary government. As a result, half of the members of the provisional government were regents under the Orangist regime, and the chief political appointees under the old regime as well as the officers of the old civic guard simply stayed in office. But the popular frustration and discontent that had been evident in the 1780s remained to plague the new regime. Leaders of an informal popular assembly insisted, by means of traditional petition campaigns, on more radical changes in local government – for example, the creation of a revolutionary militia, and the adoption of a new democratic constitution for local government – but were consistently outmaneuvered by those who defended the municipal privileges and political deference of the past. Finally, however, popular agitation took a new form when *wijkvergaderingen*, neighborhood assemblies mandated by the National Assembly, provided a venue and framework for meaningful and on-going popular political action. Thus, in February 1796, more than a year after the beginning of the process, the last of the holdover regents of the Orangist regime were removed from office in an election that, for the first time, brought the leaders of a dissident popular movement to power in Kampen.[21]

Far from resolving the political tensions within Kampen's population, the victory of those who had come to dominate the *wijkvergaderingen* instead ushered in a period of deep division and conflict in Kampen – a period in which first one faction, then the other triumphed by soliciting the support of the National Assembly. Though the social dimensions of this continuing conflict are not clear, the circumstances under which it finally emerged reflect the peculiar political legacy of the 1780s for Kampen. In the absence of strong and independent guilds to serve as a foundation for collective action as in Deventer and Zwolle, popular mobilization remained weak and sporadic in Kampen in the 1780s – this despite the expression of numerous urgent grievances in local pamphlets and petitions. In the beginning of the Batavian Revolution, popular mobilization was again weak and sporadic, though dramatic crowd actions did at critical junctures give the popular movement some temporary leverage over the conservative regime. But it was not until the institution of the *wijkvergadering* – not unlike the French *sections* – offered an alternative mode of popular collective action that the popular movement could become revolutionary in the sense of mounting a significant challenge to the old-regime elite. Ironically, then, the very weakness of its early mobilization induced the popular revolutionary movement in Kampen to embrace with unusual enthusiasm and success the new forms of popular politics that were created by more successful revolutionaries elsewhere. Thus did Kampen gain a new reputation after 1796, not as a haven of moderation and tranquillity, but as a hotbed of radicalism and strife.

In broad outline, the various political outcomes of the municipal revolutions in Overijssel's principal cities can be summarized by the interaction of the two

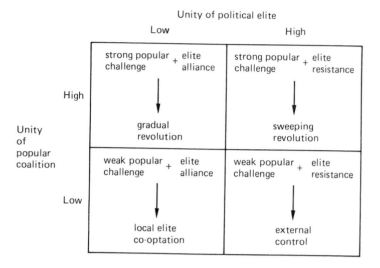

Figure 8.1   Political outcomes of municipal revolutions.

variables presented in figure 8.1. In all three cities, the political process of revolution was cut short in September of 1787 by Prussian invasion and was restarted again in January of 1795 under the impact of French invasion; in all three, the local history of the Patriot Revolution was clearly reflected in the local history of the Batavian Revolution. In Zwolle, where the struggles of the Patriot Revolution had divided the political elite and the broad Patriot coalition remained united (upper left quadrant in figure 8.1), the first provisional Batavian government included a number of Patriot regents who had been removed from office in 1787, but their cautious politics were soon challenged by a strong popular coalition that picked up where its Patriot predecessor had left off. By May, a more radical regime had come to power in Zwolle. This we might call a gradual revolution. In Kampen, by contrast, where the old-regime elite remained united and generally resistant to internal political change while the popular coalition was weak and divided during the Patriot Revolution (lower right quadrant), the elite continued to dominate local politics in the absence of a strong and united popular movement to challenge it in the first year of the Batavian Revolution. Not until the Batavian National Assembly had mandated the restructuring of local politics did a forceful popular movement emerge to install Kampen's first radical regime in 1796. In this case, because of the local stalemate the community was vulnerable to external control.

As we have seen, the situation in Deventer was particularly volatile in the 1780s because of the divisions both within the old-regime elite and within the popular coalition (lower left quadrant), and in 1795, without the support of those who had defected in 1786, the popular coalition failed to mount a strong revolutionary challenge to the Patriot regents who had been removed from office in 1787. Thus, the Batavian Revolution remained a relatively quiet and moderate affair in Deventer as the popular movement was co-opted by local elites who had allied themselves with the revolution. By extension, this analysis suggests, only where the old-regime political elite remained united in the face of a durable popular coalition in the 1780s would we expect to find a sweeping revolutionary displacement of the old-regime elite on the strength of a strong popular challenge in 1795 (upper right quadrant). This scenario probably comes closest to conforming to our most romantic notions of revolutionary class conflict: a broad and durable coalition of the oppressed rises up to defeat resoundingly the implacable forces of oppression. Yet, given the concrete historical grounds for divisions within popular revolutionary coalitions as well as old-regime elites, this must be seen as the least likely outcome of local revolutionary conflict at the end of the eighteenth century.

This comparative analysis of municipal revolution in Overijssel also suggests several broader conclusions about the revolutionary processes at work in Europe and North America in the last quarter of the eighteenth century. In the first place, it underscores the fundamental importance of the politicization and mobilization of traditional urban artisans and shopkeepers for the emergence of strong revolutionary coalitions. This is a familiar refrain in the literature not only on the French and American revolutions but also on the Belgian and English conflicts of the same period.[22] What the revolutionary experience of Deventer highlights, however, is the critical importance of prior institutional arrangements. The many independent guilds of Deventer provided invaluable organizational resources and experience which were, in the crisis occasioned by the Fourth English War, easily converted to political uses. But in the most developed areas of Europe and North America the organization of urban artisans and shopkeepers into guilds, confraternities or fraternal societies varied considerably, and as we have seen, even slight variations in a fairly standard form, such as the corporative guild, could be critically important in the development of revolutionary conflict. The ability to organize independently in order to protect common interests is surely important, but as the case of Deventer suggests, the exclusiveness which might enhance the *esprit de corps* of guildsmen could also be costly in political terms. While the aggressive independence of the leaders of Deventer's guilds undoubtedly contributed, in the short run, to their political power, their exclusion of "outsiders" resulted ultimately in political isolation, disillusionment, and failure.

The defection of many guildsmen from revolutionary activism in Deventer underscores, in turn, the importance of large-scale structural changes for our understanding of the realignment of local politics during the revolutionary period. In Deventer, the combined effect of the rise of the Amsterdam entrepôt and the growth of protoindustrial manufacturing was the growing political division between those, whether capitalists or petty-bourgeois, who were oriented to the local market and throve on protection and those, whether merchants or manufacturers, who sought to open larger markets for their entrepreneurial activity. While these transformations were not unique to Deventer or the Dutch Republic, the complex geography of capitalist expansion in the early modern period also does not conform neatly to the patterns of European state formation in the same period.[23] In absolutist France, for example, the political position of guildsmen was greatly complicated by the long-standing ties among monopoly, privilege, municipal power, state finance/ credit, and royal protection that were the legacy of Louis XIV's war-making. It would be as mistaken to generalize the experience of Deventer's guildsmen as it has been misleading to look at Paris without looking at Lille.[24] Thus, it is important, in further developing international comparisons, to supplement R. R. Palmer's political/constitutional analysis of the age of the democratic revolution with regionally and locally specific economic/institutional analysis.

Still, at the risk of overstepping the bounds of reasonable speculation, one is tempted to suggest that urban artisans and shopkeepers played a similar role in the democratic revolutions of the eighteenth century as Eric Wolf has suggested middle peasants have played in the peasant wars of the twentieth century.[25] In reacting to the pressures of long-term economic and social change, independent artisans and shopkeepers – as distinct from wholesale merchants and wage laborers – had both something to lose by the continued growth of commercial and protoindustrial capitalism and, in many cases, the ready means to defend their interests collectively. Their mobilization might be considered the *sine qua non* of effective revolutionary challenges in the eighteenth century; yet, like the middle peasants of the twentieth century peasant revolutions, the petty-bourgeois artisans and shopkeepers of the eighteenth-century municipal revolutions were often either rejected by their coalition partners in the short run (as in Deventer) or overtaken by broader political and economic changes in the long run (as in Zwolle). In either case, skilled artisans and shopkeepers, like middle peasants in the twentieth century, seemed to lose in the long run no matter which side won the immediate struggle for state power.

This analysis of municipal revolution in the Dutch Republic also underscores the development of political ideology as an unintended and somewhat surprising consequence of the revolutionary conflicts of the eighteenth century. In her recent interpretation of the French Revolution, Lynn Hunt gives particularly clear expression to a common argument that struggles within the revolutionary coalition in France "brought ideology into being;" she argues specifically that democratic republicanism was the most important legacy of the French Revolution.[26] The experience of Deventer's municipal revolution illustrates the same process by which sharpening conflicts within a broad revolutionary coalition led to the development of a particularly radical and revolutionary conception of representative democracy which, in its explicit rejection of the corporative interests and institutions of traditional artisans and shopkeepers, divided the polity and deprived the revolution of its original core of popular support. But Deventer's conflicts also highlight the variability of this explosive interaction between issues and actors.

In the Dutch Republic, republicanism, as such, was neither new nor particularly revolutionary; nor was the project of democratic reform divisive when it was paired with an obvious concern for the economic problems and interests of guild-based artisans and shopkeepers, as was the case in Zwolle. Rather, the explosive ideological connection of representative democracy with the precepts of economic liberalism – especially, the freedom of the labor market and the expansion of economic competition – was the product of the special circumstances, social, economic, and institutional, that shaped the development of revolutionary conflict in Deventer. Here, then, we are reminded that particular political ideologies, like the radical republicanism of the French Revolution or the liberal constitutionalism of the American Revolution, are not universally revolutionary; rather, they are revolutionary in specific historical contexts only to the extent that they actually divide people in often subtle, though not unpredictable ways. Within the broad, international context of democratic revolution, the task of comparative historical analysis is to continue to refine our understanding of the subtle interaction of ideas and actors within variable regional and local contexts, not just within "national" polities.

Finally, this analysis of municipal revolution in Deventer underscores the important results or consequences of democratic revolutionary conflict in the eighteenth century. The destruction of old-regime paternalism, the transformation of popular politics through the development of explicitly political voluntary associations, and the emergence of the rhetoric or vocabulary of modern politics constitutes nothing short of a fundamental revolution in political culture. But Deventer's experience of municipal revolution, in particular, calls into question some conventional notions about the nature of revolutionary change – that is, of revolutionary outcomes. The immediate failure of the Patriots' revolutionary coalition to maintain control in 1787 did not constitute a failure to transform municipal politics; rather, counterrevolution in Deventer confirmed the transformation of political culture along lines that were first predicted by the revolution itself. To be sure, important differences in political culture will always be evident: Van der Capellen's relation to *het Volk* was, after all, a more sober version of John Wilkes's relation to London's crowds. But the fundamental point is that in the most developed regions of western Europe and North America, the critical processes of revolutionary conflict – politicization, mobilization, and the emergence of multiple sovereignty – tended to work in the same direction whether, in the short run, the revolutionary coalition "won" or "lost"; whether national constitutions were created and endured or not. To do justice to that story, which is to a great extent the story of ordinary people in obscure places, we will have to move a long way away from a tale of two cities.

NOTES

1 Alfred Cobban, *Ambassadors and Secret Agents. The Diplomacy of the First Earl of Malmesbury at The Hague* (London, 1954), p. 178.
2 *Voorlopig Berigt van Everhard Herman Putman, Burgemeester der Stad Deventer* (Amsterdam, 1787), p. 6.
3 See, for example, the experience of W. H. Droghoorn and two other young men in Ootmarsum; P. H. L. Spee, "Ootmarsum," in *Herstel, Hervorming, of Behoud? Tien Overijsselse steden in de Patriottentijd, 1780–1787*, ed. M. A. M. Franken and R. M. Kemperink (Zwolle, 1985), p. 135.
4 Putman, *Voorlopig Berigt*, p. 10.
5 On the politics of the Kattenburg in Amsterdam, see P. Geyl, *De Patriottenbeweging* (Amsterdam, 1947).
6 Putman, *Voorlopig Berigt*, p. 5.
7 *NNJ*, 1787, pp. 5602–5, and [J. de Chalmot, ed.,] *Verzameling van Placaaten, Resolutien en andere authentieke stukken enz* (50 vols, Campen, 1788–93), vol. 9, pp. 197–227.
8 See J. Theunisz, *Overijssel in 1795, vanaf het uitbreken der revolutie tot het bijeenkomen van de Eerste National Vergadering* (Amsterdam, 1943).
9 GA Deventer, Rechterlijk Archief, 124: "Boek van Memoriën. Lijste van het getal van stemmen, zoals uit de respective agt Wijken alhier nauwkeurig bijeengebragt zijn geworden en wel op den 31 Maart 1795." The former Burgemeesters who were elected were W. H. Cost, G. D. Jordens, Gerrit Jacob Dumbar (not to be confused with his cousin, Gerhard Dumbar), C. A. Jordens, J. D. van Duren, A. Vijfhuis, and J. W. Tichler; the former Councilors were Gerrit Schimmelpenninck, Lambert Bannier, and W. H. van Hoëvell.
10 For the events surrounding the Orangist restoration, see *NNJ*, 1787, *passim*, and De Chalmot, *Verzameling*, esp. volumes 6, 8–10, and 12.
11 De Chalmot, *Verzameling*, vol. 6, pp. 25–7, 53–9.
12 Ibid., vol. 6, pp. 269–87, vol. 9, pp. 167–210.
13 Ibid., vol. 10, pp. 298–311, vol. 12, pp. 282–90.
14 See C. Wiskerke, *De Afschaffing der Gilden in Nederland* (Amsterdam, 1938).
15 The city remained tense for months after the Prussian invasion, and there were numerous clashes between the Prussian troops and the local population; see P. J. Lettinga, "Zwolle," in *Herstel, Hervorming of Behoud?*, pp. 63–7.
16 This may be a reflection of the institutional weakness of the Sworn Council in Zwolle; it was not worth risking the wrath of the local population since the Council constituted very little threat to the counter-revolutionary Magistracy.
17 J. Theunisz, "De regeering van de Provisionele Burger-Representanten van Zwolle (30 January–3 Mei 1795)," *Tijdschrift voor Geschiedenis*, 55 (1940), pp. 254–71.
18 Wiskerke, *Afschaffing*, pp. 110–12.
19 Cf. ibid., pp. 128–54, and S. Schama, *Patriots and Liberators. Revolution in the Netherlands, 1780–1813* (New York, 1977).

20 W. A. Fasel, "De Democratisch-Patriotische woelingen te Kampen," *VMORG*, 74 (1959), pp. 103–4.
21 Ibid., pp. 104–30, and C. L. Vitringa, *Staatkundige geschiedenis der Bataafsche Republiek*, vol. 3 (Arnhem, 1864), pp. 120–95.
22 In addition to the works on the American, French, and British conflicts cited earlier, see for the mobilization of artisans and shopkeepers in the southern Netherlands, Janet Polasky, *Revolution in Brussels, 1789–1793* (Hanover, NH, 1987), Y. van den Berghe, *Jacobijnen en traditionalisten. De reacties van de Bruggelingen in de revolutietijd (1780–1794)*, 2 vols (Brussels, 1972), and Van den Berghe, *Brugge in de revolutietijd, 1770–1794* (Brugge, 1978).
23 Charles Tilly, "Cities and states in Europe, 1000–1800," Working Paper no. 51, Center for Studies of Social Change, New School for Social Research, New York, October 1987.
24 Gail Bossenga, "City and state: an urban perspective on the origins of the French Revolution," in *The French Revolution and the Creation of Modern Political Culture*, vol. 1, *The Political Culture of the Old Regime*, ed. Keith Michael Baker (Oxford, 1987).
25 Eric Wolf, *Peasant Wars of the Twentieth Century* (New York, 1969).
26 Lynn Hunt, *Politics, Culture and Class in the French Revolution* (Berkeley, Ca, 1985).

Appendix I Occupational Classification

In analyzing the working population of Deventer and compiling the occupational profiles of the Patriot and Orangist movements in Deventer and more generally in Overijssel, I followed as much as possible the occupational classifications used by B. H. Slicher van Bath in *Een samenleving onder spanning. Geschiedenis van het platteland in Overijssel* (Assen, 1957), pp. 137–54. The only significant change had to do with the classification of day laborers (*daghuurders*). Slicher van Bath, whose research was concerned primarily with the rural population of Overijssel, classified day laborers as agricultural workers. For the urban population of Deventer especially, it seems necessary to classify them as common laborers or unskilled workers along with those called *arbeiders*. The following, then, is a list of the most common components of each of the occupational categories that I have used throughout this book.

MANUFACTURING

Wood:

cooper (*kuiper, kuipersbaas, kuipersknegt*)
chair-maker (*stoelmaker, stoeldraijer, stoeldraijersknegt, stoelmatter*)
cabinetmaker (*kastenmaker*)
wooden shoemaker (*klompmaker*)
cork cutter (*kurksnijder*)
sawyer (*houtzager*)

Metal:

silversmith (*silversmit*)
coppersmith (*koperslager*)
tinsmith (*tinnegieter, tinnegietersknegt*)
blacksmith (*smit, smitsbaas, smitsknegt*)

Leather:

shoemaker (*schoenmaker, schoenmakersbaas, schoenmakersknegt, schoenlapper*)
leather-dresser (*leertouwer, leertouwersbaas, leertouwersknegt*)
tanner (*looier*)
chamois-dresser (*seembereyder, zeemtouder*)
saddlemaker (*sadelmaker, sadelmakersknegt*)

Textiles:

weaver (*wever, weversbaas, weversknegt*)
spinner (*wolspinder, wolspindersbaas, wolspindersknegt, spinster*)
knitter (*breyder*)
bleacher (*bleeker*)
ropemaker (*touwslager*)

Garments:

tailor (*kleermaker, kleermakersbaas, kleermakersknegt*)
wig-maker (*paruikmaker*)
hat-maker (*hoedmaker, hoedmakersknegt, mutsopmaakster*)
seamstress (*naaister, linnennaaister*)

Food:

baker (*bakker, bakkersknegt, banketbakker, koekbakker*)
butcher (*slagter*)
corn chandler (*grutter*)
miller (*mulder, molenaar, molenaarsbaas, molenaarsknegt*)
brewer (*brouwer, brouwersknegt*)
distiller (*geneverstoker, geneverstokersknegt*)

Construction:

carpenter (*timmerman, timmermansbaas, timmermansknegt*)
mason (*metselaar, metselaarsknegt*)
hod-carrier (*opperman*)
ship's carpenter (*scheepstimmerman, scheepstimmermansknegt*)

Miscellaneous trades:

basket-maker (*mandemaker, mandemakersknegt*)
broom-maker (*bezembinder*)
brush-maker (*borstelmaker*)
wagon-maker (*wagenmaker*)
clock-maker (*horlogemaker*)

button-maker (*knoopmaker*)
candle-maker (*caarsmaker*)
ivory turner (*yvoordraijer, yvoordraijersknegt*)

TRADE AND TRANSPORTATION

Trade:

merchant (*koopman*)
shopkeeper (*winkelier*)
grocer (*kruidenier*)
wine merchant (*wijnkoper*)
sugar merchant (*suikerkoper*)
bookseller (*boekverkoper*)

Transportation:

innkeeper (*castelein, herbergier*)
tavernkeeper (*tapper*)
boatman (*schipper, schippersknegt*)
carter, porter (*caarman, voerman, sjouwer, cruijer*)

SOCIAL SERVICES

Education and liberal professions:

schoolmaster (*schoolmeester*)
professor (*professor, rector, lector*)
surgeon (*chirurgyn*)
doctor (*doctor, medecyn doctor*)
lawyer (*advocaat*)
musician (*musicant, trompetter, orgelist*)

Office-holders and politicians:

elected officials (*municipaal, representant*)
appointed officials (*Burgemeester, secretaris, scholtus, commissaris*)
municipal employees (*lantarn opsteker, klepperman, bode, doodgraver*)

Religious:

minister, pastor (*predikant*)
priest (*vader*)
sexton (*custos, verwalter custos*)

AGRICULTURE AND FISHING

Agriculture:

farmer, peasant (*boer, bouman*)
gardener (*hovenier, tuinier*)

Fishing:

fisherman (*visscher*)

UNSKILLED LABOR

worker (*arbeider*)
day laborer (*daghuurder*)
maid, domestic worker (*meid, wasvrouwe, werkvrouwe, strykster*)

INACTIVE

rentier (*rentenier*)
disabled (*gegazeerd*)
on poor relief (*bedeeld*)
no occupation listed

Appendix II Identifying the Actors: a Research Note

The process by which I assembled the occupational profiles of the Patriot coalition in Deventer divided into several distinct phases. The first stage involved compiling a file of the names of active Patriots. I began with the membership list of the Vrijcorps because it was very carefully constructed and the names on it were easily legible. I entered the name of each member on an index card and recorded all the information available from the membership list (company, rank, and in most cases age). Then I worked through the four petitions in chronological order. If the signatory was a member of the Vrijcorps, I noted this on his card; if he was not, I entered his name on a new card. Deciphering the signatures was often difficult, but in some cases, as problematic signatures reappeared, it was possible to transcribe them with greater certainty. Proceeding in this way, I accumulated an alphabetical file of nearly 2,000 names of Patriots with varying records of political involvement.

The second step was to create a separate alphabetical file for the names of all the heads of households that were listed in the occupational census of 1795, and to record on each card the information in the census (most importantly, occupation and size of household). The third stage – linking the names from the two lists – was the most critical. At this point, I naturally encountered a number of difficult problems, the most serious of which were the duplication of common names and variant spellings for the same name in the various sources. In some cases, for example, when the people with identical names had the same occupation, or when the census-taker simply exchanged a "c" for a "k" or shortened a double vowel to a single vowel, it was possible to overcome these difficulties. My general rule of thumb was, however, to be cautious in matching names from the two files and to exclude the doubtful cases. The results were as follows:

	No. of signatures	No. of legible names	No. of names in census	% of names in census
October 1782	1,460	1,160	536	46
December 1782	384	368	214	58
February 1783	714	645	358	56
February 1787	740	710	372	52
Vrijcorps	—	349	153	44

In all, compiling the occupational profile of the Patriot movement by hand was a long and tedious operation fraught with uncertainties at every stage. Still, it yielded a coherent measure over a period of nearly five years of the political activities of 800 identifiable individuals. These individual records were then tabulated and analyzed with the help of a micro-computer to produce the evidence that undergirds this study of revolutionary conflict in Deventer. What the results suggest is that even if one is cautious in linking names from multiple sources, it is possible to identify large percentages of those who were politically active during the revolutionary upheaval. If anything, the problems of name duplication and variant spellings would seem to bias the sample against the inclusion of lower-class people with unfixed surnames and marginal literacy. Still, as it happened, the results indicate a far greater level of participation of these very people than the traditional historiography would suggest. In any case, it seems to be true that applying this procedure, however primitive, to the analysis of petitions, membership lists, and census records yields a broader and less biased picture of the opposing coalitions than might ever be obtained from eyewitness reports, journalistic accounts, or police arrest records.

Bibliography

ARCHIVAL SOURCES

The specific archival sources used in this study are cited individually in the notes to the text. The following is a list of the principal archival collections that were used.

Algemeen Rijksarchief, Den Haag
  Binnenlandsche Zaken, 1795–1813
Rijksarchief in Overijssel, Zwolle
  Staten Archief (1578–1795)
  Rechterlijke Archieven (before 1795)
    includes records of many *stadsgerichten*
  Archief van de Ridderschap van Overijssel
  Marken Archief
  Collectie Aanwinsten (1839–1962)
  Handschriften toebehorende aan de Vereeniging tot Beoefening van Overijsselsch
    Recht en Geschiedenis
Gemeente Archief Deventer
  Republiek I
  Republiek II
  Rechterlijk Archief
  Collectie Dumbar
  Familie Archief Jordens
  Familie Archief Besier
Gemeente Archief Kampen
  Oud Archief
  Rechterlijk Archief
Gemeente Archief Zwolle
  Oud Archief
Gemeente Archief Hasselt
  Oud Archief
Gemeente Archief Oldenzaal
  Oud Archief
Gemeente Archief Ommen
  Oud Archief

Gemeente Archief Ootmarsum
Oud Archief
Gemeente Archief Steenwijk
Oud Archief
Oudheidkamer Twente, Enschede
Stad Ootmarsum

PRINTED PRIMARY SOURCES

BIBLIOGRAPHIC AIDS

Doorninck, M. van, "Van der Capellen tot den Pol (bibliographische proeve)," *Bijdragen tot the Geschiedenis van Overijssel*, 2 (1877), pp. 125–50.
Doorninck, M. van, "Staatkundige Vlugschriften, 1782–1799," *Bijdragen tot de Geschiedenis van Overijssel*, 7 (1883), pp. 34–135.
Knuttel, W. (ed.), *Catalagus van de Pamphletten-verzameling berustende in de Koninklijke Bibliotheek*, 9 vols, 's-Gravenhage, 1899–1920.

PERIODICALS

Blaadje zonder titel voor burger en boer in Overijssel, 1 vol., Deventer, 1785–6. (Complete copy in the Rijksarchief in Overijssel, Zwolle.)
De Politieke Kruyer, 10 vols, Amsterdam, 1782–7.
De Post van de Neder-Rhyn, 11 vols, Utrecht, 1781–7.
Nederlandsche Jaarboeken, 10 vols, Leiden/Amsterdam, 1750–9.
Nieuwe Nederlandsche Jaarboeken, 29 vols, Leiden/Amsterdam, 1760–88.
De Volksvriend, 1 vol., Zwolle, 1786–7. (Complete copy in the Atheneum Bibliotheek, Deventer.)

PAMPHLETS AND PUBLISHED DOCUMENTS

Many of the pamphlets cited below are not listed in the Knuttel catalog of the well-known pamphlet collection of the Koninklijke Bibliotheek in The Hague. These I have located in the Atheneum Bibliotheek in Deventer, where they are cataloged separately in the general catalog, and in the special pamphlet collection relating to the history of the American Revolution in the William L. Clements Library at the University of Michigan, Ann Arbor.

Aan het Volk van Nederland, Ostende, 1781. (Modern Dutch edition, Weesp, 1981.)
Aanmerkingen en Vragen aan de Burger-commissie der stad Zwolle over derzelver Aanspraak aan de Burgerij, Zwolle, 1786.
Aanmerkingen op het Rapport van de Commissie uit Raad en Meente te Zwolle over de bezwaren, door een Zwolsch Burger, Zwolle, 1786.
Aanmerkingen op het werkje, genoemd: het politiek systema van de regeering van Amsterdam . . . (n.p.), 1781.
Aanmerkingen op zommigen van de Overysselsche Steede bezwaren, byzonder op die van Zwolle . . . Zwolle, 1786.

Aanmerkingen over het adres en de Denkwys van veele Leden der respectieve Gilden te Deventer, Deventer, 1787.

Aanspraak aan de burgers, boeren, en verdere in- en opgezetenen van Overyssel . . . Amsterdam, 1782.

Aanspraak aan de Zwolsche Burgerye nevens twee Concept-reglementen zoo van de Keure en Verlating der Gemeenslieden als die der Magistraat der Stad Zwolle . . . Zwolle, 1786.

Aanspraak en opwekking aan den Burgery van Deventer, Om, in navolging der vrye Stigtenaars, de Banden van een onwettig ingevoerd Regeerings-reglement los te maken, en een verbeterd . . . in te voeren, Utrecht, 1785.

Aanspraak van een Deventers Gildebroeder, aan zyne Medeburgers en Gildebroeders, Deventer, 1787.

Aanspraak van een Overysselschen landman aan alle brave Nederlanderen, (n.p.), 1781.

Addres aan de Gezworen Gemeente van Deventer op naam van Gildens en Stemgeregtigde Burgerij door 26 personen gepresenteerd den 19 Jan. 1787 met de Resolutie van Raad een Gemeente van den 20 ditto, Deventer, 1787.

Advis en Consideratien van de Gezworene Gemeente der Stad Campen. Over het Rapport ter verbetering van de Regeerings bestelling deezer Stad . . . Kampen, 1787.

Advis van de Heeren Burgemeesteren Theussink, van Sonsbeek, Geldernman, van der Wyk en van Marle. Over het Rapport van de Commissie uit Raad en Meente tot de burger bezwaren, Kampen, 1786.

Advis van Otto Nicolaas Westenink, Lid der Gezworen Gemeente der Stad Deventer – ter Vergadering overgegeven den — October 1786, Deventer, 1787.

Algemeene Staatkundige Stellingen, betrekkelyk op de verandering van het Regeerings-reglement in Overyssel, Dord, 1785.

Antwoord aan den Schryver van het Onderzoek, of de oprigting van vaste of permanente Collegien van Burger-Committeerden, in de Overysselsche Steden, nuttig zy, dan niet, Dord, 1786.

Antwoord aan een Burger te Campen, over de bezwaren die in de hoofd-steden geoppert worden, tegens het Regeerings-reglement in Overijssel, door een burger te Zwolle, Zwolle, 1787.

Antwoord aan een jong onderdaan, op eenige weinige vragen, door een oud regent, voorgestelt aan zijne landgenooten, Nymweegen, 1779.

Antwoord aan een Vriend te Deventer, over de verandering van het Regeerings-reglement in Overyssel, Utrecht, 1785.

Antwoord op de missive van J. V. Z. bevattende een verslag van de merkwardigste bezonderheden op den jongst afgelopen Overysselschen Landdag voorgevallen, Amsterdam, 1784.

Artikelen opgedragen ter beoordeling aan de Burgers en Ingezetenen van Deventer, Deventer, 1787.

Beaufort, W. H., de (ed.), *Brieven van een aan Joan Derck van der Capellen van de Poll* (Werken uitgegeven door het Historisch Genootschap te Utrecht, new series, no. 27), Utrecht, 1879.

Bekeering van een Patriot of belydenis van een vrycorpist: gedaan door eenen Pruissischen Huzaar by hunnen inmarsch in Overyssel, Deventer, 1788.

Bericht van de Burger Commissie der Stad Campen, Betreffende de Inlevering van Bezwaren aan de Commissie uit Raad en Meente Gedaan den 31 January 1786, Campen, 1787.

Brief aan een vriend, over de Noodzaakelykheid van de verandering van het Regeerings-reglement in Overyssel, Dord, 1785.

Brief over de waere oorzaak van 's Lands ongeval . . . (n.p.), 1782.

Brief van een Burger uit Campen, aan een Burger te Deventer, Campen, 1786.

Brief van een heer te Utrecht, aan zijn vriend te Amsterdam, Amsterdam, 1779.

Brief van een oprechten Fries aan den heer V. D. H., (n.p.), 1779.

Brief van een vriend te Zwolle over den onlangs door den druk gemeen gemaakten Brief aangaande de verandering van 't Regeerings-reglement in Overyssel, Deventer, 1785.

Capellen, J. D. van der, *Vertoog over de onwettigheid der Drostendiensten in Overijssel,* Leyden, 1778.

Claessen, Johannes, *Nederlands werkloosheid in den oorlog als een gevolg van Gods toorn . . .* Utrecht, 1782.

Concept-Reglement op de Regeering van de stad Deventer, Deventer, 1787.

Concept-Reglement op de Regeerings-Bestelling der stad Campen, Campen, 1787.

Concept-Reglement van Regeering voor de stad Zwolle. Uitgebragt door de Burger-Committeerden, En aan derzelver gezamentlyke Committenten ter beoordeeling aangeboden, Zwolle, 1787.

Crimineel Process, tegen W. L. van Warmelo, Predikant te Wijhe in Overijssel . . . Amsterdam, 1792.

Dagverhaal en Verzameling van Handelingen en Stukken . . . rakende het punt van overstemminge ter Staatsvergaderinge der provincie Overijssel, sedert . . . 22 December 1784, Deventer, 1785.

De Burger-gecommitteerden der stad Zwolle aan hunne Committenten, Zwolle, 1787.

De Burgerij te Zwolle opgewekt tot een spoedig herstel van hare onderdrukt vrijheid, (n.p.), 1786.

De heersch- en plunderzucht der Engelschen geroskamd; ter aanmoediging van regtschapen vaderlanders . . . Straatsburg, 1779.

De vryheid der drukpers, onafscheidelyk verknogt aan de vryheid der republiek . . . Amsterdam, 1782.

De wenscch van Utrechts-burgery, vernietigt door den raadsman van Willem den vyfden . . . (n.p.), 1781.

Derde Rapport van Gecommitteerden uit Raad en Gemeente rakende zekere Adressen door pretense Gecommitteerden uit de Burgerij aan Schepenen en Raad geadresseed, Deventer, 1787.

Egte stukkeen betreffende het voorgevallene te Deventer, Deventer, 1783.

Geschiedenis van het exercitie-genootschap der stad Almelo, in de provincie van Overijssel en het landschap Twenthe, (n.p., n.d.).

Het Engelsche en Americaansche Kaartspel, vertoond in drie bedrijven, Utrecht, 1778.

Het politiek systema van de regeering van Amsterdam, in een waar daglicht voorgesteld, en haar gedrag . . . verdedigt in een brief aan een heer van regeering in Zeeland, Middelburg, 1781.

Het verraad ondekt, en de verraaders genoemd . . . (n.p.), 1782.

Iets noodzakelyks aan de Burgery van Zwol over het recuseren van hare tegenwoordige Gemeentslieden, Zwolle, 1787.

Iets voor Deventers Burgery en Ingezeetenen, door een vriend van Eendragt, Orde en Vrijheid, (n.p.), 1787.

Jonkheer Johan Derk van der Capellen van den Pol, beschreven in de Ridderschap van Overijssel, Regent . . . Leiden, 1779.

Memorie wegens het commercieele belang deezer republicq in het sluiten van een tractaat van commercie met de Vereenigde Staaten van Noord-Amerika, Rotterdam, 1781.

Meulen, W. W. van der (ed.), "Brieven van J. D. van der Capellen tot den Pol,"

Bijdragen en Mededelingen van het Historisch Genootschap, 28 (1907), pp. 103–341.

Missive behelzende een Betoog, dat de heeren Erfstadhouderen van Overyssel het regt Niet hebben om de keuren van Raad en Gezwooren Gemeente in de steden van die provincie . . . te veranderen, Zwolle, 1783.

Missive van een Amsterdamsch koopman, aan zyne vriend in Gelderland. Over de behandelingen der Engelschen; de memorien der Engelsche en Francsche ministers, en verdere zaaken heir toe betrekkelyk, Dordrecht, 1778.

Naam-Register van alle Heeren leden der Regeering in de Provincie Overijssel . . . voor den Jare 1787, Zwolle, 1787.

Naam-Register van alle Heeren leden der Regeering in de Provincie Overijssel . . . voor den Jare 1788, Zwolle, 1788.

Nieuwe spiegel der jeugd, of Britsche tyranny, voorgestelde in een samenspraak tusschen vader en zoon . . . Harlingen, 1779.

Onderzoek, of de oprigting van vaste of permanente Collegien van Burger-Committeerden, in de Overysselsche Steeden nuttig zy, dan niet, Dord, 1786.

Onpartijdige raadgevinge tot eensgezindheid en moderatie, van Batavus, aan alle waare liefhebberen des vaderlands, Utrecht, 1779.

Price, Richard, *Aanmerkingen over den aart der Burgerlyke vryheid, over de gronden der Regeering, en over de regtvaardigheid en staatkunde van den oorlog met America*, Leyden, 1776.

Price, Richard, *Nader aanmerkingen over den arrt en waarde der burgerlyke vryheid en eene vrye regeering*, Leyden, 1777.

Priestly, Joseph, *Proeve over de algmeene gronden van regeering en over den aart van politieke en burgerlyke vryheid*, Leyden, 1783.

Rapport over de ingeleverde Provinciale Bezwaren . . . door Raad en Meente der Stad Campen goedgekeud, den 28 Juny 1786, Campen, 1786.

Rapport over de verbetering van de Provinciale Regeeringswyze door de heeren, by Concordaat van Schepenen en Raad en de Gezworen Gemeente der Stad Deventer op den 21. September 1785 gecommitteerd, uitgebragt, en by Concordaat van den 8. Maart 1786. geapprobeerd, Deventer, 1786.

Rapport over de verbetering van de Regeeringsbestelling der Stad Campen, Door Heeren Gecommitteerden uit Raad en Gezworene Gemeente uitgebragt in November 1786, Campen, 1787.

Rapport van de Commissie uit Raad en Gemeente tot de Burger Bezwaren, en Concept Reglement van Regeering voor de stad Zwol, Zwolle, 1787.

Rapport van Heeren Gecommitteerden uit Raad en Gemeente der Stad Deventer, Rakende Het Addres, den 19 Jan. 1787 aan de Ed. Achtb. Gezw. Gemeente van Deventer gedaan door 26 Personen . . . Deventer, 1787.

Redenvoering van F. A. van der Marck, over de liefde tot het Vaderland, te bestuuren overeenkomstig met de redelyke en gezellige natuur der menschen of over den waaren aard van het zogenaamde Patriotismus . . . Deventer, 1783.

Reglementen op de Begeving van Ampten en Commissien, in de Provincie van Overijssel, Gearresteerd by Resolutie van Ridderschap en Steden den 14 Mei 1787, Campen, 1787.

Requesten en adressen van de burgerye der stad Zwolle, Zwolle, 1784.

Resolutie van de Heeren van de Magistraat der Stad Zwolle . . . over Het Rapport door de Commissie uit Raad en Meente tot de bezwaren uitgebragt . . . Deventer, 1787.

Samenspraak (in 't ryk der dooden) tusschen Prins Willem den I, en den Generaal Montgommery.

Over de eertyds voorgevalalen omwenteling in de Nederlanden, en de tegenwoordige gesteldheid der zaaken in Amerika, Amsterdam, 1778.

Suermond, W., *Leerrede gehouden op den Keurdag der Regeering van Deventer den 22 Febr. 1786,* Deventer, 1786.

Tweede Rapport . . . over de Verbetering van de Stedelyke Regeeringswyze uitgebragt in Augustus des jaars 1786, Deventer, 1786.

Verzameling van Placaaten, Resolutien en andere authenieke stukken enz. betrekking hebbende tot de gewigtige gebeurentissen, in den Maand September [1787] . . . en vervolgens in het gemeenbest der . . . Nederlanden voorgevallen (ed. J. de Chalmot), 50 vols, Campen, 1788–93.

Voorlopig Berigt van Everhard Herman Putman, Burgemeester der Stad Deventer, Amsterdam, 1787.

Zeven dorpen in brand door de onvoorzigtighid van een schout en een secretaris of Historie van de Oliekoeken . . . (n.p.), 1781.

SECONDARY SOURCES

Acquoy, J. "De admissie in de Ridderschap van Overijssel gedurende de Republiek," *Bijdragen voor Vaderlandsche Geschiedenis en Oudheidkunde,* 4e reeks, 6: 258ff.

"Ampten, Beneficiën, Officien, Tractementen, enz. door de regeering van Zwolle begeven," *Bijdragen tot de Geschiedenis van Overijssel,* 1 (1874): 49–71, 134–68, 269–78.

Aya, R., "Popular intervention in revolutionary situations: a research agenda," *Symposion,* 1 (1979): 124–51.

Aya, R., "Theories of revolution reconsidered: contrasting models of collective violence," *Theory and Society,* 8 (1979): 39–99.

Bartstra, J. S., *Vlootherstel en Legeraugmentatie, 1770–1780.* Assen, 1952.

Bercé, Yves-Marie, *Revoltes et revolutions dans l'Europe moderne, XVIe–XVIIIe siècles.* Paris, 1980.

Berghe, Y. van den, *Jacobijnen en traditionalisten. De reacties van de Bruggelingen in de revolutietijd (1780–1794),* 2 vols. Brussels, 1972.

Berghe, Y. van den, *Brugge in de revolutietijd, 1770–1794.* Brugge, 1978.

Black, Anthony, *Guilds and Civil Society in European Political Thought. From the twelfth century to the present.* London, 1983.

Blanning, T. C. W., *Reform and Revolution in Mainz, 1743–1803.* London, 1974.

Blécourt, A. S. de, "Burgerwapening in de Patriottentijd," *Groningsche Volksalmanak voor het jaar 1897,* 1896: 145–90.

Bloch, Marc, "A contribution towards a comparative history of European societies," *Land and Work in Medieval Europe,* New York, 1969.

Boot, J. A. P. G., "Fabriekeur en textielzaken omstreeks 1750," *Textielhistorische Bijdragen,* 5 (1964): 18–51.

Boot, J. A. P. G., "Het linnenbedrijf in Twente omstreeks 1700," *Textielhistorische Bijdragen,* 7 (1965): 21–64.

Boot, J. A. P. G., "De markt voor twents-achterhoekse weefsels in de tweede helft van de 18e eeuw," *Textielhistorische Bijdragen,* 16 (1975): 21–28.

Bossenga, Gail, "City and state: an urban perspective on the origins of the French Revolution," *The French Revolution and the Creation of Modern Political Culture,* vol. 1,

The Political Culture of the Old Regime, ed. Keith Michael Baker. Oxford, 1987.

Bruin, G. de, "De souvereiniteit in de republiek: een machtsprobleem," *Bijdragen en Mededelingen betreffende de geschiedenis der Nederlanden*, 94 (1979): 110–21.

Bruin, G. de, "Geschiedschrijving over de Gouden Eeuw," *Kantelend Geschiedbeeld*, ed. W. W. Mijnhardt. Utrecht/Antwerpen, 1983.

Bruin, R. E. de, *Burgers op het kussen. Volkssoevereiniteit en bestuurssamenstelling in de stad Utrecht, 1795–1813*. Zutphen, 1986.

Bruinenberg, H., *Duizend jaar Steenwyk*. Steenwyk, 1966.

Buijnsters, P. J., *Nederlandse literatuur van de achttiende eeuw*. Utrecht, 1984.

Bussemaker, C. H. T., *Geschiedenis van Overijssel gedurende het Eerste Stadhouderloze Tijdperk*. 's Gravenhage, 1888.

Bussemaker, Th., "J. D. van der Capellen tot den Pol," *Tijdspiegel*, 3 (1891).

Calhoun, Craig Jackson, "The radicalism of tradition: community strength or venerable disguise and borrowed language?," *American Journal of Sociology*, 88 (1983): 886–915.

Carter, Alice Clair, *Neutrality or Commitment: The Evolution of Dutch Foreign Policy, 1667–1795*. London, 1975.

Cobban, A., *Ambassadors and Secret Agents. The Diplomacy of the First Earl of Malmesbury at The Hague*. London, 1954.

Colenbrander, H. T., *De Patriottentijd. Hoofdzakelijk naar buitenlansche bescheiden*, 3 vols. 's-Gravenhage, 1897–99.

Colenbrander, H. T., "Aantekeningen betreffende de Vergadering van Vaderlandsche Regenten te Amsterdam, 1783–1787," *Bijdragen en Mededelingen van het Historisch Genootschap*, 20 (1899): 77–192.

Colmjon, Gerben, "Een blik op het dagelijks leven te Deventer in de 17e eeuw," *VMORG*, 80 (1965): 23–40.

"Contracten van Correspondentie [Zwolle]," *VMORG*, 9 (1874).

Countryman, Edward, *The American Revolution*. New York, 1985.

Croockewit, J. F., *De Patriotten te Wijk-bij-Duurstede in de jaren 1783–1787*, Wijk-bij-Duurstede, 1889.

Dekker, R. M., *Holland in beroering. Oproeren in de 17e en 18e eeuw*. Baarn, 1982.

Dekker, R. M., "'Politiek geweld' en het process van staatsvorming in de geschiedenis van de Nederlanden," *Sociologicsh tijdschrift*, 10 (1983): 335–53.

Dekker, R. M., "Women in revolt. Popular protest and its social basis in Holland in the seventeenth and eighteenth centuries," *Theory and Society*, 16 (1987): 337–62.

"Deventer in de Patriottentijd III," *Salland*, 29: 30 (April 16, 1935).

Dickens, Charles, *A Tale of Two Cities*. Penguin English Library edn, New York, 1970.

Dijk, H. van, and D. J. Roorda, "Sociale mobiliteit onder regenten van de Republiek," *Tijdschrift voor Geschiedenis*, 74 (1971): 309–28.

Dillen, J. G. van, *Van Rijkdom en regenten: Handboek tot de economische en sociale geschiedenis van Nederland tijdens de Republiek*. Den Haag, 1970.

Doeve, E., *De Laatste Dagen van het Boerenbolwerk* (Drentse Historische Studiën, VI). Assen, 1983.

Doorninck, J. I. van, "De omwenteling van 1787 te Deventer," *Kleine Bijdragen tot de Geschiedenis van Overijssel*, 11 (n.d.).

Doorninck, J. I. van, *Geslachtkundige aantekeningen ten aanzien van de gecommitteerden ten landdage van Overijssel sedert 1610–1794*. Zwolle, 1871.

Doorninck, J. I. van, "Oude regeeringsgebruiken te Deventer," *Bijdragen tot de*

Geschiedenis van Overijssel, 2 (1875): 226–40, 300–21 and 3 (1876): 249–58.

Doorninck, J. I. van, "Deventer contracten van correspondentie (1709–1710)," *VMORG*, 13 (1883): 48–55.

Doorninck, J. I. van, "Touren der Commissien," *VMORG*, 13 (1883): 45–8.

Dubbe, B., "Het tinnegietersambacht te Deventer," *VMORG*, 77 (1962): 37–148.

Dubbe, B., "Deventer geelgieters in de 17e en 18e eeuw," *VMORG*, 78 (1963): 119–30.

Dumbar, G., *Het Kerkelijk en Wereldlijk Deventer*. Deventer, 1732.

Dumbar, G., *Tegenwoordige Staat van Overijssel*, 4 vols. Amsterdam, 1781–1803 (reprint edition, 8 vols, Zaltbommel, 1964).

Eeghen, I. H. van, *De Gilden, theorie en praktijk*. Bussum, 1965.

Elias, Norbert, "Towards a theory of communities," *The Sociology of Community. A Selection of Readings*, ed. Colin Bell and Howard Newby. London, 1974.

Faber, J. A., "Dure tijden en hongersnoden in preindustrieel Nederland," Inaugural lecture, Amsterdam, 1976.

Faber, J. A. et al., "Population changes and economic developments in the Netherlands: a historical survey," *A. A. G. Bijdragen*, 12 (1965): 47–113.

Fasel, W. A., "De Democratisch-Patriotische woelingen te Kampen," *VMORG*, 74 (1959): 89–130.

Fehrman, C. N., "Mr. Jacob Abraham Uitenhage de Mist, 1749–1823," *Overijsselse Portretten*, Zwolle, 1958.

Fockema Andreae, S. J., *De Nederlandse staat onder de Republiek*, 2nd. edn Amsterdam, 1962.

Formsma, W. J., "De revolutie van 1795 in Ootmarsum," *VMORG*, 54 (1938): 137–48.

Formsma, W. J., "Hasselt in de gewestelijke geschiedenis," *VMORG*, 58 (1942): 31–48.

Formsma, W. J., "De windhandel van 1720 in Overijssel," *VMORG*, 60 (1945): 110–24.

Formsma, W. J., "Vormen van bestuur ten platteland in de Noordoostelijke Provincies voor 1795," *Bijdragen voor de Geschiedenis der Nederlanden*, 3 (1948): 21–41 and 161–78.

Formsma, W. J., "Van reformatie tot revolutie," *Geschiedenis van Overijssel*, ed. B. H. Slicher van Bath. Deventer, 1970.

Franken, M. A. M. and R. M. Kemperink (eds), *Herstel, Hervorming of Behoud? Tien Overijsselse steden in de Patriottentijd, 1780–1787* [*Overijsslse Historische Bijdragen*, 99 (1984)]. Zwolle, 1985.

Frijhoff, Willem, "Deventer en zijn gemiste universiteit. Het Atheneum in de sociaalculturele geschiedenis van Overijssel," *Overijsselse historische bijdragen*, 97 (1982): 45–79.

Frijhoff, Willem, "Dutch Enlightenment in front of popular belief and practice: an interpretation," paper presented to the symposium "Decline, Enlightenment, and Revolution: The Dutch Republic in the Eighteenth Century," Washington, DC, March 1987.

Fruin, Robert, *Geschiedenis der Staatsinstellingen in Nederland tot den val der Republiek*, 2nd edn 's-Gravenhage, 1922.

Geyl, P. *Revolutiedagen te Amsterdam*. 's-Gravenhage, 1936.

Geyl, P., *De Patriottenbeweging 1780–1787*. Amsterdam, 1947.

Geyl, P., "Noord-Nederlandse Patriottenbeweging en Brabantse Revolutie," *Studies en Strijdschriften*. Groningen, 1958.

Geyl, P., *Geschiedenis der Nederlandse stam*, vol. 5. Amsterdam/Antwerpen, 1962.

Godechot, Jacques, *La grande nation, l'expansion revolutionaire de la France dans la monde, 1789–1799*, 2 vols. Paris, 1956.

Godechot, Jacques, *The Counter-Revolution. Doctrine and Action, 1789–1799*. London, 1972.

Goldstone, Jack A., "The comparative and historical study of revolutions," *Annual Review of Sociology*, 8 (1982): 187–207.

Goudsblom, Johan, "De nederlandse samenleving in een ontwikkelingsperspectief," *Symposion*, 1 (1979): 8–79.

Graaf, J. de, "Sallandse markedagen," *VMORG*, 61 (1946): 52–60.

Grever, John H., "Committees and deputations in the Assemblies of the Dutch Republic," *Parliaments, Estates and Representation*, 1 (1981): 13–33.

Groeneveld, S. and H. L. Ph. Leeuwenberg (eds), *De Unie van Utrecht. Wording en werking van een verbond en een verbondsacte*. Den Haag, 1979.

Guibal, C. J., *Democratie en Oligarchie in Friesland tijdens de Republiek*. Assen, 1934.

Gutmann, Myron P., *Toward the Modern Economy. Early Industry in Europe, 1500–1800*. New York, 1988.

Haitsma Mulier, E. O. G., "De geschiedschrijving over de Patriottentijd en de Betaafse Tijd," *Kantelend geschiedbeeld. Nederlandse historiografie sinds 1945*, ed. W. W. Mijnhardt. Utrecht/Antwerpen, 1983.

Harsin, P., *La Revolution Liegeoise de 1789*. Brussels, 1953.

Hart, M 't, "Cities and statemaking in the Dutch Republic, 1580–1680," *Theory and Society*, forthcoming.

Hartog, J., *De Patriotten en Oranje van 1747 tot 1787*. Amsterdam, 1882.

Hattink, R. E., "Roomsche kerkgemeenten en priesters in Twente in de 18e eeuw," *VMORG*, 24 (1909): 57–89.

Hazewinkel, H. C., *Geschiedenis van Rotterdam*, vol. 1 (reprint edn). Zaltbommel, 1974.

Heijden, M. van der, *De dageraad van de emancipatie der Katholieken in Nederland*. Nijmegen, 1947.

Hendriks, G., *Een stad en haar boeren*. Kampen, 1953.

Heuven-Bruggeman, M. van, "Een rekest in Zwolle in de nazomer van 1785," *VMORG*, 91 (1976): 70–95.

Hildebrand, K., "De Patriottentijd in Stad en Lande 1780–1787," *Groningse Volksalmanak* 1950: 1–71.

Himbergen, E. J. van, "Grondwettig Herstelling," *Kleio*, 19 (1978): 265–75.

Hoerder, Dirk, *Crowd Action in Revolutionary Massachusetts, 1765–1780*. New York, 1977.

Hohenberg, Paul M. and Lynn Hollen Lees, *The Making of Urban Europe, 1000–1950*. Cambridge, Mass., 1985.

Holtrop, P. N., *Tussen Piëtisme en Réveil. Het "Deutsche Christentumsgesellschaft" in Nederland, 1784–1833*. Amsterdam, 1975.

Hufton, Olwen, *Europe: Privilege and Protest, 1730–1789*. London, 1980.

Hulzen, A. van, *Utrecht in de Patriottentijd*. Zaltbommel, 1966.

Hunt, David, "Peasant politics in the French Revolution," *Social History*, 9 (1984): 277–99.

Hunt, Lynn, "Committees and communes: local politics and national revolution in

1789," *Comparative Studies in Society and History*, 18 (1976): 321–46.

Hunt, Lynn, *Revolution and Urban Politics in Provincial France. Troyes and Reims, 1786–1790*. Stanford, Ca, 1978.

Hunt, Lynn, *Politics, Culture, and Class in the French Revolution*. Berkeley, Ca, 1984.

Isaac, Rhys, "Preachers and Patriots: popular culture and the revolution in Virginia," *The American Revolution: Explorations in the History of American Radicalism*, ed. Alfred F. Young. De Kalb, Ill., 1976.

Jappe Alberts, W., *De Nederlandse Hanzesteden*. Bussum, 1969.

Jong, M. de, Hzn, *Joan Derk van der Capellen, Staatkundig levensbeeld uit de wordings tijd van de moderne democratie*. Groningen/Den Haag, 1921.

Jongkees, A. G., "De Nederlandse laat-middeleeuwse cultuur in Europese samenhang," *AGN*, vol. 4, Haarlem, 1980.

Jongste, J. A. F. de, *Onrust aan het Spaarne. Haarlem in de jaren 1747–1751* (Hollandse Historische reeks, 2). Amsterdam, 1984.

Keune, W. Th., "Gebeurtenissen rondom de verkeiezing van Schepenen en Raad en de Gezworen Gemeente van Deventer in 1703," *VMORG*, 81 (1966): 119–29.

Kieft, C. van de, et al., *500 jaren Staten-Generaal in de Nederlanden. Van Statenvergadering tot Volksvertegenwoordiging*. Assen, 1964.

Knoops, W. A., and F. Ch. Meijer, *Goejanverwellesluis, De aanhouding van de princes van Oranje op 28 juni 1787 door het vrijcorps van Gouda*. Amsterdam, 1987.

Koch, A. C. F., "The Reformation at Deventer in 1579–1580. Size and structure of the Catholic section of the population during the religious peace," *Acta Historiae Neerlandica*, 6 (1973): 27–66.

Kossmann, E. H., "The crisis of the Dutch State 1780–1813: Nationalism, federalism, unitarism," in J. S. Bromley and E. H. Kossmann (eds), *Britain and the Netherlands*, vol. 4, *Metropolis, Dominion, Province*. The Hague, 1971.

Kossmann, E. H., *The Low Countries, 1780–1940*. Oxford, 1978.

Kriedte, Peter, et al., *Industrialization before Industrialization*. Cambridge, 1981.

Kroes-Ligtenberg, Christina, *Dr. Wybo Fijnje (1750–1809). Belevenissen van een journalist in de Patriottentijd*. Assen, 1957.

Kronenberg, H., "Grootburgerrechten te Deventer," *VMORG*, 26 (1910): 195–202.

Kronenberg, H., "Schepenen, Raden en Gezworen Gemeente te Deventer van 1787–1795," *VMORG*, 38 (1921): 79–87.

Kronenberg, H., "In en om de Deventer Magistraat, 1591–1795," *VMORG*, 44 (1927): 73–92.

Kronenberg, H., "Het kasboek van Mr. Arnold Weerts," *VMORG*, 47 (1930): 11–25.

Kronenberg, H., "Verhouding tussen adel en patriciaat in Deventer," *VMORG*, 65 (1950): 84–9.

Kuile, G. J. ter, "De heerlijkheid Almelo, 1236–1798," *Tijdschrift voor Rechtsgeschiedenis*, 17 (1941): 365–411.

Kuile, G. J. ter, "Overijssel in de 18e eeuw," *Tijdschrift voor Rechtsgeschiedenis*, 19 (1951): 263–95.

Kuile, G. J. ter, "Rechtspraak en bestuur in Overijssel ten tijde van de Republiek der Vereenigde Nederlanden," *VMORG*, 67 (1952): 141–68 and 68 (1953): 69–97.

Kuile, G. J. ter, "Rechtskundige verschijnselen in de nieuwere tijd," *Geschiedenis van Overijssel*, ed. B. H. Slicher van Bath. Deventer, 1970.

Kuiper, W. H., "De Almelose doopsgezinden en het beginsel der weerloosheid in de patriottentijd," *VMORG*, 88 (1973): 60–6.

Leeb, I. L., *The Ideological Origins of the Batavian Revolution. History and Politics in the Dutch Republic, 1747–1800*. The Hague, 1973.

Lindeboom, J., "Het Deventer Professoraat van F. A. van der Marck," *VMORG*, 54 (1938): 115–37.

Lintum, C. te, "Mr. J. W. Racer als Patriot," *VMORG*, 21 (1900): 89–128.

Lutje Schipholt, A. H., "Over landloperij en haar bestrijding." *VMORG*, 64 (1949): 129–49.

Manen, I. van and K. Vermeulen, "Het lagere volk van Amsterdam in de strijd tussen Patriotten en Oranjegezinden, 1780–1800," *Tijdschrift voor sociale geschiedenis*, 6 (1980): 331–56 and 7 (1981): 3–42.

Marshall, Sherrin, *The Dutch Gentry, 1500–1650. Family, Faith, and Fortune*. New York, 1987.

Mendels, F. and P. Deyon, "Protoindustrialization: theorie et realité," *Revue du Nord*, 63 (1981): 11–19.

Mendels, Franklin, "Proto-industrialization: the first phase of the industrialization process," *Journal of Economic History*, 32 (1972): 241–61.

Meulen, W. W. van der, *Coert Lambertus van Beijma. Een bijdrage tot de kennis van Frieslands geschiedenis tijdens den patriottentijd*. Leeuwaarden, 1894.

Mijnhardt, W. W., "De Nederlandse Verlichting: een tereinverkenning," *Kleio*, 19 (1978): 245–63.

Mijnhardt, W. W., "The Dutch Enlightenment: humanism, nationalism, and decline," paper presented to the symposium "Decline, Enlightenment, and Revolution: The Dutch Republic in the Eighteenth Century," Washington, DC, March 1987.

Mulder, Lambert A., *De Revolte der Fijnen. De Afscheiding van 1834 als sociaal conflict en sociale beweging*. Meppel, 1973.

Nagtglas, F., *Voor honderd jaren*. Utrecht, 1886.

Nauwelaerts, M. A., "Scholen en Onderwijs," *AGN*, vol. 4. Haarlem, 1980.

Nieuwenhuis, Tom, *Keeshonden en Prinsmannen. Durgerdam, Ransdorp en Holisloot, 1780–1813*. Amsterdam, 1986.

Obbema, P. F. J. and A. Derolez, "De productie en verspreiding van het boek," *AGN*, vol. 4. Haarlem, 1980.

Palmer, R. R., *The Age of the Democratic Revolution*, 2 vols. Princeton, NJ, 1959–64.

Palmer, R. R., "The Great Inversion: America and Europe in the eighteenth-century revolution," *Ideas in History. Essays Presented to Louis Gottschalk*, ed. R. Herr and H. T. Parker. Durham, NC, 1965.

Parker, Geoffrey, *The Army of Flanders and the Spanish Road, 1567–1659*. Cambridge, 1972.

Polasky, Janet, *Revolution in Brussels, 1787–1793*. Hanover, NH, 1984.

Popkin, Jeremy, "Print culture in the Netherlands on the eve of the revolution," paper presented to the symposium "Decline, Enlightenment, and Revolution: The Dutch Republic in the Eighteenth Century," Washington, DC, March 1987.

Pot, C. W. van der, "De twee Dumbar's 1680–1744, 1743–1802," *Overijsselse Portretten*. Zwolle, 1958.

Prevenier, W. and W. Blockmans, *The Burgundian Netherlands*. Cambridge, 1986.

Reitsma, R., *Centrifugal and Centripetal Forces in the Early Dutch Republic. The States of Overijssel, 1566–1600.* Amsterdam, 1982.

Rijn, G. van, "Kaat Mossel," *Rotterdams Jaarboekje,* 1890: 159–231.

Rijndorp, J. L., "Gerrit Willem van Marle," *Overijsselse Portretten.* Zwolle, 1958.

Riley, James, "The Dutch economy after 1650: decline or growth?", *Journal of European Economic History,* 13 (1984): 521–69.

Rogghé, P., "De omwenteling van 1789. Het aandeel van Vlaanderen," *Bijdragen tot de Geschiedenis en Oudhiedkunde* (Verhandelingen Maatschappij voor Geschiedenis en Oudheidkunde te Gent, 4), 1943: 143–79.

Romein, Jan, "Joan Derk van der Capellen," *Erflaters van onze beschaving.* Amsterdam, 1956.

Rooden, P. T. van, "De plunderingen op Schouwen en te Zierikzee, 1786–1788," *Archief van het Koninklijk Zeeuwsch Genootschap der Wetenschappen,* (1983): 173–99.

Rooijakkers, Gerard and Theo van der Zee (eds), *Religieuze volkscultuur. De spanning tussen de voorgeschreven orde en de geleefde praktijk.* Nijmegen, 1986.

Roorda, D. J., *Partij en Factie. De Oproeren van 1672 in de steden van Holland en Zeeland, een krachtmeting tussen patrijen en facties,* 2nd edn. Groningen, 1978.

Roorda, D. J., "William III and the Utrecht 'Government-Regulation': background, events and problems," *The Low Countries History Yearbook,* 12 (1979): 85–109.

Roorda, D. J., "Het onderzoek naar het stedelijk patriciaat in Nederland," *Kantelend geschiedbeeld,* ed. W. W. Mijnhardt. Utrecht/Antwerpen, 1983.

Rowen, H. H., "The revolution that wasn't: The coup d'etat of 1650 in Holland," *European Studies Review,* 4 (1974): 99–117.

Rowen, H. H., "Neither fish nor fowl: the Stadholderate in the Dutch Republic," *Political Ideas and Institutions in the Dutch Republic.* Los Angeles, 1985.

Rowen, H. H., *The Princes of Orange. The Stadholders in the Republic.* Cambridge, 1988.

Rudé, George, *Wilkes and Liberty.* Oxford, 1962.

Sas, N. C. F. van, "Joan Derk van der Capellen, 'Aan het volk van Nederland,'" *Theoretische Geschiedenis,* 10 (1983): 409–11.

Sas, N. C. F. van, "The Patriot Revolution: new perspectives," paper presented to the symposium "Decline, Enlightenment, and Revolution: The Dutch Republic in the Eighteenth Century," Washington, DC, March 1987.

Schaik, P. van, "De economische betekenis van de turfwinning in Nederland," *Economish-Historisch Jaarboek,* 32 (1967/8): 141–205 and 33 (1969/70): 186–235.

Schama, Simon, *Patriots and Liberators, Revolution in the Netherlands, 1780–1813.* New York, 1977.

Schelven, A. L. van, "Een overzicht van Twentse fabriqueurs uit 1795," *Textielhistorische Bijdragen,* 4 (1963).

Schulte Nordholt, J. W., *Voorbeeld in de Verte, De invloed van de Amerikaanse revolutie in Nederland.* Baarn, 1979.

Sillem, J. A. van, "Joan Derk van der Capellen tot den Poll," *De Gids,* 2–3 (1882).

Skocpol, Theda, *States and Social Revolutions. A comparative Analysis of France, Russia, and China.* Cambridge, 1979.

Slee, J. C. van, *De Illustre School te Deventer, 1630–1878,* 2 vols. 's-Gravenhage, 1916.

Slicher van Bath, B. H., "Manor, mark and village in the Eastern Netherlands," *Speculum,* 21 (1946): 115–48.

Slicher van Bath. B. H., *Een samenleving onder spanning. Geschiedenis van het platteland in Overijssel*. Assen, 1957.

Slicher van Bath, B. H., "Historische ontwikkeling van de textielnijverheid in Twente," *Textielhistorische Bijdragen*, 2 (1961): 21–39.

Sneller, Z. W., "De Twentsche weefnijverheid omstreefs het jaar 1800," *Tijdschrift voor Geschiedenis*, 41 (1926): 395–419.

Sneller, Z. W., "De opkomst van de plattelandsnijverheid in Nederland in de 17e en 18e eeuw," *De economist*, 1928: 691–702.

Sneller, Z. W., "De opkomst der Nederlandsche katoenindustrie," *Bijdragen tot de economische geschiedenis*. Utrecht/Antwerpen, 1968.

Snuif, C. J., "Het gewapend Burger-Vrijcorps van Ootmarsum," *VMORG*, 44 (1927): 106–17.

Snuif, C. J., "De burgerwapening in Goor," *VMORG*, 45 (1928): 260–1.

Soboul, Albert, *The French Revolution, 1787–1799. From the Storming of the Bastille to Napoleon*, trans. Alan Forrest and Colin Jones. New York, 1975.

Soly, H., "Social aspects of structural changes in the urban industries of eighteenth-century Brabant and Flanders," *The Rise and Decline of Urban Industries in Italy and the Low Countries During the Late Middle Ages and the Early Modern Times*. Leuven, 1988.

Soly, H. and C. Lis, *Poverty and Capitalism in Pre-Industrial Europe*. Atlantic Highlands, NJ, 1979.

Sonenscher, Michael, "The sans-culottes of the Year II: rethinking the language of labour in revolutionary France," *Social History*, 9 (1984): 301–28.

Steen, G. and W. Veldsink, *De geschiedenis van Ommen*. Ommen, 1948.

Stoeffler, F. Ernest, *The Rise of Evangelical Pietism*. Leiden, 1965.

Taylor, G., "Les cahiers de 1789: aspects révolutionaires et non-révolutionaires," *Annales: Economies, Sociétés, Civilisations*, 28 (1973): 1495–514.

Te Brake, Wayne, "Revolution and the rural community in the Eastern Netherlands," *Class Conflict and Collective Action*, ed. Louise A. and Charles Tilly. Beverly Hills, Ca/London, 1981.

Te Brake, W. P., "Van der Capellen en de Patriottisch Revolutie in Overijssel," *De wekker van de Nederlandse natie*, ed. E. A. van Dijk, et al. Zwolle, 1984.

Te Brake, Wayne P., "Popular politics and the Dutch Patriot Revolution," *Theory and Society*, 14 (1985): 199–222.

Te Brake, Wayne P., "Provincial histories and national revolution: the Dutch Republic in the 1780s," paper presented to the symposium "Decline, Enlightenment, and Revolution: The Dutch Republic in the Eighteenth Century," Washington, DC March, 1987.

Te Brake, W. Ph., "*Burgers* and *boeren* in the Dutch Patriot Revolution," *1787: De Nederlandse Revolutie?*, ed. Th. S. M. van der Zee et al. Amsterdam, 1988.

Te Brake, Wayne P., "Violence in the Dutch Patriot Revolution," *Comparative Studies in Society and History*, 30 (1988): 143–63.

Theunisz, J., "De regeering van de Provisionele Burger-Representanten van Zwolle (30 Januari–3 Mei 1795)," *Tijdschrift voor Geschiedenis*, 55 (1940): 254–71.

Theunisz, J., *Overijssel in 1795, vanaf het uitbreken der revolutie tot het bijeenkomen van de Eerste Nationale Vergadering*. Amsterdam, 1943.

Thompson, E. P., "The moral economy of the English crowd in the eighteenth century," *Past and Present*, n. 50 (1971): 76–136.

Tilly, Charles, "Revolutions and collective violence," *Handbook of Political Science*, vol. 3, ed. F. Greenstein and N. Polsby. Reading, Mass., 1975.

Tilly, Charles, *From Mobilization to Revolution*. Reading, Mass., 1978.

Tilly, Charles, "The web of contention in eighteenth-century cities," *Class Conflict and Collective Action*, ed. Louise A. and Charles Tilly. Beverly Hills, Ca/London, 1981.

Tilly, Charles, "Flows of capital and forms of industry in Europe, 1500–1900," *Theory and Society*, 12 (1983): 123–42.

Tilly, Charles, "Retrieving European lives," *Reliving the Past. The Worlds of Social History*, ed. Olivier Zunz. Chapel Hill, NC, 1985.

Tilly, Charles, "Cities and states in Europe, 1000–1800," Working Paper No. 51, Center for Studies of Social Change, New School for Social Research, New York, 1987.

Tracy, James D., *A Financial Revolution in the Habsburg Netherlands. Renten and Renteniers in the County of Holland, 1515–1565*. Berkeley, Ca, 1985.

Vijlbrief, I., *Van anti-aristocratie tot democratie. Een bijdrage tot de politieke en sociale geschiedenis der stad Utrecht*. Amsterdam, 1950.

Vijlbrief, I., "De Patriottencrisis," *Algemene Geschiedenis der Nederlanden*, vol. 8: *De Revolutie Tegemoet, 1748–1795*. Utrecht/Antwerpen, 1955.

Vitringa, C. L., *Staatkundige geschiedenis der Bataafsche Republiek*, vol. 3. Arnhem, 1864.

Vos van Steenwijk, A. N. de, "Een Overijsslse Patriot," *VMORG*, 86 (1971): 35–72.

Vos van Steenwijk, A. N. de, "Een Drents patriot," *Nieuwe drentse volksalmanak*, 29 (1975): 25–44.

Vries, Jan de, "The decline and rise of the Dutch economy, 1675–1900," *Research in Economic History*, Supplement 3 (*Technique, Spirit and Form in the Making of Modern Economies: Essays in Honor of William N. Parker*) (1984): 149–89.

Vries, Jan de, *European Urbanization, 1500–1800*. Cambridge, Mass., 1984.

Vries, Johan de, *De economische achteruitgang der Republiek in de achttiende eeuw*. Amsterdam, 1959.

Vries, K. de, "De Overijsselse stad in de middeleeuwen, een rechtssociologische verkenning." *VMORG*, 73 (1958): 45–56.

Vries, O., "Geschappen tot een ieders nut. Een verkennend onderzoek naar de Noord-nederlandse ambtenaar in de tijd van het Ancien Regime," *Tijdschrift voor Geschiedenis*, 90 (1977): 328–49.

Vries, Th. de, *Geschiedenis van Zwolle*, 2 vols. Zwolle, 1954–61.

Walker, Mack, *German Home Towns*. Ithaca, NY, 1971.

Wallerstein, Immanuel, *The Modern World System*, 2 vols. New York, 1974–80.

Wansink, H., "Holland and Six Allies: the Republic of the Seven United Provinces," *Britain and the Netherlands*, vol. 4, ed. J. S. Bromley and E. H. Kossmann. The Hague, 1971.

Wertheim, W. F., and A. H. Wertheim-Gijse Weenink, *Burgers in verzet tegen regenten-heerschappij. Onrust in Sticht en Oversticht, 1703–1706*. Amsterdam, 1976.

Wertheim-Gijse Weenink, A. H., *Democratische bewegingen in Gelderland, 1672–1795*. Amsterdam, 1973.

Wertheim-Gijse Weenink, A. H., "Early 18th century uprisings in the Low Countries: prelude to the Democratic Revolution," *History Workshop*, 15 (1983): 95–116.

Wessels, L. H. M., "Tussen Ratio en Revelatio. De Nederlandse Verlichting beoordeeld: enkele historiographische notities betreffende cultuur, mentaliteit en religie in de achttiende eeuw," *De Periferie in het Centrum. Opstellen aangeboden aan M. G. Spiertz*. Nijmegen, 1986.

Westendorp Boerma, J. J., "Volksoplopen in de 18de eeuw," *Tijdschrift voor Geschiedenis*, 52 (1937): 382–96.

Westrate, H. A., *Gelderland in de Patriottentijd*. Arnhem, 1903.

Williams, Gwyn A., *Artisans and Sans-Culottes. Popular Movements in France and Britain during the French Revolution*. New York, 1969.

Wilson, C. H., "The economic decline of the Netherlands," *Economic History Review*, 9 (1939): 111–27.

Wiskerke, C., *De Afschaffing der Gilden in Nederland*. Amsterdam, 1938.

Wit, C. H. E. de, *De Strijd tussen aristocratie en democratie in Nederland, 1780–1848*. Heerlen, 1965.

Wit, C. H. E. de, "De Nederlandse revolutie van de 18e eeuw en Frankrijk," *Documentatieblad Werkgroup 18e Eeuw*, 11/12 (1971): 29–51.

Wit, C. H. E. de, *De Nederlandse Revolutie van de Achttiende Eeuw*. Oirsbeek, 1974.

Wolf, Eric, *Peasant Wars of the Twentieth Century*. New York, 1969.

Wood, Gordon S., "A note on mobs in the American Revolution," *William and Mary Quarterly*, 23 (1966): 635–42.

Wood, Gordon S., *The Creation of the American Republic, 1776–1787*. Chapel Hill, NC, 1969.

Wulfften Palthe, A. A. W. van, *Levenschets van Mr. J. W. Racer*. Zwolle, 1886.

Wulfften Palthe, A. A. W. van, "Onderhandelingen omtrent het regeeringsreglement van Overijssel in 1786," *VMORG*, 18 (1891): 57–68.

Young, Alfred F. (ed.), *The American Revolution. Explorations in the History of American Radicalism*. De Kalb, Ill., 1976.

Zagorin, Perez, "Prolegomena to the comparative history of revolution in early modern Europe," *Comparative Studies in Society and History*, 18 (1976): 151–74.

Zilverberg, S. B. J., "Kerk en Verlichting in Noord-Nederland," *AGN*, vol. 9. Bussum, 1980.

Zwaan, Ton, "Politiek geweld, maatschappelijk structuur en burgerlijk civilisatie. Een verkenning van de binnenstatelijke geweldpleging in de ontwikkeling van de Nederlandse samenleving 1648–1960," *Sociologisch Tijdschrift*, 9 (1982): 433–75.

Glossary

Batavian Republic revolutionary regime established in the northern Netherlands following the invasion of French troops and the exile of William V in January 1795.

boeren yeoman farmers, peasants

burger generally, a citizen of a chartered town; more restrictively, one who has either inherited or purchased the *burgerrechten* of a city, as opposed to a mere resident.

Burgemeester ruling magistrate of a chartered town; in Deventer, either one of twelve *schepenen*, who served in pairs as chief executives and judges on a rotating basis for two months each year, or one of four *raden*, who constituted an advisory council. Collectively, the *schepenen* and *raden* were known as the Magistracy (*Magistraat*).

Burgerij collectively, the citizens of a chartered town; also generally meaning the "middle class" as distinct from the patriciate or the nobility, on the one hand, and the *grauw*, on the other.

Burgercommittee an ad hoc citizens' vigilance or correspondence committee.

burgerrechten formally the rights of citizenship in a chartered town, acquired either through inheritance or by formal purchase; a precondition for guild membership or appointment to municipal office.

civic guard (*schutterij*) municipal militia under the control of the magistracy.

drost in Overijssel, a regional official with administrative and judicial authority appointed by the provincial Estates; superior to the *schouten* and *richters*.

drostendiensten a *corvée* or unpaid labor service required of the rural inhabitants of Overijssel for the benefit of the *drosten*.

Dutch Revolt the sixteenth-century revolt against Philip II of Spain which resulted in the independence of the seven United Provinces or the Dutch Republic.

Economische Tak   one of many reforming societies concerned with the problem of economic decline in the Dutch Republic; established in 1777 as a "branch" of the Holland Society of Sciences.

Estates (*Staten*)   in Overijssel, collectively the delegates of the *hoofdsteden* and the members of the Ridderschap, who claimed sovereignty over the province following the Dutch Revolt.

Estates General (*Staten Generaal*)   collectively the delegates of the seven sovereign provinces who, under provisions of the Union of Utrecht, provided for a common coinage and defense and ruled directly over the Generality Lands.

exercitie genootschappen   "exercise associations" or voluntary militias outside the direct control of the magistracy; also called *vrijcorpsen*.

fabrieken   entrepreneurial manufactures outside the control or regulation of guilds.

generale ouderlieden   the two "elders" or general spokesmen of the guilds, collectively, in Deventer.

Governmental Regulation (*Regeerings Reglement*)   rules of government, concerned especially with appointments to provincial and local offices, imposed on Overijssel in 1675 by Stadhouder William III, following a period of foreign occupation; the Regulation was abolished after William's death in 1702, but was reinstated in 1747 by William IV.

grauw   rabble or mob; the commons.

grietenij   rural district in the province of Friesland.

gunstelingen   favorites or clients.

hoofdsteden   in Overijssel, the principal or capital cities – Deventer, Kampen, and Zwolle – which sent delegates to the provincial Estates.

hoofdgeld   "head" tax levied on all adults, excepting indigents, in Overijssel.

Kleine steden   in Overijssel, the smaller chartered towns which did not send delegates to the provincial Estates.

koopman   merchant, either wholesale or retail.

Landdag   official meeting of the provincial Estates.

Orange, House of   the princely dynasty from which most of the Dutch provinces chose their Stadhouders under the Republic after William the Silent had united the opposition to Philip II of Spain in the 1570s; following the death of William III in 1702, the lineage passed to the Nassau branch of the family, which descended from a brother of William the Silent and had traditionally supplied the Stadhouders of Friesland.

Orangist (*Oranjegezind*)   party label applied to the partisans of the Prince of Orange.

overstemming   decision by majority vote, that is, over the opposition of a minority; in the provincial Estates of Overijssel, decision-making by consensus was so much the norm that until the Patriots forced the issue in the

1780s, it was never clear, for example, whether the votes of the three cities plus the vote of a single nobleman constituted a valid majority or whether the votes of one-third of the Ridderschap would be required for *overstemming*.

particulieren   individuals or private persons, as distinct from members of corps like guilds.

Patriot   title appropriated by the political opponents of the Prince of Orange during the 1770s and 1780s.

Petrikeur   the annual election (*keur*) of Burgemeesters and Sworn Councilors in Deventer held on February 22 (*Petri ad Cathedrum*).

Pensionary   councilor or advocate who served as spokesman for the provincial Estates of Holland or one of its constituent cities; the Pensionaries of Holland were often the Stadhouders' most prominent competitors for leadership in national affairs.

regents   broadly, the members of the governing oligarchy in the Dutch provinces; in the cities of Overijssel, the Burgemeesters and Sworn Councilors.

Ridderschap   in Overijssel, the corps of the provincial nobility which, together with the delegates of the *hoofdsteden*, constituted the provincial Estates; internally, the members of the Ridderschap were subdivided according to their residence in one of the three "quarters" (*kwartieren*) or regions within the province – Vollenhove, Salland, and Twente.

Rijkstad   Imperial Free City, chartered by the Holy Roman Emperor.

schout   official with administrative and policing responsibilities within the rural districts of Overijssel; in Twente, this official was called the *richter*.

Stadhouder   originally, the provincial governor appointed by the "Landsheer" or sovereign; under the Republic, the Stadhouders, who might also be appointed Captains-General and Admirals-General of the Union, were appointed by the provinces severally. In Overijssel, the Stadhouder was given extensive patronage powers under the provisions of the Governmental Regulation.

Sworn Council (*Gezworen Gemeente*)   in the cities of Overijssel, the broad municipal council which annually elected the corps of Burgemeesters and shared legislative authority with the Magistracy; the members of the Sworn Council served for life and were elected by co-optation.

Union of Utrecht   defensive alliance concluded in 1579 which eventually formed the basis for the confederation of the seven United Provinces; it provided for a common defense but guaranteed the sovereignty of each of the provinces admitted to the Union.

Vroedschap   the municipal council in the maritime provinces.

Vaderlandsche Regenten   a national association of "patriotic" regents who in the 1780s openly identified with the Patriot movement in opposition to the Prince of Orange.

Vrijheid   Liberty, Freedom.

vrijcorpsen   "free corps" or voluntary militias outside the direct control of the magistrates; also called *exercitie genootschappen.*

wijkvergaderingen   neighborhood assemblies, similar to the French *sections*, created under the Batavian Republic.

Index